SYNASTRY

UNDERSTANDING HUMAN RELATIONS THROUGH ASTROLOGY

By the same author

Astrology
The Technique of Prediction

RONALD DAVISON

is England's foremost living astrologer. He has been president of the Astrological Lodge of the Theosophical Society in England since 1952 and editor of *The Astrologer's Quarterly* since 1959. Numerous articles of his have been published in many of the world's astrological journals including: *American Astrology, The Aquarian Agent, The Astrologer's Quarterly, Horoscope Magazine* and *Spica*. His previous books **Astrology** and **The Technique of Prediction** have achieved wide international acclaim for both their information content and lucid style.

Jacket design: Alden Cole

SYNASTRY

UNDERSTANDING HUMAN RELATIONS THROUGH ASTROLOGY

RONALD DAVISON

AURORA PRESS

P.O. Box 573   Santa Fe, N.M. 87504

Copyright © 1983 by Aurora Press, Inc.

No part of this book may be reproduced by any mechanical, photographic, or electronic process, or in the form of a phonographic recording, nor may it be stored in a retrieval system, transmitted, or otherwise copied for public or private use, excepting brief passages quoted for purposes of review, without the written permission of the publisher.

Aurora Press, Inc.
P.O. Box 573
Santa Fe, N.M. 87504

Library of Congress Cataloging in Publication Data

Davison, Ronald C.
    Synastry.

Bibliography: p. 352
1. Astrology.   2. Horoscopes.   I. Title
BF1708.1.D38   133.5'4   76-28731
ISBN 0-943358-05-1

CONTENTS

INTRODUCTION . . . . *i*

Chapter 1
MARRIAGE AND OTHER RELATIONSHIPS 1
                                              Planets in the Seventh House   12
                                                        Multiple Marriages   23
                                                           Planets in Libra   24
                                                           Part of Marriage   28

Chapter 2
MARRIAGE HOROSCOPES 35
                                                       The Marriage Horoscope   38
                                                    Other Inceptional Charts   42

Chapter 3
GENERAL NOTES ON COMPARISON 45

CHAPTER 4
VARIOUS METHODS OF CHART COMPARISON 55
                                                           Planetary Patterns   62

Chapter 5
SUN SIGN COMPATIBILITY 67
                                                              The Triplicities   70
                                                           The Quadriplicities   81
                                                      Planetary House Groups   85

Chapter 6
BENEFIC AND MALEFIC PLANETS 89
                                    Harmonious and Discordant Aspects   89

Chapter 7
INTERACTION BETWEEN NATIVITIES . . . . Part One   97
                                                                  The Planets   100

Chapter 8
INTERACTION BETWEEN NATIVITIES . . . . Part Two   159
                                           The Houses   161

Chapter 9
THE RELATIONSHIP HOROSCOPE   244

Chapter 10
EXAMPLES OF HOROSCOPE COMPARISON   249
                                    The Windsors   249
                                Freud, Adler, Jung   268
                                 The Manson Family   282
                          A Male-Female Relationship   297
                          Adolph Hitler and Eva Braun   308

Chapter 11
CONCLUSION   315

GLOSSARY   319

BIBLIOGRAPHY   323

INDEX   325

INTRODUCTION

No man is an island entire of itself; every man
is a piece of the Continent, a part of the main.
JOHN DONNE

All religions teach the Wholeness of humanity. The human race stands or falls as a single unit. In order to be fully responsible members of the community, individuals need to develop their potential to their full capacity. By functioning at the highest level of their capabilities they can contribute something to the community that is uniquely theirs, something that another cannot precisely duplicate. The strength of a group depends upon the quality of those who compose it, upon the extent to which they are fully integrated individuals. The achievement of such self-integration can only be at the cost of much striving and the eventual surmounting of numerous pitfalls. The temptation to exploit developing talents for selfish ends and to maintain personal independence to a degree that impairs the capacity or willingness to co-operate with others may cause many an earnest attempt at self-development to falter. The needs of the community often require that individuals should be prepared to adapt or modify their personal aims and aspirations in the cause of the greater good. At the same time there are forces at play in the world today which exalt the community to such a degree that individuals are denied the freedom of self-expression that is not only theirs by right but which is necessary to allow them to make a more effective and more inspiring contribution to the community of which they are members.

The two greatest powers in the world today, the United States of America and the Union of Soviet Socialist Republics represent the two poles of this exercise in integrating the individual with the community. There are those who believe that in America the emphasis on the idea of personal freedom and the exaltation of the spirit of private enterprise is carried too far, while in Russia the need for individuals to devote themselves unstintingly to the welfare of the community is overstressed to the extent that personal freedom is limited to a degree that would appear to inhibit true self-expression. The resolution of this problem—how to balance individual freedom against the communal need for some measure of conformity—is one of the major concerns of the remaining two or three hundred years of the Piscean Age in which we are now living. Pisces is the sign of Atonement (At-one-ment) in which people learn to lose their own identity in the oneness of all being, not really losing anything in the process, but rather expanding their own consciousness until all the parts which separate them from the oneness of all being are transformed and transcended, until all the limits which they have hitherto imposed upon themselves are removed and all boundaries dissolved. Long before we can reach this stage we need to become better acquainted with ourselves, to see ourselves as we really are and not as we think we are. To assist us to get a better and less biased perspective of the way in which we are developing our qualities, there is nothing more effective and often nothing more salutary than the discipline of having to live and work with other people who may not always completely share our good opinion of ourselves.

Living in a community has been recognized by most of the great religions as a way of making aspirants aware of their own shortcomings and speeding up the process whereby they may become more complete human beings. Not everyone is inclined to submit to the rather demanding discipline of life in a monastic community and indeed there is such a great variation in the progress made in achieving self-mastery, both at the individual and the national level, that the rough and tumble of everyday life provides more than adequate opportunities for most of us to be confronted with the less socially acceptable sides of our character. The social unit of the family provides us with an early experience of some of the more obvious advantages and disadvantages of living in close proximity to others. Soon the experiences gained within the rather enclosed unit of the family become augmented, as we are required to gain our education in company with our contemporaries in considerably larger social units, where the usually benevolent supervision of parents is replaced by the more impersonal and less indulgent guidance of the teachers. At the age of puberty, there is a growing awareness of the opposite sex and the need to develop additional social accomplishments in order to create a good impression. The eventual need to earn a living usually brings us into contact with another type of community, which often requires us to demonstrate our abilities and usefulness in a certain direction, while personal choice and the operation of circumstance combine to provide numerous other contacts through the agency of which we may discover fresh facets of our being. Only through the constant interplay of human relationship can we become truly aware of our psychological strengths and weaknesses. Each new contact brings with it the possibility of learning more about ourselves, and those relationships which require a more thoroughgoing effort on our part to maintain harmony may in the long run teach us more about ourselves than those which are less demanding.

A doting parent may, for instance, fail to see or turn a blind eye to some of our more obvious shortcomings, while chance acquaintances who pride themselves upon their outspokenness may give us more cause to reflect than many a more indulgent observer.

Just as no two human beings are alike, so no two human relationships are alike. Every contact we make has the possibility of bringing out a quality in ourselves that may not be apparent to others and which may hitherto have remained as a latent potential not called forth by the requirements of previous relationships. Consequently no two people see us in exactly the same light. If the type of response they evoke from us is sufficiently varied their impressions of us may differ greatly from each other. It is this possibility that occasionally leads people to remark: "I can't think what he sees in her!", not realizing that "he" by some subtle chemistry, has been able to evoke in "her" a deeper and more dynamic response than others would have dreamed possible.

Authors and dramatists, realizing this tendency of others to endow us with a kind of multiple personality, however inaccurately, have constructed plots based on the possibility that we may appear very differently to different people, and have presented five versions of the same person, as seen through five different pairs of eyes, each version differing so much from the other as to be almost incongruous.

This may be better understood when we realize that, astrologically, a man's wife, daughter or girl friend may tend to bring out more of the Venus and the Moon in his astrological makeup, while young people may bring out more of his Mercury, and nephews and nieces cause him to play the Jupiterian role of uncle, and so on, the response in each case being modified by cross-aspects to these planets in his nativity from planets in the nativities of those with whom he has these relationships.

Because of this variety of response levels that can be evoked, those with latent neurotic tendencies are particularly vulnerable when placed in the position of having to maintain a close relationship with those whose insensitivity and lack of sympathy have the effect of aggravating such psychological tensions. Much useful therapeutic work has been done by astrologers who have been able to demonstrate to the sufferer through the medium of chart comparison, how certain contacts in their life had operated, without them realizing it, in such a way as to exacerbate any over-sensitive area of their psyche.

Family relationships are often the source of unwelcome discord (especially when inheritance is involved) and the fact that family connections as a group are known as "relations" may well be a somewhat cynical commentary on the fact that it is sometimes more difficult to maintain a high degree of concord within the family unit than outside it. Some have suggested that the family is a salutory karmic device in order to make us more aware of our own shortcomings, while others emphasize that the Higher Self, before reincarnating, carefully chooses the parents who are to provide its physical vehicle. From that point of view we get the family we deserve!

By a detailed comparison of the horoscopes of two people we can estimate the degree of compatibility between them and the type of adjustment each will need to make in order to achieve a truly harmonious relationship with the other. The comparison of horoscopes is known as Synastry, from the Greek prefix *syn,* which has the meaning of a mutual bringing together, and *astron,* a star.

Those who ask an astrologer to make such a comparison between their own horoscope and that of another usually do so because they are planning to get married, realizing perhaps that though love may not be so blind as the proverb suggests, it is not capable of the kind of detached analysis that can be derived from a scientific study of the compatibility potentials indicated by the interplay of their horoscopes.

Astrology teaches that everyone has the potential to create harmony within themselves and that they are able to live in harmony with others to the extent that they are truly at peace with themselves. Most of our relationships fall short of perfection since it is given to very few to achieve such perfect inner harmony. Indeed, there are some who are so bedevilled by inner discords that there may be a question mark against their ability to achieve any kind of rapport with another. The discerning astrologer will therefore look first to the individual nativities to determine the capacity of each to create harmony around him, knowing that the quality of our personal relationships is determined by the extent to which we have developed our own inner being. This does not mean that highly evolved individuals will have no enemies, for the more uncompromising their attitude towards those factors which have a disintegrative effect upon the wholeness of their being, the more they may find that those who identify themselves psychologically with such disintegrative factors are apt to recognize in them their "Enemy."

Theoretically it is possible to assess astrologically, if we wish to do so, the type of relationship we might establish with any other individual provided his or her birth-time is known. Such an individual need not even be a contemporary and it is often possible to discover interesting links between an historical personage and those who have subsequently found him to be a source of inspiration. Any type of relationship may be subjected to such astrological scrutiny, from the partnership between husband and wife to the rapport existing between teacher and pupil or to the relationship between employer and employee, between partners in business and between members of a family, be they grandparent, parent, child or grandchild, provided due allowance is made for the difference in age of the respective parties. The relationship of individuals to larger units of the community may also be studied. The nativity of pupils can be compared with the foundation horoscope of the school which they attend, the members' horoscopes can be compared with the foundation chart of the club to which they belong, and so on. The effect of environment may also be assessed by noting the interplay between the horoscopes of individuals and the chart of the town in which they reside and the country where they live. At the national level, the amount of rapport between nations can be assessed and a better appreciation gained of the obstacles, to effect a more complete understanding between countries whose aims appear inimical to each other.

Perhaps it is not too much to hope that before long the value of astrology in assessing the capacity for harmonious relationship between people will be more widely recognized by those engaged in all kinds of public relations activities, and those whose work entails the need to establish as close a rapport as possible with their fellows.

The greatest value of Synastry probably lies in its ability to assess the compatibility of prospective partners in marriage. Until recently it was frequently the custom in India for children of very tender years to be betrothed and married to each other. Many uninitiated westerners have decried such child marriages, not realizing that these unions were never concluded until a conscientious astrological survey of the nativities of the two prospective partners had been completed. Far from the ensuing union being haphazard or ill-assorted, it stood more chance of success than some of the irresponsible mating in the Western world between immature adults, whose liaisons sometimes owed their origin to a passing physical attraction, a desire to improve financial status on the part of one of the partners, an infatuation with the idea of "getting married" or to some other unworthy reason. While those uninitiated in the more intricate techniques of astrology may well be excused for imagining, because of the amount of popular literature on the subject, that an astrological assessment of compatibility depends mainly or entirely on a comparison of the Sun signs of those concerned, based mainly on the assumption that like attracts like, it cannot be too strongly stressed that the art of Synastry requires a careful comparison of many horoscopical details. In the chapters that follow, consideration will be given to the traditional rules governing compatibility, together with an exploration of a number of additional techniques that have been devised over the years to enable a more complete assessment to be made. Finally, the author presents for the first time a system which he discovered some years ago when experimenting with a number of new ideas and which he has found to be invaluable in assessing the degree of affinity between partners.

CHAPTER 1

Marriage and other Relationships as Shown in the Nativity

I married a wife, oh then!
I married a wife, oh then!
I married a wife, the plague of my life
And I longed to be single again.

I married a second, oh then!
I married a second, oh then!
I married another far worse than the other
And longed for the old one again.

Again and again and again
I married another, oh then!
I married another far worse than the other
And longed for the first one again.
Anonymous

It is probably the most important maxim in astrology that nothing can come to pass that is not shown in the nativity. Before comparing the horoscopes of two individuals it is therefore advisable to see what their nativities indicate, not only about their own attitude towards that area of relationship which is to be investigated, but also about the probable course of events in which such an attitude will be likely to involve them.

The basic attitude towards friends, relatives, employers, employees, enemies (if any!) and the marriage partner(s), are all shown by the condition of the appropriate houses, planets and signs in the nativity.

Astrologers are most frequently called upon to compare the nativities of couples who wish to know before marriage whether they are suited to each other, or to advise marriage partners who are finding problems in their relationship, which they hope may be solved more easily by an astrological assessment of the strengths and weaknesses of their relationship. Those intending to marry may wish for some reassurance as to their compatibility, though history records few cases of those who have been judged astrologically incompatible accepting such a verdict and calling off the engagement. In such cases it may well be that each partner needs the experience of failing to achieve married happiness in order to gain in wisdom and stature. However, such experiences are no guarantee of ultimate wisdom, as the rather cynical verses at the head of the chapter suggest! It has even been recorded that an astrologer admitted, in the course of a television interview, that she very much regretted not having looked at the indications in her own chart prior to having embarked upon a disastrous marriage.

When judging the compatibility of intending marriage partners, it is first necessary to decide whether the nativities of both indicate marriage and whether either party is "divorce prone." It may also be advisable to bear in mind the motives underlying the desire to marry.

A recent survey by Soviet sociologists pronounced that those who marry for love are likely to be less happy than those who marry for money or companionship. Marriage is a sacrament of the Church and although today the influence of the Church appears to be negligible in the lives of many citizens, it is worth noting that many couples still prefer a Church wedding, even if they do not enter such a building again, except for baptisms, funerals and their friends' weddings. There is therefore some kind of tacit acknowledgment of the Christian view of the purposes of marriage which, broadly speaking, reflect the twin requirements of matter and spirit. On the material side, the Church recognizes marriage as a union for the procreation of children (the race has a right to perpetuate itself) and as a way of satisfying the physical needs of each partner, within a framework most socially acceptable to the community; while on the spiritual side, the Church upholds marriage as a discipline in which man and wife may prove of mutual support, aiding each other's spiritual development, and as a union symbolic of the perfect alliance between the Masculine and Feminine principles of the Universe.

Some marry for security, others to avoid loneliness, to reduce income tax liability or to qualify for residence in a foreign country. Marriage on the basis of sexual attraction alone is the least likely to prove enduring. Such motives are rarely admitted openly and most couples would claim to be marrying for love, not only because it is widely recognized as the most respectable motive for marrying, but also because it is often difficult to make an objective analysis of the romantic glow that surrounds many such attachments.

The institution of marriage is universal and while, at various times, in different parts of the world, polyandry and polygamy have been practised, monogamy is by far the most prevalent from of marriage to be found. While customs may vary according to the religious and ethical background of the community involved, and while the roles of the respective partners may have fluctuated according to the varying conditions of society at the time, it has always been a feature of the institution of marriage and of the rules governing pre-marital behaviour, even when these did not enjoin chastity before marriage, that they should be subject to the approval of the community and that those about to marry should be seen to conform to those rules.

While at one time it might have been safe to assume that a couple would not marry until they had reached a certain stage of maturity as well as some degree of financial security, these considerations no longer apply to such a great extent. In those Eastern areas of the world where child marriages have been customary, the practice has probably been much less likely to produce marital unhappiness than many uninitiated Western observers might have supposed, since the choice of partners was usually entrusted to the local astrologers. In the West, however, no such scrutiny is customarily made and the hazards are likely to be greater. It has been said that the younger generation is maturing earlier, but the signs of such maturity have only been estimated at a very superficial level. In terms of actual maturity the progress may have been largely illusory and merely the result of the immaturity of their elders, who thoughtlessly expose them to the impact of ideas portrayed through the media of the press, films and television, where commercial considerations encourage an undesirable emphasis on the sensational aspects of sex and violence, with the result that they are almost brain-washed into early imitation of the less desirable features of the distorted world which is presented to them, and into accepting false standards of value that exalt personal freedom and independence at the expense of self-discipline. Thus it is that a section of the younger generation consider it desirable to set aside established conventions in relation to sex and marriage, engaging in pre-marital sex and living with the partner of their choice without having first entered into any legal contract or gone through any form of ceremony. Even so, in spite of the present climate of social behaviour which has resulted in the coining of the phrase, "the permissive society," it is doubtful whether morals are really any more lax today than they have been in the past.

Earlier generations have been less open about their marital infidelities and pre-marital escapades. In a social atmosphere where any moral laxities of this nature were frowned upon it was considered discreet to keep such activities as secret as possible. The conventions in this respect were faithfully observed. Present day conventions rarely involve much pretence of secrecy, so that there is more openness and less hypocrisy about sexual behaviour than formerly. In addition, methods of birth control are now more sophisticated. If these had been available to previous generations there would no doubt have been a good deal more promiscuity. It has been observed that greater sexual freedom has not resulted in a corresponding increase in happiness, and it would appear that when it comes to solving problems arising from sex relationships, the present generation are no more mature than their forbears.

Because one of the main reasons for the existence of marriage is the procreation of children, there is a general tendency for married couples to belong to a similar age group, though notable exceptions will no doubt spring to mind in which the husband is much older than the wife. When companionship and mutual help is the main purpose of the marriage there may sometimes be a considerable age gap between the partners. The woman who marries an older man often has a strong Father image that she wants to see personified in her partner, while the man who marries a much older woman often has a similarly well developed Mother image.

It is therefore unwise, particularly at the present time, to assume that a person is too young or too old to marry or that where there is a disparity of age between intending partners, or a difference of race, marriage is not likely to take place.

When arriving at a judgment concerning other people's love and marriage problems, the astrologer should not concern himself with the external aspects of the case except insofar as the couple may be making difficulties for themselves by not complying with the law or by openly flouting convention.

We may now turn to an examination of those factors in the nativity which indicate whether or not the native is likely to marry, the kind of partner he or she is likely to choose and the experiences likely to be encountered in the marriage partnership. Since the urge to mate is a natural instinct, it follows that unless there are strong indications to the contrary, the native is likely to marry. People who do not marry are usually those who value their independence highly (though some marry and find a way of maintaining a satisfactory degree of independence!), those with a highly developed sense of service who find themselves called upon to look after aged or infirm relatives (although such duties need not preclude marriage, as I have at least one case on my files of a woman—with the luminaries in conjunction in Virgo in her fourth house—who was married for a number of years and then, after her husband's death, spent the later years of her life caring for an aged mother) or those who are prevented from doing so by circumstances outside their control. The independent types sometimes have a well-developed ambition so that all their time is devoted to self-promotion. Even so, if the career can be furthered by the right type of marriage, they may be prepared to put aside their objections in the cause of self-advancement!

Good looks and physical attractiveness can bring greater opportunities for romance and marriage, though not necessarily so, for there are very few who are so lacking in appeal that nobody regards them as attractive. In some cases, outstanding physical beauty, especially when a well developed sense of integrity is lacking, may prove an attribute of rather doubtful worth as far as the attainment of happiness is concerned. Physical magnetism is usually most strongly accentuated when the fixed signs are tenanted and there are planets in the fifth and eighth houses. When a fifth or eighth house planet in one nativity falls on the Ascendant of another person of the opposite sex, the latter is likely to be fully aware of the other's magnetic qualities.

Aspects between Venus and Uranus are usually an indication of physical attractiveness. The connection between these aspects and the possibility of divorce underlines the fact that physical charms are an attribute that can provide problems for the unevolved. Although a strong and prominent Venus does not necessarily signify that the native is endowed with more than a fair share of good looks, it usually denotes the ability to inspire affection. In cases of abnormal sexual activity, Uranus, which is said to rule the sex glands, is usually prominent.

Charles Carter once pointed out that Landru, the "French Bluebeard," and Madame Steinheil were both born within four days of each other, and both seemed to possess the power to exercise a tremendous fascination over the opposite sex. In both cases, Venus was in Aries, in aspect to every other body in the horoscope except Pluto. The preponderance of fire signs points to the probability that this element may provide the greatest degree of physical attractiveness, though an over-accentuation can indicate much vanity.

Venus is often referred to as the planet of love. This generalization can be very misleading, not only because the word is used nowadays in a variety of different contexts, but because such a generalization tends to draw attention away from the basic principle of Venus, which is the power to establish harmony. Marriage is an exercise in maintaining harmony. If Venus is afflicted in the natus, one may have difficulty in creating an harmonious atmosphere, because of a disinclination to make the extra effort required or the tension created by trying too hard or because circumstances conspire to defeat one's best attempts to live in harmony with others. On the other hand, if Mars is also in aspect to Venus, or the two bodies are in mutual reception, such a combination of the masculine and feminine principles will incline the native to seek the company of the opposite sex, even if not to marry.

While Venus shows, by its sign position and aspectual strength, the native's capacity to create and maintain harmony, the general attitude towards marriage and partnership is shown by the condition of the seventh house of the horoscope, particularly when there is a planet in this house. There may, of course be more than one planet so placed. Aspects to the horizon also play a major role in defining attitudes and the likely course of events in relation to partnerships.

In a male horoscope, the Moon and Venus are the significators of the feminine side of the native's nature and, by extension, of the type of woman to whom he is likely to be attracted. If either body is much afflicted by the malefics, marriage is less likely. In general, aspects from Saturn tend to delay marriage, if not to deny it, while aspects from Uranus introduce a tendency to succumb to sudden attractions (with the possibility of equally sudden disenchantments) and to generally erratic behaviour in sexual relationships, which can bring about sudden changes of emotional allegiance that may well disrupt an existing partnership. Neptunian aspects introduce the possibility of yearning for some ideal emotional experience which may remain elusive and illusionary, unless Saturn is blended harmoniously with Neptune. The desire to realize an ideal is a natural and praise-worthy aim, but if the native fails to understand that the attainment of an ideal is only possible to those who earnestly strive to fit themselves to be worthy of such a blessing, the ultimate result is likely to be a sense of disillusion and complete frustration.

In a female horoscope the Sun and Mars represent the masculine side of the nature and, by extension, the type of man to whom the native is likely to be attracted. When either body is much afflicted by malefic planets, marriage is less likely or the experiences in marriage may call for the exercise of tolerance and fortitude.

Even when, in horoscopes of either sex, there are strong afflictions to the appropriate significators, but the Sun and Moon are harmoniously related by aspect and Venus and Mars are also similarly linked, marriage may still take place. Discordant aspects to marriage significators do not necessarily indicate that a marriage will fail, but it may mean that each partner will have to work that much harder to solve any problems which may arise and will have to make greater sacrifices, with greater efforts towards self-adjustment in order to make the marriage a success.

Traditionally, the first exact aspect to a natal planet formed by the appropriate luminary, as it moves forward in the zodiac on the days after birth, signifies the type of partner and in a general sense, the circumstances of the first meeting and the general character of the marriage. Should no aspect be formed before the Moon in a male horoscope or the Sun in a female horoscope changes signs, this indicates a good deal of difficulty in bringing marriage about. A useful point to bear in mind when comparing the horoscopes of prospective marriage partners is that the planet to which the appropriate luminary first applies (this planet does not have to be in aspect to the luminary at birth) is often rising or prominently placed in the partner's horoscope or it may link with the partner's Sun sign or rising sign. A man in whose horoscope the Moon first applies to Mercury may find that his marriage partner has her Sun or Ascendant in Gemini or Virgo. The application of the luminaries to a retrograde planet does not render this rule less valid, though circumstances may make it less easy for the native to marry. However, men born when Venus is retrograde and women born with Mars retrograde are less inclined to seek the company of the opposite sex.

The first application of the luminaries can only be used as a general guide, for it excludes the possibility in a male horoscope of a lunar type of partner being indicated as the Moon cannot apply to itself! The Moon's first application to a planet in Cancer may, however, go some way towards remedying this deficiency. Similarly, in a female horoscope, a solar type of partner cannot be indicated, unless by the Sun's first application to a planet in Leo.

The associative temperament is most prominent in the water signs, which have been termed fruitful signs. The appropriate significators in these signs usually indicate that marriage will take place. When the sign Libra is well accentuated there is usually a desire for marriage, although strong afflictions involving the sign may deny this.

When the Sun is in Aries, Taurus, Leo and Capricorn there is often an eagerness to marry, which is only slightly less when the Sun is in Libra or Sagittarius. Potentially, Libra is the Sun sign that instinctively realizes the inner purpose of marriage, with the result that any afflictions involving the sign may bring a keener sense of disappointment than other signs would experience over the failure of a marriage.

Certain Gemini and Sagittarius types are restless, difficult to pin down and may lack the stability or inner desire to make a success of marriage and therefore remain bachelors, while some Cancerians prefer the feeling of domestic freedom that comes from living on their own. However, the majority of Cancerians have a strong feeling for family life and will wish to found a family of their own. Afflictions to bodies in Cancer or to its ruler, the Moon, can upset the domestic atmosphere, and if Saturn afflicts the Moon, family ties may intervene to delay marriage. In a male horoscope, this may indicate marriage to an older woman. Similarly, Sun-Saturn aspects in a female nativity can delay marriage or signify an older partner.

It has been observed that in a male horoscope, aspects between the Sun and Uranus tend to denote a rugged individualist who prefers to carve his own way through life. He may therefore regard marriage as a hindrance that prevents him from realizing his appointed destiny.

He wants to be free to display and to enhance his individuality. On the other hand, those with the Sun in aspect to Neptune are more inclined to place much less importance on demonstrating their individuality openly and are more concerned with enlarging their experience by involving themselves more closely with other people. In some cases, they may allow this involvement to reach the stage where they become infatuated with others and even identify themselves with them. If a Sun-Neptune aspect is prominently accentuated there may well be some sympathy with the ideal of polygamy.

In the case of Martian aspects to Uranus and Neptune the situation is reversed. The combination of Mars and Uranus usually indicates a man who is able to project his masculinity in a dynamic way, through a desire to demonstrate his manliness. On this account he is likely to attract the attention of the opposite sex and will take a wife in order to show that he is successfully playing his masculine role. When Mars is in aspect to Neptune, a disproportionate amount of energy may be used up in trying to put ideals into practice and in making dreams come true. The native's wish to have his own way often leads him to over-dramatize issues and exaggerate his troubles, so that problems arise out of incidents that other more stable types might take in their stride. These tendencies can produce difficulties in the marriage relationship, where it is normally the woman's role to provide the more obviously emotional elements. In some cases, when a man with a prominent Mars-Neptune aspect does marry, his wife may find herself in the position of having to compete for first place in his affections with a number of interests and hobbies in which he becomes thoroughly involved.

Aspects to Mercury are often revealing. This planet, which represents the native's intelligence and mental powers, has the quicksilver responses that its name suggests, so that of itself it betokens a restless alertness and ready impressionability. It needs control and guidance, hence it has been referred to as the "Divine Child."

When there is not a sufficiently well disciplined response to the Mercurial ray, there may well be tendencies towards immaturity and restlessness that are not conducive to taking on the responsibilities of marriage and the maintenance of a stable establishment. If Jupiter is in aspect to Mercury, such tendencies may be magnified, while if Saturn is in aspect, they are likely to be diminished. When there is a prominent Jupiter-Mercury aspect, one may be driven by a continual desire to expand one's intellectual horizons, reaching out all the time to acquire fresh knowledge and learn more about the world in which one lives. Such types may regard marriage as something that may severely handicap this perpetual search for knowledge. On the other hand, an aspect from Saturn to Mercury encourages the development of a sense of responsibility and an acceptance of the necessity to establish a stable routine in order to have a firm foundation on which to build, consequently there is a marked inclination to settle down.

Unfortunately, life patterns do not always coincide exactly with text-book interpretations (or there would be no art in delineating horoscopes) and there may be overriding factors which cancel out indications to the contrary suggested by one or two prominent configurations. The Sun, for instance, may be configured with both Uranus and Neptune, which suggests a very special kind of sensitivity that may or may not assist living in close partnership. Mars may be in aspect with both Uranus and Neptune, Mercury with both Jupiter and Saturn. In such cases, other indications will need to be carefully weighed.

As a general rule, men with the Moon and Venus in aspect tend to marry, as do women with the Sun and Mars in aspect. Indeed, the Sun-Mars aspect inclines towards marriage in the nativities of both sexes, since Mars rules the corporeal desires. When it is in aspect to the Sun there is a need to find a suitable outlet for these energies in a satisfying sexual relationship.

The rulers of the first and seventh houses (and of the fifth and seventh houses) in good aspect point to the likelihood of marriage. The same is true if the luminaries are in good aspect to each other, especially as this aspect promises the ability to remove inner psychological discord, thus increasing the power to project an atmosphere of harmony that will attract others.

The Sun in good aspect to Saturn augurs well for loyalty in marriage in the nativities of both sexes, but adverse aspects between the two bodies in a female horoscope may indicate that the husband will be too self-centered, too narrow-minded or apt to suffer from ill health. When Mars afflicts the Sun, some inner disharmony in the native may be reflected in a husband who is inclined to be over-impulsive, quick tempered and aggressive. Jupiter afflictions to the woman's Sun may bring an over-optimistic partner whose high hopes are never matched by his performance, who may squander good opportunities through carelessness or who may be very extravagant. Uranian afflictions suggest a husband whose need for independence may not always allow him to adapt easily to the demands of partnership and who tends to be somewhat restless and unpredictable. Neptunian afflictions are apt to introduce an element of impracticability into the partner's make-up. He may retreat into a world of his own, in some cases resorting to alcohol as a means of forgetting his problems.

Afflictions to the Moon in a man's horoscope tend to work out in a similar way to solar afflictions in a woman's horoscope, as far as his wife's temperament is concerned.

If the appropriate luminary is afflicted by Saturn, Mars and Pluto or by any two of these, marriage may be to a widow or widower.

Aspects between Saturn and Venus may need careful evaluation, as a strong Saturn can inhibit the Venusian capacity for affection and sometimes produce a rather narrow and selfish emotional nature. The emotions may be difficult to arouse or they may run deep, so that the evolved native is capable of much self-sacrificing devotion and loyalty. Sometimes the affliction denotes a very hardheaded attitude towards marriage, so that financial considerations can outweigh all others. In general, the contact favors a lasting marriage with much loyalty and affection if the planets are well placed, but little real harmony and often some coldness if Venus is poorly placed and afflicted.

Aspects from Uranus to Venus sometimes tend to disrupt harmony and can indicate a susceptibility to sudden infatuations that temporarily and sometimes permanently spoil domestic harmony. If either body is in the seventh house (see Elizabeth Taylor's horoscope in Chapter 10) the possibility of divorce is increased. When Venus is aspected by both Saturn and Uranus a situation can arise where the couple decide to separate without formally severing the marriage bond.

Sometimes the elevation of one luminary over another will show which party makes the running in courtship. The man with the Sun elevated and the woman with the Moon elevated will want to take the initiative in seeking a partner, while if the man has the Moon elevated above his Sun and the woman has the Sun elevated above her Moon, they will be inclined to let the opposite sex make the first overtures. The situation will, of course, be modified if the man has the Sun elevated and the woman has the Moon elevated, when each may wish to take the initiative in making their choice. On the other hand, if the positions are exactly reversed, it may be some time before a firm declaration of intent is forthcoming.

PLANETS IN THE SEVENTH HOUSE

One of the clearest indications of the type of partner the native is likely to attract is given by planets in the seventh house. The seventh house of the horoscope represents the not-self. Planets in the seventh indicate qualities that we either do not possess in sufficient strength or that we like to pretend that we do not possess. In an attempt to compensate for this we are likely to seek out those who can encourage or challenge us to develop these qualities in greater measure. We are therefore likely to choose a marriage partner who appears to embody the characteristics of a planet in the seventh house (there may of course be more than one planet here) or of the sign on the cusp if the house is untenanted, as a means of fortifying what may appear to us to be a deficiency in our own make-up. A rising planet denotes a quality that we wish to demonstrate to the world that we possess. A setting planet represents a quality that we are asking the world to supply us with. This is why the seventh house, besides ruling partners, also represents open enemies, who will have no compunction in taking advantage of our weakest points.

When the Sun is in the seventh house, marriage and partnership are likely to assume a paramount role in the life. If the Sun is well aspected, especially by the Moon or Jupiter, a solid and lasting marriage with much domestic happiness may result.

These natives are inclined to seek a partner who can encourage them to be their real self and who may, by example, encourage them to develop more fully powers of inspiration. They will be challenged to display a greater degree of confidence and to exercise authority more effectively and with greater magnanimity.

When the Sun is in the seventh house there can be a tendency to seek a "father figure" and, as the natives may be inclined to surrender the initiative to their partners, they are rather more likely to react than act first themselves, so that their partners may assume a dominant role. If the Sun is much afflicted, there can be a tendency for the partner to be egotistical and autocratic. When the Sun is well supported, the partner is likely to be proud, firm-minded, self-confident, ambitious, honorable, frank and generous, with a well-developed personality.

In some way the native's sense of pride is involved in the choosing of a marriage partner. There may be a wish to gain social prestige and to marry someone who can be admired and respected. If the Sun is much afflicted, an element of jealousy or rivalry may impair the marriage relationship. The need for a partner who is manifestly successful in life may delay marriage, or the successful culmination of the partnership may not arrive until middle life.

To get the best results from any co-operative enterprise these natives must learn to sacrifice any selfish pride and too much desire to have their own way.

The above remarks apply to a lesser degree when the sign Leo is on the seventh cusp.

When the Moon is in the seventh house there may be some indecisiveness in choosing a partner, especially as the native's feelings are somewhat apt to be easily influenced by those with whom he or she comes into contact.

These natives are inclined to seek partners who can bring out their sympathetic side and play on their emotions. With men there is often a tendency to seek a "mother figure" and to bring out in others a desire to mother and protect him. He is therefore likely to attract a partner who is kind and domesticated, though if the Moon is not in a fixed sign she may sometimes want to make changes or travel and, if there are strong afflictions to the Moon, these tendencies could prove rather unsettling. Both partners may need to be on their guard against moody or fickle behaviour. If the Moon is afflicted by Mars or Uranus there may be occasions when difficult emotional situations arise that call for very tactful handling.

Marriage may be undertaken with the object of establishing a home. As a result the domestic qualifications and the family and social background of a prospective partner may acquire a disproportionate priority in the native's reasons for choosing a partner. Often there will be several opportunities for marriage.

When the Moon is afflicted an over-fastidious attitude towards choosing a partner may be a cause of delay in marriage. Nevertheless, marriage tends to be early unless the Moon is aspected by Saturn, while aspects to Uranus may bring sudden developments, so that marriage occurs when the native's friends least expect it, or the alliance may surprisingly break up when there was no apparent sign of a prior rift in the partnership. With an active seventh house Moon the possibility of more than one marriage is likely.

There is usually a compelling emotional need for a partner. In order to get the best results from any co-operative enterprise these natives must learn to control any tendency to be continually at the mercy of their moods, which may result from over-vulnerable feelings. They should try to keep within bounds a tendency to be too dependent on others for their emotional stimuli and they should try to check a constant desire for changes in the nature of the relationship.

The above remarks apply to a lesser degree when the sign Cancer is on the seventh cusp.

When Mercury is in the seventh house much thought may be given to the subject of partnership and marriage and these natives may be inclined to look to marriage principally to provide mental satisfaction. They may therefore seek a partner who can assist them to function more effectively on the intellectual level and who can bring out their ability to adapt and communicate with others. They are likely to look for someone with a lively flow of ideas that challenge them to formulate their own thoughts with greater definition and to express them with greater freedom so that they are able to become increasingly aware of their own intellectual potential. The partner may be volatile, quick-witted and fluent in speech, though under affliction, there is some tendency to attract a restless, highly strung type, who can be outspoken and highly critical. If the afflictions are severe, there may be a high degree of nervousness and even mental unbalance. The partner may be connected with education, or a writer, traveler, salesman, interpreter, secretary or typist.

In order to get the best results from any co-operative enterprise, these natives should learn to control their argumentativeness and desire to criticize, and should endeavor to seek a deep-level foundation for a mutual understanding.

The above remarks apply to a lesser degree when the sign Gemini or Virgo is on the seventh cusp.

When Venus is in the seventh house there is usually much appreciation of the value of relationships, but there can be an inordinate craving for affection which places the partnership on a rather fragile basis. Thus an apparently ideal position for Venus does not invariably bring happiness in marriage, particularly when Venus is much afflicted. The desire for an harmonious marriage may be so strong that any imperfections in the relationship appear larger than life size. These natives are inclined to seek partners who can order their lives harmoniously and who can introduce an element of beauty into their environment. This latter requirement may be represented at least in part, by their partner's attractive physical characteristics. Their sense of emotional well-being depends to a large extent on the smooth co-operation of their partner. This is more likely to be forthcoming if their own affectionate approach is sufficiently demonstrative to draw forth an affectionate response, in which case their partner is more likely to adopt an indulgent attitude towards any shortcomings in their behaviour.

When Venus is well aspected the whole life may be specially enriched by marriage, and there will be a tendency to attract a talented and fortunate partner who will bring the native both material and social benefits. If Venus is debilitated, the partner's moral standards may be open to question or the union may be irregular in some way. Afflictions from Saturn can delay marriage or indicate a union where there is little sexual interest.

Through an over-dependence on the partner to provide the element of harmony, there is a tendency for each to leave it to the other to make the first move towards restoring harmony after a dispute. Should both partners have Venus in the seventh there can be problems, especially when Venus is in a fixed sign and a greater element of pride is involved. In order to get the best results from marriage and partnership, the native should exercise as much control as possible over any tendencies to self-indulgence and avoid over-emphasizing the sensual side of life.

These remarks apply to a lesser degree when the sign Taurus or Libra is on the seventh cusp.

With Mars in the seventh house the energies are most naturally mobilized in seeking to adjust to others and a good deal of stimulus is expected from social contacts. The natives are inclined to seek partners who can rouse them to a more active participation in the world around them, and who can challenge them to show more initiative and increase their sense of combativeness: in other words, a sparring partner! It is difficult for them to exclude the element of challenge from activities involving others. There may be a tendency to play on other people's sense of aggression so that they can see how well they can stand up to another's antagonism. Consequently, the marriage relationship may never run smoothly and indeed, they may regard an unruffled partnership as too dull and boring. They may, therefore, not mind losing battles to a partner who is prepared to carry the fight to them. Insofar as men are traditionally expected to play the dominant role in marriage, this placement may be more suited to a female horoscope where the tendency is to attract a man who is energetic and enterprising. Men with this position tend to attract women who like to lay down the law and generally take the initiative, managing the family finances and making the major decisions as a matter of course. The partner is likely to be very ardent, positive, active, capable and courageous, with a will of her own.

There is a desire for someone who can play the role of a champion or a crusader. Sometimes, this position indicates marriage to a member of the armed forces, the police, or to an athlete or an adventurer. A well placed Mars in the seventh house makes for an association where the passions have full play and a love match with much devotion is possible. The tendency is to marry early, often as a result of love at first sight, although under affliction the native may "marry in haste and repent at leisure."

Afflictions to Mars in the seventh are somewhat critical and may operate to delay or prevent marriage. They may indicate strife and friction in marriage as a result of the partner's hasty temper, intemperance, extravagance, brashness, intolerance (when in aspect to Jupiter) or over-demanding attitude (especially when afflicted by Saturn). When afflictions to Mars from malefics are present partnerships may as a result be short-lived. Sometimes there is a danger of a serious accident to the partner or even their early death.

In order to get the best results from marriage and partnership, the native should try to be as co-operative and easy-going as possible, practicing gentleness and diplomacy rather than allowing any assertive or quarrelsome impluses to gain the upper hand.

These remarks apply to a lesser degree when the sign Aries or Scorpio is on the seventh cusp.

When Jupiter is in the seventh house there are chances of a fruitful, prosperous and successful marriage (especially under good directions) though this position does not automatically guarantee marital happiness. These natives are inclined to seek a partner who can give them the urge to develop a more expansive attitude to life, and to strengthen their faith, deepen their philosophical awareness and understanding and multiply their resources on all levels. They feel that they need a partner's co-operation to help them further develop their moral outlook and social conscience. When both partners have a well placed Jupiter, the marriage may benefit greatly from their desire to place their relationship on the highest possible level of concord and each may bring great comfort to the other.

The partner, who is often a member of one of the professions, may be more affluent than the native and, when Jupiter is well placed and aspected, may possess many sterling qualities. An afflicted, debilitated Jupiter may indicate that the partner is somewhat opinionated, indolent, self-indulgent, extravagant and self-willed, sometimes untrustworthy and profligate. An unreliable partner can be a source of expense, and it has been known for a wife with this position to have to become the breadwinner as the result of her husband losing his job through being an alcoholic.

When Jupiter is afflicted this position can indicate delay in marriage (usually if there is an aspect from Saturn) or strife, disputes and legal battles. In spite of these experiences the native is usually ready to try again when the marriage tie is broken by death or divorce. Adverse aspects from the luminaries to a seventh house Jupiter may deny marriage, but in a female nativity a good aspect to Jupiter from the Sun can indicate marriage to a wealthy widower.

This position indicates that the native is able to bring out the generous and good-natured impulses in others, but in order to get the best results from the marriage partnership he or she may need to control any extravagant tendencies and to prevent pride from unduly affecting the smooth course of the relationship.

These remarks apply to a lesser degree when the sign Sagittarius or Pisces is on the seventh cusp.

When Saturn is in the seventh house there may be a very self-controlled and sometimes calculating attitude towards all forms of partnership. These natives are inclined to seek a partner who will awaken their sense of responsibility and give them a greater sense of purpose and will to succeed. With a woman there may be a subconscious desire to marry a "father figure" and the partner may well feel an urge to organise the native's life on a more effective basis. Other people feel it incumbent upon themselves to supply a steadying influence in the native's life and to provide the element of discipline that seems to be lacking. There is therefore a tendency to attract a more mature type of partner and a possible reluctance to take on the responsibilities of marriage. Alternatively, a fear of being exploited by the partner may operate to delay marriage.

Wherever Saturn is placed we are made more aware of our duty, and when the aspects are favourable and Saturn is not debilitated, this position usually indicates that one loyally abides by marriage vows and faithfully carries out marital duties. This is a position which puts a high premium on the neglect of duty towards the partner, so that if we fall short of our obligations, inevitable retribution will follow.

Under affliction there is a tendency to endure an unhappy marriage rather than to lose face by breaking up an established partnership: "Better the devil you know than the devil you don't!"

Saturn is exalted in the seventh house and requires us to "do unto others as we would be done by." We weigh ourselves in the balance and if we neglect to make our partner happy, our own happiness will be affected in the same proportion.

There may be a tendency to attract a partner to whom one owes a karmic debt in the form of service. Unless there are other indications to the contrary, real enthusiasm for the state of marriage is rarely present and the discipline of marriage may in some cases appear to be an unwelcome restriction. This position is consistent with the possibility of having undertaken a vow of chastity in a previous life.

With a well placed and well aspected Saturn in the seventh house, the partner is likely to be a person of much integrity, faithful, steady, reliable, industrious, persevering and economical, perhaps not over-demonstrative and preferring deeds to words, and providing a real anchor for the partnership. When Saturn is poorly placed and adversely aspected, the partner may act in such a way as to become a burden, and may be uncommunicative, narrow in outlook, cold, over-critical and apt to leave the native to make all the running. In some cases the spouse may be much loved but prone to ill health and may die before the native. Sometimes this situation may arise as a result of having neglected or let down a partner in a previous life. Marriage to a widow or widower is possible.

In order to get the best results from the marriage partnership there is a need to make a special effort to understand the partner as well as possible and to sacrifice all thoughts of self-interest.

These remarks apply to a lesser degree when the sign Capricorn or Aquarius is on the seventh cusp.

When Uranus is in the seventh house there are likely to be some elements in the partnership which are out of the ordinary. Uranus has been identified, and rightly so, as one of the main indicators of divorce, but this does not mean that a seventh house Uranus will inevitably break up a partnership, any more than a seventh house Venus guarantees a permanent or everlastingly blissful marriage. It does suggest, however, that both partners may need greater "elbow room" than most people, so that they do not feel that their liberty is being too much eroded by the need to conform to the normal conventions of the marriage partnership. Their relationship must be capable of growth and the partners should be prepared to take any startling new developments in the relationship in their stride. The greatest threat to the marriage may occur when one partner's capacity for self-development expands at a speed greatly in excess of the other's, so that the spouse may no longer be recognizable as the person he or she was when the marriage took place.

Those with Uranus in the seventh are likely to seek a partner who can supply a dynamic factor in their life, challenging them to become less conventional, more original and inventive and more willing to adopt an experimental approach to the world at large. Marriage may be regarded as an opportunity to extend the frontiers of their experience by enlisting the aid of a partner who can make some unique and creative contribution to the union. Thus they are likely to choose a mate who is something of an individualist, with an unconventional approach to life and an original way of dealing with life's problems. The partner may possess considerable personal magnetism and occasionally a degree of genius, but if Uranus is much afflicted, eccentricities, erratic tendencies and even fanaticism may be present.

The approach to marriage may be highly idealistic or utopian and there may be an inclination to favour platonic unions. On the other hand there may be a tendency to seek excitement in partnerships and, if other indications agree, a marked interest in romantic adventures may result in passing infatuations that can cause a rift with the marriage partner. Sometimes the circumstances of the marriage are such that one of the partners is away from home for long periods, or the husband and wife may maintain separate establishments even although happily married. Cases have been recorded with this position of Uranus where one or both partners have still been at school at the time of the marriage ceremony, returning to their respective schools to be re-united only on week-ends. Other cases have occurred where couples have married purely for companionship, only to discover later that they were truly in love.

The partner may be of a different religion or belong to a different race, and tension may develop as a result of external pressures due to the prejudice and intolerance of the communities concerned.

When Uranus is afflicted, the marriage bond is difficult to maintain. Sometimes the native is not sufficiently tolerant or farseeing to allow his partner sufficient freedom, or to make allowances for the tensions to which a highly strung mate may occasionally be subject. In some cases it seems as if the native goes out of his way to choose a partner who will be unfaithful!

Uranus in the seventh house tests the native's capacity to transcend the ordinary and orthodox view of marriage. Thus it tends to indicate the break-up of a loveless marriage and to exaggerate any tensions which arise through incompatibility of temperament.

In order to get the best results from the marriage partnership, there is a need to go more than halfway to accept the partner's advanced or unorthodox ideas, to appreciate the advisability of not trying to tie the partner down, especially for the sake of "appearances" and to understand the true inner meaning of the marriage relationship and the real nature of true love.

These remarks apply to a lesser degree when the sign Aquarius is on the seventh cusp.

When Neptune is in the seventh house very much depends on the native's real motives for getting married. There is a tendency to idealise marriage and to seek a "soul mate." Unfortunately the cherished ideal may not exist in reality, because the native has not developed to the stage where he or she is worthy to claim such a partner and bring such ideals into practical reality, although a good aspect from Saturn can indicate the possibility of so doing. There may sometimes be a yearning for someone who is inaccessible on account of differences of status, wealth or race.

These natives are likely to seek a partner who can provide a source of inspiration and bring out their capacity for compassion and loving understanding. There can be a tendency to see a prospective partner through rose-colored spectacles or to weave imaginative fantasies about new contacts or hoped for encounters. Consequently there is a possibility that the partner may not be the type of person conjured up by the native's imagination. Cases have been recorded of marriages to bigamists, to those with homosexual tendencies, to alcoholics and to drug addicts. In most of these cases, the native had no previous suspicion of the partner's weaknesses.

There is some tendency to form alliances based on admiration or pity. If Neptune is afflicted or weak by sign, such admiration may have resulted from the native having been dazzled by glamorous externals, while an over-active sense of pity may be exploited by a prospective partner so that the native marries out of sentiment or misplaced sympathy. Sometimes the partner is an invalid.

When Neptune is well placed and well aspected the partner may have sensitive emotional responses which need to be treated tenderly, and a well developed sense of altruism with some talent for artistic self-expression and an interest in the less material side of life, or be connected with activities where the projection of glamour and illusion are a vital factor as, for instance, in the entertainment industry. The partner may have Pisces strongly represented. When Neptune is badly placed and afflicted, there is a tendency to become involved with unreliable, inconstant and somewhat shiftless types whose sympathies may largely be focused upon themselves, or they may be underprivileged in some way, or neurotic, or invalids suffering from chronic ill health.

Sometimes the partner may not be what he or she seems or pretends to be although this can be due in part to the native's unconscious willingness to indulge in self-deception. This position is consistent with a platonic union. Experiences encountered in marriage may be designed to enable the native to take a more compassionate view of the failings of others. With an afflicted Neptune in the seventh some types may instinctively suspect that the marriage relationship could bring disappointments and unhappiness, so they remain single. Should they marry, the union may not be consummated or may fall short of what might reasonably have been expected.

In order to get the best results from the marriage relationship the native must learn to sacrifice vague yearnings for an unattainable ideal, to control any tendency to be carried away by shallow romanticism and to be as clear-headed and practical as possible when assessing the virtues and attractions of prospective mates.

These remarks also apply to a lesser degree when the sign Pisces is on the seventh cusp.

When Pluto is in the seventh house an element of inevitability may enter into the partnerships formed by these natives. They are inclined to seek a partner who will provide a challenge to discover new resources within themselves that will give them the power to transcend previous performances and to transform certain aspects of their being. The partner's intrinsic qualities and way of going about things may cause the discarding of some of the more superficial aspects of the personality in order to discover more of the real individual underneath. There is a tendency to admire well developed will power in others, with the result that the natives may attract those who tend to dominate them, possibly feeling that if they have to cope with a somewhat overpowering personality they may discover more effectively the full extent of their own resources. When these natives feel that they are not able to handle such a partner with sufficient skill, they may resent their predicament and place the blame for it squarely on their partner. Sometimes there may be a "Svengali" type of relationship.

Pluto is a planet which encourages total commitment, so that the partner is likely to react strongly if the native falls short in this respect. Psychologically, natives with Pluto in the seventh have a vital need to co-operate with others and they sense that in some way partnership will contribute to their growth as individuals and enable them to develop an inner strength. Consequently they are likely to attract those who are capable of having a dynamic impact on their life, eventually compelling in them some form of metamorphosis.

An afflicted Pluto in the seventh may pose searching problems and much will depend on the nature of the planets in aspect to Pluto, because the qualities denoted by these planets are apt to be intensified, so that any shortcomings on either side may be difficult to cope with unless both partners are prepared to make a determined effort to work on themselves in order to remedy such defects.

When Pluto is well placed and aspected the partner may be rather self-contained and self-sufficient, with a strong sense of purpose, and with those qualities denoted by the sign in which Pluto is placed, well developed and accentuated. If Pluto is badly placed and aspected, the spouse's iconoclastic attitude and cynical disregard for any considerations other than his or her own welfare or special interests may involve the native in cliff-hanging situations that require taking over all the partner's responsibilities or having to clear up the wreckage of the marriage after the partner has decamped. Pluto in the seventh house challenges the native to find a thoroughly secure and deep-level basis for partnership. It may sometimes happen that before this can be achieved, unfinished business from a relationship occurring in a previous life has first to be satisfactorily cleared up. In order to get the best results from the marriage partnership these natives must learn to recognize their own inner and essential nature, observing themselves with enough objectivity and detachment to place a correct evaluation on all their motives, especially when they find that their partner leads them into liaisons which are not in their best interests. They must be prepared to "stretch themselves" and to utilise all their resources to the full, dedicating themselves to the task of self-development particularly insofar as their ability to relate to others is concerned.

These remarks apply in a lesser degree when the sign Scorpio is on the seventh cusp.

MULTIPLE MARRIAGES

Multiple marriages may occur when the Moon or Venus in a male nativity are in Gemini, Sagittarius and Pisces, especially when they are in aspect to other bodies in mutable signs, and when Uranus is in aspect to Venus. Tommy Manville, whose numerous marriages caused him to be the subject of considerable publicity, was born with Venus in Pisces in square to the Moon, Jupiter, Neptune and Pluto in Gemini. Henry VIII had Venus in Gemini, with the Moon's North Node, and at the mid-point of Mars and Saturn, denoting the violent end of two of his wives and the natural but untimely death of another.

In a female nativity, more than one marriage may take place if the Sun or Mars are in Gemini, Sagittarius or Pisces, especially if they are in aspect to other bodies in mutable signs, and when Venus is in aspect to Uranus. Elizabeth Taylor has the conjunction of Venus and

Uranus in the seventh house (see page 302). Mary Anita Loos was born with Venus on the Midheaven in square to Uranus in the seventh.

A double-bodied sign on the seventh cusp can indicate more than one marriage and several planets in the seventh can sometimes indicate the number of partners. William Lilly had Neptune on the seventh cusp and Mars and Jupiter in the seventh house. He described his second wife as being "of the nature of Mars." The appropriate luminary applying to aspects of more than one planet before it leaves the sign it is in may be an additional testimony that the native will marry more than once. A second marriage partner is said to be ruled by the ninth house, a third by the eleventh and so on.

Separation and divorce may occur when the Moon in a male chart, and the Sun in a female nativity, applies to an adverse aspect of a malefic, especially when Venus is afflicted. Uranus in the seventh house can denote a sudden termination to a relationship, especially when adversely aspected and in aspect to the seventh cusp. Uranus afflicting the Moon in a male horoscope or the Sun in a female horoscope can also denote divorce, though this will be more likely when the seventh house is involved in some way or the sign Libra is tenanted by one of the two bodies.

PLANETS IN LIBRA

Planets in Libra, the seventh sign, give an indication of how one is likely to apply one's various drives and resources in order to maintain harmony in relationships.

When the Sun is in Libra, the establishment of harmony can become a major aim in the life, as these natives tend to identify this activity with their sense of pride and self-esteem as well as with their need for achievement. Thus, if the Sun is well aspected there is every chance of building smooth relationships, while adverse aspects are likely to denote difficulties arising as a result of their wounded pride and the belief that they have been unfairly treated.

The Moon in Libra indicates that the feelings are very much involved in the creation of an harmonious atmosphere. An ability to sense instinctively how best to adjust to others can greatly assist in putting them at their ease. Social acceptance is important, and partnership is appreciated as something that can confer mutual benefits, so that even when the feelings are hurt there can be a tendency to "put a good face on it." When the Moon is much afflicted this capacity, even if not diminished, may have well-defined limits, beyond which these natives are not prepared to go. They may abandon their efforts to maintain harmony because too much emotional stress is involved.

With Mercury in Libra, harmony is largely an intellectual concept. The meeting of minds is important and mental compatibility may be the quality most desired in partnership. There may be a tendency to believe that any disharmony can be removed "if only we can talk it over," while if Mercury is much afflicted, there may be too little attention to the partner's point of view, or the partner may be argumentative or quarrelsome, especially if these natives try too frequently to score intellectual points in their discussions.

Venus in Libra is, theoretically speaking, ideally placed. The natives seek to express their affections in the most harmonious way they can. An inner desire for peace can make for an excellent marriage relationship if Venus is strong and well aspected. Under affliction, there may be a tendency to seek peace at any price, to make a habit of being nice to everyone and of not being able to say "no." Thus jealousy may be aroused in the partner. There is sometimes a love of romance for its own sake, so that partnerships are entered upon just to indulge this need.

There may be a tendency to over-idealize the concept of marriage or the kind of partner envisaged, especially if Venus is aspected by Neptune, so that any falling short in the realization of this cherished ideal can produce considerable disappointment or frustration. There is sometimes a need for a wide variety of emotional experience, while a well developed tactical sense may be used to play one prospective partner off against another. The power to arouse an affectionate response from others may not always be used widely.

When Mars is in Libra the energies are totally committed to the establishment of a satisfactory state of equilibrium in the life and the passions require fulfillment through a spirited response from the partner. There may be a wish to take the lead in all co-operative enterprises as well as to make the running in courtship and to take the major initiative in marriage. Under affliction, these natives may become quarrelsome when they feel that they are losing the initiative.

The very fact that they are prepared to put so much energy into building an harmonious relationship may rebound against them in the form of energetic opposition from those who do not appreciate the forthright method of approach. This position of Mars can make these natives resentful if they feel they are receiving less than justice from their partners.

Jupiter in Libra is theoretically another excellent testimony of an ability to build an harmonious atmosphere around one's self, but in practice it often happens that the so-called benefic planets can produce more psychological difficulties than the malefics. An expansive attitude to the establishment of harmony and a well-developed sense of proportion can often result in a prosperous and fruitful union, so that this position tends to diminish the chances of marriage ending in divorce. A desire to improve the status through marriage often results in the native choosing a partner from one of the professions. Under affliction there may be a tendency to place a greater value on the improvement of social status than upon the establishment of a union based on true love. There may be more concern to demonstrate to the world that the marriage has been successful rather than that it has been a happy one. Much expense may be incurred through partnership, perhaps on account of the marriage partner's extravagant tastes.

Saturn in Libra natives enlist their security drives to help them establish partnerships on as sound and practical a basis as possible. A strong sense of duty can make them very much aware of their obligations as a partner. They may take great trouble to find a mate who is able to demonstrate a similar integrity. They may therefore marry at a later age than most, or choose an older partner or a contemporary who is apt to be austere or undemonstrative. A desire for perfection may make them too demanding in the marriage relationship or their view of marriage may be too conventional or old fashioned. When Saturn is afflicted they may be cold or regard marriage as a yoke with which they do not care to burden themselves. Alternatively, they may tell themselves that they will never find a partner who will measure up to their requirements. A parent may interfere in the marriage. If Saturn is much afflicted the partner may die or the marriage may break up, not necessarily leading to divorce. When well aspected, Saturn in Libra is likely to indicate an enduring relationship.

Uranus in Libra natives will hope to gain some extra stimulus through partnership that will provide them with a new level of experience and enable them to feel in some way that they have gained a greater degree of freedom. The wider horizons that they seek may merely result in a belief that they should be free to change partners when they feel that they have outgrown a relationship. A desire to experiment in partnership may cause them to regard the conventional forms of marriage as too restricting, if not actually obsolete. An extreme example occurred when Uranus last entered Libra a few years ago and in Copenhagen (ruled by 1° Libra) the Danish parliament introduced a Bill to legalise "marriage" between homosexuals. This position of Uranus can bring an idealistic and forward looking attitude to marriage and a desire to invest the union with something more than the conventional significance, so that when the native is completely in tune with the Uranian vibration a most rewarding union is possible. However, this is rather a crucial position for Uranus, which tests the native's inner balance and demands a fair degree of moral integrity and native wisdom. Under much affliction this position may indicate difficulty in maintaining a stable partnership and may best be described as "divorce prone."

Neptune in Libra signifies that these natives channel their sense of idealism and any desire to seek transcendental experiences in their search to establish a significant rapport with those around them. Neptune represents the native's capacity for compassionate understanding and the raising of the sympathies to hypersensitive levels, so that the need to establish a partnership where there is no disharmony to disturb the perfect balance of the partnership is therefore paramount. It follows that any imperfections in a marriage relationship may give rise to the keenest feelings of disillusion and disappointment if the native has failed to accept that ideals are seldom realized at the physical level without being considerably modified, and only as a result of much effort at self-purification. Marriage is envisaged ideally as the perfect merging of two individuals in some form of mystical union. The quest for a soul mate may result in the relinquishing of any hope of finding true compatibility, or in a tendency to invest any contemplated partnership with an aura of blissful unreality that does not make for a firm and lasting relationship. There may be a highly spiritual union or a platonic marriage.

Unless a clear-sighted and practical view of marriage is cultivated, these natives may be self-deceived about the true nature of their partners or they may be deceived by their spouses. When Neptune is much afflicted the partner may be subject to much illness or predecease the native by some considerable time.

When Pluto is in Libra the native has a paramount need to establish harmony in relationships. The marriage partnership may appear to be the most effective channel through which these natives can achieve some form of regeneration, bringing all their inner resources of character to bear on the task of building a truly meaningful relationship. This position places a premium on successfully adjusting to others, so that if Pluto is much afflicted there may be a tendency for these natives to disassociate themselves from all relationships where true harmony is lacking. The marriage relationship can dominate the whole life, and any imperfections may be keenly felt with the result that these natives may feel compelled to dig deep within themselves to discover the cause. If Pluto is much afflicted, relationships are apt to be terminated with great finality. Occasionally this may be brought about by the death of the partner, or in other cases these natives may have no compunction in blaming their partners for the failure of the marriage. There is a great need for harmony and therefore a happy marriage can be a particularly rewarding experience, while a disastrous union can have a correspondingly adverse effect. Much will depend upon the aspects to Pluto.

Planets in Cancer give some idea of the approach to domestic life and the native's ability to settle down to establishing a home and family. When there are squares between planets in Cancer and Libra, the chances of building a really firm foundation for marriage are to some extent diminished.

PART OF MARRIAGE

Aspects to the Part of Marriage are often indicative of the chances of a successful and happy marriage, according to the sign tenanted and which planets are in closest aspect to the Part which is located as many degrees from the seventh cusp of a nativity as Venus is distant from the Ascendant but on the same side of the horizon as Venus. Thus, if Venus is ten degrees below the Ascendant, the Part of Marriage will be located ten degrees below the Descendant. If Venus is 22 degrees above the Descendant, the Part of Marriage will then fall twenty-two degrees above the Ascendant. The Part can be calculated from the formula: Longitude of Ascendant + Longitude of Descendant - Longitude of Venus, though with a little practice its position will be obvious from a visual inspection.

If Venus is in square to the Ascendant, it follows that the Part will also be in square to the Ascendant. If Venus is on the Ascendant, the Part will be in opposition to Venus. In these situations, the strength of Venus and the aspects to it are crucial and unless Venus is well supported, its aspects to the Part of Marriage are not necessarily productive of harmony.

The use of the seventh cusp in determining where the Part falls, suggests that this Part shows how others are likely to respond to the way in which we project our desire to achieve harmony. Aspects to the Part (and they should be close) will then indicate how marriage will be likely to work out. As in other branches of astrology, favorable aspects from well placed planets are helpful and unfavorable aspects from badly placed planets can be interpreted as danger signals. Such contacts with the Part represent those elements in our psyche which will help to consolidate, or provide a threat to, our marriage. Additionally they may also indicate karmic factors that have a bearing upon the marriage relationship.

In astrology it is often the extreme cases which throw most light on the subject. Nicholas Culpeper, the famous herbalist, suffered a shattering blow on the eve of his marriage when his bride to be was struck dead by lightning while on her way to the marriage rendezvous. His Part of Marriage on the eighth cusp was five degrees from Mars, but its antiscion fell on his Lower Meridian in between a close conjunction of Saturn and Pluto. The fourth house affliction also had some relationship to the marriage of his parents, since his mother was widowed after only a year of marriage.

In the horoscope of a lesbian, who turned against men because of her intense dislike of her father, shown by a close Sun-Saturn conjunction in Capricorn, the Part of Marriage fell at the mid-point of this conjunction.

An aspect of the Sun to the Part appears to have a stabilizing effect, showing a whole-hearted involvement in the business of living harmoniously with a partner. If the Sun is much afflicted, pride may prove to be a stumbling block. In any case marriage is likely to be regarded as a most important factor in the life and much emphasis may be placed on the partner's worldly standing. In one instance a woman with the Part in close conjunction with the Sun, announced her express intention of marrying a millionaire!

A contact with Jupiter is usually helpful. Saturn, while providing a stabilising influence, can introduce an element of delay, as in the cases of Hitler and Eva Braun, whose legal union did not take place until hours before their suicide. In another case a trine to the Part of Marriage from a debilitated seventh house Saturn signified a disastrous marriage, due in part to the frigidity and coldness of the native.

An aspect from Uranus can, though not invariably, indicate divorce, while Neptune, which can introduce an element of idealism, is often not a very stabilising factor. Sometimes the partner may become an invalid. Pope Paul IV, sworn to celibacy by the nature of his calling, had the Part conjoined Mars and trine Neptune, so that a dedication to the ideal of marriage was transmuted and symbolically translated into a wedding with Mother Church. An aspect with Pluto is not always helpful, seeming to introduce an element of intensity which is hard to handle.

Aspects from Mars depend greatly upon this planet's condition by sign and aspect and reflect the extent to which the native's passions are likely to be satisfied or frustrated by the marriage relationship. In one instance, a trine from Mars in Scorpio to the Part in Pisces was the indicator of an early widowhood.

Mercury does not appear to play a large part in influencing the circumstances of the marriage though it can sometimes signify marriage to a younger partner. Aspects to the Moon depend a great deal upon the sign and house in which that luminary is placed. Norma Shearer, who married her employer, had the Part sextile the Moon in Leo in her tenth house. Edith Piaf, whose husband was considerably younger, had the Part in sextile to the Moon in Gemini in the seventh house.

Aspects to the Part from planets in Libra can be crucial, while the placement of the Part itself in Libra also seems to give it greater emphasis. The Part does not appear to be well placed in Pisces, where some element of sacrifice may be called for.

One would expect to find significant aspects to the Part of Marriage in the actual marriage horoscope and the charts in my files suggest that this may indeed be so. Again, much depends on the radical position of the planets concerned. A trine of an unafflicted Saturn to the Part occurs in a long and well established marriage, but the same aspect from a debilitated and afflicted seventh house Saturn reflects a disastrous union between another couple. In a marriage where the death of the husband occurred after only a few years, the Part is at the mid-point of a Venus-Pluto conjunction, and in another case where the wife considerably pre-deceased her husband, the Part was conjunct Mars and in sextile to the mid-point of a Sun-Pluto conjunction. There was also a trine to Neptune in Libra and the couple appeared to be ideally suited to each other. Another marriage chart with Neptune in Libra in square to the Part related to a marriage which was soon dissolved.

In two rather extreme cases, the Part was severely afflicted. In one case the wife was constantly nagging her husband and at times resorted to physical violence. Eventually the husband obtained a divorce on the grounds of his wife's persistent cruelty. The Part was in square to a Sun-Pluto conjunction. In the other case, the newly married husband took his wife to their new home where she found that his mistress was already installed. He told them that he loved them both. The new wife walked out after just one hour. The Part was conjunct the Moon and Uranus in Gemini!

In general the quality of the aspects to the Part appears to reflect the quality of the marriage and the general remarks as to the nature of aspects to the Part of Marriage in individual nativities can be applied also to the aspects present in the Marriage horoscope.

One might reasonably expect to find significant aspects to the Part in "First Meeting" horoscopes but I do not have enough of these to assert categorically that this is so. On the other hand it will be found that there are significant contacts with the Part from the marriage partner's horoscope.

The fact that the seventh house, besides being the house of marriage, is also the house of open enemies may at first sight appear incongruous, except to a mysoginist, but this is a logical pairing since we tend instinctively to seek in a partner those qualities that we may neglect to develop in ourselves or that we may actually lack. Therefore these qualities are the very ones that can damage us most when used against us by an enemy. The seventh house represents our attitude towards co-operation so that malefics in the seventh, and in Libra, especially when afflicted, may signify the occasional breakdown of amicable relations.

The course of other relationships in the horoscope may be traced by an examination of the appropriate houses and planets. Friends come under the eleventh house. Our capacity for making friends and our experiences in friendship may be estimated from the condition of planets in the eleventh house and in Aquarius (if any), from the nature of the sign on the eleventh cusp and the aspects to the cusp and its ruler. Benefics in the fifth and eleventh houses, unless afflicted or debilitated by sign, augur well for the formation of rewarding friendships that remain a lasting source of satisfaction.

If we work for others, our employer and those whom he delegates to serve in a supervisory capacity are shown in general way by the Sun, by the condition of any planets in the tenth house or Capricorn (if any), by the sign on the Midheaven and the aspects to the planet ruling that sign. Strong close aspects to the Midheaven may also be significant. If we employ others or supervise their labors, our experiences in the relationship are determined by the condition of any planets in the sixth house or in Virgo, by the sign on the sixth house cusp, aspects to the cusp and its ruler, and in a general way by aspects to Mercury. Relationships with neighbors are shown by the condition of Mercury, and any planets in Gemini or in the third house, together with the sign on the third house cusp, the aspects to the cusp and its ruler.

Relatives are indicated in the horoscope by various houses. Parents are shown by the fourth and tenth houses and, in a general way, the Sun and Saturn represent the father and the Moon represents the mother. Brothers and sisters are represented by Mercury and the third house, uncles and aunts by Jupiter and the sixth house (which is the third house counting from the fourth cusp, therefore the parents' brothers and sisters). This method of deriving subsidiary house rulerships is a technique derived from horary astrology, and it is open to question as to how far it is possible to keep going round the houses in order to derive subsidiary meanings. In theory we could arrive at a house which signified our brother's neighbour's employer's wife (which will be the eighth house of our horoscope) but this type of re-allocation is not particularly effective or even desirable.

The point may not have escaped readers that the third house, for instance, can represent brothers and sisters (or more accurately our attitude to them and the type of response it is likely to evoke) as well as neighbours, with Mercury also representing both in a general way. If we further extend the significance of the third house, according to the practice outlined above, it can also represent any secret enemies of the parents, the wife of a brother-in-law and so on. This means that the same few significators have to do duty for a wide variety of relationships and comparatively casual contacts.

Should we require to examine the quality of a relationship with one of the many individuals signified by the third house, we can much more effectively deal with the matter (provided we have the necessary birth data) by applying the rules of synastry in a comparison of our own horoscope with that of the individual concerned.

CHAPTER 2

Marriage Horoscopes and other Inceptional Charts

It is a fundamental principle of astrology that the birth moment of any project contains within it all the potentials for development that may arise from that particular happening or action. It is for this reason that the horoscope for the start of a human life is so important, although it might be argued that the horoscope for conception is even more significant. Unfortunately it is almost impossible to determine the correct time of this event (which is not the same time as that determined by the Pre-Natal Epoch) although a formula may one day be discovered.

A horoscope cast for the time when we first meet somebody will indicate the whole course of that relationship and such a chart can be an invaluable guide should the contact develop into one of particular significance. Unfortunately very few of us take the trouble to acquire the habit of recording the time when we first meet a new acquaintance, and it is not always possible to note the exact details if we are introduced to a large group of people within a comparatively short time. Only a small proportion of contacts may prove to have an important effect on the life, and it is therefore understandable that astrologers often neglect to register the time of first meetings, since much of the data thus accumulated would be of little value. However, when two people consult an astrologer in order to know more about the potentialities of their relationship, a great deal of additional astrological information about the quality of their relationship will be available if they are able to recall the moment when they first met.

The planetary positions in the horoscope for the moment of first meeting will, of course, be the transits operative in the horoscopes of the two parties involved and so the significance of the meeting horoscope cannot be fully appreciated unless the nativities of the couple are carefully compared with it. If the transits should favourably aspect one nativity and not the other, it may be that the attraction will not be mutual and one of the parties will wish to develop the association while the other may not. The progressed positions in the individual nativities should give further indications about the potentials of the association, especially as some of the transits at the time of meeting may trigger off significant directions.

The horoscope for the time of first meeting can often be judged accurately without reference to the nativities of those involved. In a case well known to the writer, a man first met the woman whom he subsequently married when the Sun was almost exactly in conjunction with Uranus and in trine to Jupiter in Libra. The Sun ruled the ascendant of the chart and Pluto was rising in Leo. The man in the case, although an astrologer, was not at the time particularly aware of the importance of the moment of first meeting, nor did he sense that the relationship might later turn out to be one of the most highly significant in his life. Soon after the first meeting circumstances decreed that the couple should go their separate ways for some three years. In the meantime the astrologer formed the opinion that his own directions indicated he was soon likely to marry, and had even decided upon an exact date and made a written prediction which he placed in a sealed envelope and deposited with a third party. There was only one point which remained uncertain; at that time he had no prospective partner in mind! Suddenly, out of the blue, he received a letter from the young lady he had first met three years earlier, suggesting that it would be pleasant if they could arrange to meet again. Suddenly, the astrologer realised the implications of this suggestion in the light of the directions forming in his own horoscope. Carefully back-tracking, he was able to estimate with a fair degree of accuracy the moment of their first meeting. It was not long before he had established that the Sun-Uranus conjunction in the meeting horoscope fell exactly on the degree of the Moon in the young woman's nativity, while the Moon in the meeting horoscope was conjunct the woman's Mars and in opposition to her Sun. Venus in conjunction with Saturn opposed the man's Sun, which was the ruler of his natal seventh house (and by progression in trine to his own Moon and the woman's ascendant). Jupiter, in trine to the Sun and Uranus from the sign Libra in the first meeting horoscope, was also the ruler of the woman's seventh house.

Within six months of renewing their relationship, the couple were married on the actual day that the astrologer had forecast several months previous to the renewal of their friendship.

It is perhaps necessary to add that every first meeting between members of the opposite sex that takes place under beneficent Venusian and seventh house configurations does not necessarily result in marriage. Each party, for instance, may already be happily married, or differences in age or circumstances may rule out the possibility of marriage. There is, however, every chance that a rewarding companionship may be developed so that each feels very much at home in the other's company. On the other hand, there can be cases of extremely harmonious first meeting horoscopes where, probably for lack of opportunity the relationship never develops or matures, even though the two concerned may be very well disposed towards each other. In such cases the explanation will probably lie in their progressed horoscopes or else in a comparison of the two nativities which may reveal some inhibiting factor.

A first meeting horoscope between a middle-aged man and a girl in her teens shows Libra rising with Jupiter in the seventh house, in square to Venus on the Midheaven. The luminaries are in conjunction and in sextile to Mars, while Neptune is in trine to Venus. An immediate rapport was established between the two and although they are of different nationalities they have always been able to communicate freely with each other, often with a lively flow of ideas. The introduction took place through the man's niece and Jupiter, the planet ruling uncles, was in the seventh house of relationships in the first meeting chart, thus almost automatically the girl regarded their relationship as that of uncle and niece.

The first meeting horoscope can be progressed by any valid method. If the relationship is a significant one, the progressions and transits will furnish accurate indications of the unfolding pattern of that relationship.

While only a small proportion of life's contacts may turn out to be highly significant, no relationship is without a purpose. When two people meet who are subsequently to play an important role in each other's lives, the time of their first meeting is truly a "moment of destiny."

THE MARRIAGE HOROSCOPE

First meetings usually happen by chance, but the time of marriage can be chosen, not always to the minute, perhaps, as a good deal may depend upon the availability of and the amount of co-operation from the official who is to perform the ceremony. Those with a knowledge of astrology will no doubt try, as the writer did, to choose a time when the planetary indications appeared to favour a high degree of harmony and happiness. It is once again necessary to stress that nothing can come to pass that is not shown in the nativity and however favorable the time chosen may be, if a successful and happy marriage is not indicated in the birth horoscope, the choice of a "good" marriage day will not alter these natal indications.

Even so, there is no point in choosing a "difficult" day on which to marry. While thousands of couples may never give a thought as to whether the day is "propitious" or not and may gravitate instinctively towards the day most in tune with their own marriage destiny, most astrological students would like to feel that they had done all they could to give destiny a helping hand, and therefore opt for a marriage date and time that appeared to promise the best chances of success. There is no guarantee, of course, that they might not have chosen the same date without astrological guidance. Also, it might not always be possible to find an ideal day during the period within which one wishes to get married.

In a case known to the writer, an astrologer chose a time for his wedding that placed a Venus-Jupiter conjunction on the day in exact trine to his Ascendant only to find out later that his birth time was, in fact, half an hour earlier, which rendered the trine inoperative as far as his Ascendant was concerned. However, the conjunction was still in trine to his ruler, while the Moon at the time of marriage, not apparently in contact with any factor in the nativity now fell almost exactly on the Lower Meridian, so that even when making his choice on the basis of an incorrect birth time, the astrologer was still able to choose a time which fitted in most appropriately with his own true nativity.

The question is sometimes asked as to why the marriage ceremony should be regarded as of such crucial astrological importance. Generally speaking, all rituals have an importance over and beyond anything their external celebration might signify. The fact that the union receives official recognition and is duly proclaimed before all those present at the ceremony means that as far as the religious and civil authorities are concerned, and in the eyes of the community at large, the moment when the couple are pronounced man and wife is the moment when the marriage officially begins.

I well remember the case of an astrologer who told me that he was proposing to get married on a day when there was a conjunction of Mars and Saturn in Libra (with Neptune not far away) in close square to Uranus in Cancer, which was in trine to a debilitated Venus in Scorpio. When I suggested that no astrologer in his right mind would deliberately choose to marry under such configurations he replied that he regarded the time of the wedding ceremony as immaterial, since he had already had sexual relations with his bride to be and he regarded the real "marriage" horoscope as dating from that time. No amount of persuasion would change his opinion that the time of the legal ceremony was relatively unimportant. He accordingly married, as planned, and within two or three years the girl he married, who was young enough to have been his daughter, grew tired of the relationship and walked out. He did not long survive the breakup of the marriage and died of a heart disease which could well have been aggravated by his emotional distress.

In order to choose the best time to marry it is desirable to select a day when those configurations are present in the heavens which most nearly reflect the factors that one would expect to find in a nativity promising a happy marriage. A favorable aspect between the luminaries; between Venus and Mars and Venus and Jupiter; good aspects to planets in Libra or Cancer; the benefics and luminaries prominently placed; Venus dignified by sign and not combust, cadent or retrograde and free from affliction by the malefics; a good aspect to the Ascendant from the benefics; a strong seventh house free from affliction, with good aspects to the ruler of the Ascendant and the seventh house, are all desirable features, while the Moon and Fortuna should be configured as favorably as possible, with the Moon applying to a good aspect of Venus and Jupiter and preferably increasing in light and motion and, if possible, having passed the first quarter. If rising, the Moon should not be in conjunction with a malefic or a quarrelsome atmosphere may prevail.

It is unlikely that a time will be found incorporating all these features. A strong and well aspected Venus, and the rulers of the first and seventh houses well aspected, and the Moon fairly free from affliction should be given priority when a time is being selected. Because the horoscope of marriage is also a summary of the transits on the wedding day to the nativities of both husband and wife, it will become increasingly obvious that the selection of a suitable time to marry, a time that produces a horoscope indicative of a happy and lasting marriage, and one that is favorably configured in all important respects with the nativities of both partners, is not always easy to find. Since it has been said that "the course of true love seldom runs smooth," it may well be that a "too perfect" marriage chart is not as desirable as it may seem.

Wherever the Moon may be, it is better for it not be applying to an aspect of Mars or Saturn.

Although much may depend on the interaction of the marriage horoscope with the nativities of the husband and wife, it is a valid horoscope in its own right, being sensitive to transits and capable of being progressed by any valid directional system.

When progressed and converse planets in the horoscopes of both partners form aspects to planets or angles in the first meeting and marriage charts these may well indicate modifications or developments in the relationship, according to the planets involved, so that first meeting and marriage horoscopes can furnish useful additional information to the astrologer when he is estimating the possibilities and potentialities of a partnership.

The various houses of the marriage chart may be interpreted in the usual way. Afflictions involving the second house may relate to financial problems, those involving the fifth, to problems arising through the wayward behaviour or ill health of children, and so on. It follows that the malefics angular, especially when afflicted, are best avoided and a too active Uranus, involved with the luminaries, Venus or the seventh house may indicate the possibility of divorce or the break-up of the marriage.

In the horoscope for a marriage that took place on 6th October, 1945, at 2:30 p.m. G.M.T. (50N50; 0W10), 19 Capricorn rises. Mars and Saturn, eight degrees apart, bracket the seventh cusp and the Moon in 17 Libra is in square to the setting conjunction from the eighth house. Venus is in Virgo on the cusp of the eighth in square to Uranus on the cusp of the fifth house. Altogether there are five bodies in Libra in the eighth house and all the planets, plus the Sun, are within the containing trine of the Moon and Uranus. Pluto is in the seventh at the mid-point of Uranus and Neptune. It would be difficult to find a more disastrous configuration under which to start a marriage. The marriage lasted about six weeks, during which time the husband enlisted his wife's unwilling aid in carrying out a burglary. Most of the time he apparently kept her drugged (he was a qualified doctor) and she had no prior knowledge of his felonious activities. After the marriage broke up she spent a number of years trying to make restitution in respect of the goods stolen by her husband, which she regarded as an obligation that she was morally bound to discharge. Notice the six bodies, including both luminaries, in the eighth house (other people's money). Her natal Sun conjunct Saturn fell on the seventh cusp of the marriage horoscope.

Another marriage that took place a little earlier in 1945, occurred on 28th July at 10:20 a.m. Double Summer Time in London. The Ascendant of the marriage horoscope in 16° Virgo, was exactly configured with an opposition of the Moon and the square of Uranus, but at the same time Saturn was in sextile to the rising degree and therefore in trine to the Moon. In the light of subsequent events it is important to record that Saturn was debilitated in Cancer and on the cusp of the eleventh house. The Midheaven in 12° Gemini was at the mid-point of Venus and Mars. Jupiter and Venus were in angular houses but in square to each other and the rising Jupiter was debilitated. Mercury, ruling the Ascendant, was in conjunction with Mars and in trine to Neptune in Libra. The Moon was decreasing in light, in aspect to Uranus and a debilitated Saturn but applying to an opposition of Jupiter. The marriage was a happy one and from relatively humble beginnings the young couple gradually established themselves on a sound financial footing with a pleasant home and a family of three sons (one of them adopted) and a daughter.

After twenty years the secondary progressed Mars had reached the conjunction of the radical and progressed Uranus, and was therefore in square to both the Ascendant and the radical Moon. At the same time the Mars-Uranus conjunction opposed the wife's Sun-Uranus mid-point. In the previous year a conjunction of the converse luminaries had fallen on the radical Saturn and the Sun was beginning to pass through the three degree arc between the radical and converse Saturn. It was in the twentieth year of the marriage that the full impact of the radical configuration was released. After the wife was recovering from an apparently successful operation for cancer, the eldest son was killed in a car crash. The shock of this tragedy brought about a rapid deterioration in the wife's condition and she died within a few weeks. A novel feature of the marriage was the special attraction that cats held for both partners, and there were seldom less than six or seven cats strolling around their house. For a time they bred Siamese cats. There were some who suspected that the cats may have had a connection with the onset of the wife's cancer.

The mid-point of the husband's Mars-Jupiter trine fell on the Ascendant of the marriage chart as did the mid-point of his wife's close Sun-Moon and Venus-Uranus conjunctions. Uranus in the marriage chart fell on the husband's South Node, while the rising Jupiter fell on his Sun. Mars in the marriage horoscope was on his Midheaven, and the mid-point of the Sun-Neptune sextile in the marriage horoscope fell on the ruler of his Ascendant, Mercury, and in square to the mid-point between his wife's Saturn and her Venus-Uranus conjunction. This latter conjunction was squared by Mars in the wedding chart. Pluto in the wedding horoscope fell on her Jupiter-Neptune conjunction in square to her Mars. The horizon of their eldest son's nativity exactly reversed the Meridian of the marriage chart and his Sun exactly squared this axis. The son's Pluto-Neptune mid-point exactly opposed his natal Sun so that his natal horizon, forming a grand cross with his Sun and Pluto-Neptune mid-point, linked him tragically with the Meridian of the marriage horoscope and even more significantly with the fourth cusp—the end of the matter.

The daughter of the marriage had the mid-point of her Neptune-Pluto sextile exactly on the marriage Ascendant.

OTHER INCEPTIONAL CHARTS

Inceptional charts of various kinds are also useful in assessing the potentials of other types of relationship. The beginning of a business partnership, the starting of a new job, the first arrival of a relative for a long-term or semi-permanent stay, the moment of first entering a new residence, the moment of departure for a holiday and even a horoscope for the acquisition of a pet or the purchase of such household items as radio and television sets can provide an extension of the information available to the astrologer. If at any time there is a need to gain more information about such matters, the inceptional horoscopes may be progressed or compared with the native's horoscope in accordance with the usual rules of synastry.

In a case where, through force of circumstances, the native's sister and her daughter came to stay with her for a year, Venus on the day of their arrival was on the native's Midheaven and Mars on her Descendant. Jupiter was on her radical Moon in Gemini (sisters) and the Sun and Jupiter were in trine on the day of arrival. At the actual moment they arrived Jupiter was about to pass over the Upper Meridian and the trine of the Sun and Venus to this angular Jupiter registered the fact that the stay was a very happy one. At the same time Uranus was in exact opposition to the host's Sun, an indication that he found it more difficult than his wife to adjust to this sudden invasion of his home.

The first arrival of a puppy in a certain household took place on the day when the Moon formed a T-square in mutables with Mars and Mercury. Mercury ruled the Ascendant, which was almost exactly opposed by Mars. Judy's excitable temperament and seemingly inexhaustible energy were a sore trial to her mistress and her urge to chase every car in sight resulted in an extra wire mesh fence being erected all round the garden so that she could not leave the premises except under the close supervision of her owners. Within a few months Judy had grown big enough and strong enough to leap the new fence and found herself free to chase as many cars as she wanted. This was too much for her mistress's peace of mind so, reluctantly, Judy was taken back to the farm where she was born to do the work she was best suited to, that of looking after the sheep. She continued to chase cars until the end of her days and never came to any harm.

At the time of her first arrival, Fortuna was on her mistress's Midheaven and Uranus was forming a T-square with her mistress's Sun and Mars. The Sun (in trine to Neptune, in sextile to Jupiter and Pluto, and in quincunx to Saturn) fell on her mistress's Ascendant. There was a close rapport between Judy and her owner but the angular T-square in mutables at the time of her first arrival showed the early breakup of the association. Judy was born on the same day of the year as her mistress and her Venus was in close conjunction with her mistress's Moon.

When a television set was first installed in a certain household, largely on the initiative of the lady of the house, the Moon was in opposition to Uranus. This fell across the Meridian of her horoscope, while a conjunction of Venus and Pluto fell in trine to her Sun. Neptune was in close trine to her Pluto. Jupiter was in close trine to her husband's Neptune, and Mercury in close trine to his Sun, pinpointing his major interests as educational programmes, news features and football matches. In the inception chart, Fortuna was in the fifth house of pastimes and entertainments.

The first installation of a telephone in a certain household occurred under a triple conjunction in Libra of the Sun, Uranus and Mercury, all in trine to the native's fourth house Saturn in Gemini. The angles at the moment the installation was completed exactly repeated the angles of his natal chart. Jupiter in Sagittarius was almost exactly in trine with his wife's Mercury, and within hours she was receiving a long distance call from her sister (who had been given advance information about the installation) 4,000 miles away. Mars was in exact trine to her Gemini Moon. By far the greatest number of telephone conversations take place with another sister who lives not far away. At the moment the telephone was first used, the upper Meridian was exactly conjunct the husband's Mercury.

By the use of inceptional charts a good deal of useful extra information can be accumulated that will assist the astrologer's judgment of a number of situations, and by applying the rules of synastry outlined in the following chapters it will often be possible in the case of human relationships to confirm or perhaps modify judgments made purely on the basis of a straightforward comparison of the nativities involved.

It is also valid to compare the charts of individuals with certain horary charts. For instance, if the question: "Should I go into partnership?" be asked, the horoscopes of prospective business partners can be compared with the horary map and the interplay between the two horoscopes interpreted according to the usual rules. A word of warning needs to be added. It is necessary first to be absolutely sure that the horary chart is radical and accurately reflects the probable circumstances of any proposed partnership.

CHAPTER 3

General Notes on Comparison

While it is probably impossible to find two people who are totally compatible or totally incompatible, it is usually possible to decide whether they are able to create an harmonious relationship between themselves in spite of small areas of incompatibility, or whether they have so little in common that any elements of compatibility in their natures are insufficient to enable them to establish a satisfactory relationship. The astrologer who is faced with the task of judging whether two people will get on well together will therefore usually have to estimate the relative proportion of harmony and disharmony between their two nativities and, in the case of prospective marriage partners, to judge whether the degree of harmony present is sufficient to guarantee a happy and lasting union or, if a business partnership is contemplated, to ensure a sound and profitable relationship.

The value of Synastry lies in the fact that it can identify those areas of a partnership where the chances of compatibility are greatest and those areas where they are least, so that the partners can build on the strengths of the relationship in order to offset and eventually overcome the weaknesses.

As in other branches of astrology, it should be realized that the terms "harmony" and "disharmony" are not necessarily synonymous with "desirable" and "undesirable." Just as too many harmonious aspects in a nativity may denote that one does not encounter enough difficulties in life to bring out the best in oneself, so a great preponderance of favorable aspects between one nativity and another may indicate a rather placid relationship between the two, neither of whom has the capacity to "spark off" the other. On the other hand, certain

Martian types appreciate an occasional element of friendly contest in a relationship and thus often feel in need of at least an occasional verbal combat to add piquancy to the relationship. The most rewarding partnerships, generally speaking, are those where each partner has qualities which complement the qualities of the other, and where each has the ability to draw out the other's latent potentialities. In this way, each can help to develop the other's personality more fully and effectively.

People often learn more through their mistakes and through the difficulties and discords they meet in life. Hence those areas of discord that exist in personal relationships can be valued for the opportunities they bring us to learn more about ourselves. They have an educational value which may not be apparent if we allow ourselves to become frustrated or annoyed by the idiosyncrasies that we object to in others. The astrologer should bear this in mind when assessing the potentialities of a partnership. Marriage, for instance, is a partnership designed, among other things, to assist individuals to grow in spiritual stature through the interplay of the partners' characters. In the overcoming of any friction present, such growth may be accelerated. While motives for marrying vary it is hardly likely that a couple, however strong their desire for self-development may be, will go out of their way to seek a partner whose character is completely alien to their own. But it is often the case that before marriage they are apparently oblivious to defects of character in each other than could cause serious problems once the first blissfully ecstatic aura of the marriage has begun to fade away. Love is blind!

If an astrologer is consulted before marriage, his problem may lie in deciding just how much strain and friction the partnership can reasonably be expected to cope with. There are certain well-established rules by which the degree of compatibility between two partners may fairly accurately be estimated at the physical, emotional, mental and spiritual level. If there is a reasonable degree of mutual sympathy, the willingness of each partner to adjust to the other can relax the tensions suggested by a number of theoretically discordant cross-aspects, which sometimes mean that one partner may be the cause of involving the other in difficulties or added responsibilities perhaps as a result of ill health, loss of earning power or the requirements of work necessitating long absences from home.

On the other hand, a basic lack of tolerance may result in even minor annoyances assuming major proportions. In this respect, even physical compatibility becomes important as, for instance, if one of the partners is a "fresh air fiend" and the other is vulnerable to the slightest draught. And if physical attraction should play a disproportionately prominent role in the partnership it might be prudent to observe whether one partner was likely to age more quickly than the other. The possible barrenness or sterility of a partner could also be crucial in a marriage where both husband and wife desired children and there was insufficient support and mutual understanding in the partnership. Such a problem can sometimes be solved by the couple adopting a child, in which case a comparison of the child's nativity with those of the prospective foster-parents could provide very useful guidance. If the parents' nativities show, through the conditions of the fifth house, difficulties involving children, as they are very likely to do if the couple cannot achieve natural parenthood, it may not be possible to find a candidate for adoption whose horoscope is compatible to the desired degree with those of the foster-parents.

In the case of a couple who adopted two children, a boy and a girl, the husband had a conjunction of Venus and Uranus in the fifth house, with Mercury there in opposition to Neptune. His wife had Neptune in the fifth house in opposition to Uranus. The boy was wayward and difficult to bring up, and eventually had to be sent away to a school that specialized in dealing with rebellious children. After leaving school he returned home but found difficulty in establishing a satisfactory relationship with his foster-parents and eventually left home to settle in Australia. In a different way, it never seemed possible to reach an entirely satisfactory understanding with their adopted daughter. She, too, left home soon after her school days were over, to set up house with a married man. As a result of her action a quarrel ensued which resulted in a rupture of the relationship with her foster-parents.

The conjunction of Venus and Uranus in the husband's chart did not indicate separation or divorce but, occurring in his fifth house, showed the unconventional behaviour of his adopted daughter and the breaking of the contact between parents and children.

Between married couples, compatibility on the emotional level may be very well established while mental interests remain wide apart, so that much will depend on the strength of the various links between their nativities as to whether a lack of true intellectual rapport becomes a major handicap to the establishment of lasting harmony.

According to popular belief, "marriages are made in heaven," while the marriage service speaks of "those whom God hath joined together." In the opinion of the writer the mere performance of the marriage ritual, even in a church, does not guarantee that the couple concerned have established a true rapport at the spiritual level. Heaven is a state of consciousness—"heaven is within"—and so for a marriage to be made in heaven requires that true rapport must exist at the highest state of consciousness to which human beings can attain. It is that state of consciousness where man becomes truly aware of the nature of the Divine. Rapport at this level signifies a real inner union in that ideal state where all humanity is seen to be One Whole —hence those who are joined together in mutual understanding on this level are truly united by God, and this understanding can never be broken.

Those who have only established a form of harmony between themselves mainly as the result of some physical attraction, or at the emotional or intellectual level may find that this is not sufficient to enable them to build a lasting partnership. On the other hand some partnerships that endure may do so in spite of a lack of a true spiritual rapport, perhaps because the partners feel compelled to remain together through a sense of duty or for some less laudable reason.

The marriage vow is regarded by the Church as something sacred that cannot be set aside. The final vows taken by a nun are similarly binding and symbolize the nun's acceptance of the role of a "bride of Christ." Yet until the final vows are taken, the nun is given every opportunity to find out whether she is suited to her demanding role, while in the case of marriage in its worldly form no such opportunities for a "trial run" are countenanced by the Church! It is therefore hardly to be wondered at that some couples feel disinclined to go through the religious ritual, when a civil authority is less demanding in terms of the standards to which it expects the couple to conform. It also becomes easier to appreciate why some prefer to dispense altogether with the marriage ceremony. Not all such liaisons unblessed by an official wedding ceremony end ignominiously. Some may be "made in heaven" even although the partners do not go through the motions of an accepted wedding ceremony.

The astrologer takes a great deal of responsibility on his or her shoulders when agreeing to pass judgment on the degree of compatibility between prospective marriage partners. It should never be the astrologer's function to tell clients what they should do, but rather to indicate to them as clearly as possible the strong points and the weaknesses of their relationship. It follows that a preponderance of favorable indications will produce very few problems for astrologer or client, yet when the majority of the indications point to some basic incompatibility or to major difficulties in the relationship, the couple may well ignore any reference to such factors by the astrologer. They may tell themselves that these deductions could not possibly be correct, as they are so obviously made for each other, or they may try to convince themselves that perhaps astrology is just a superstition after all!

In such cases, where a couple marry in spite of there appearing to be a lack of sufficient basic harmony between their nativities, it may well be that there is some karmic link between them that has to be worked out. A "difficult marriage" may be the means of teaching both of them valauble lessons, building up their experience and strengthening their characters so that they are eventually able to work out a solution of their problems and build a truly harmonious relationship.

If, on the other hand, the marriage finally fails, one or both may, as a result of their previous experiences, be better qualified to establish an harmonious relationship with a new partner. An astrologer who attempts to dissuade an apparently incompatible couple from getting married when they appear set on it may therefore be interfering with their karma (though it is a moot point whether karma can ever be interfered with), and the best service that can be rendered is to identify as clearly as possible the temperamental idiosyncrasies most likely to be productive of discord between them.

By far the greatest proportion of marriages will have taken place without the benefit of previous astrological advice. The astrologer may find that he or she is required to give judgment on difficulties and incompatibilities that may have only become obvious to the couple after they have been living together for some time. While, once again, it is usually desirable to present a balance sheet to them, there may be cases where the obstacles to creating an atmosphere of real harmony appear to be insuperable, that all the experience that can be usefully gained from such a discordant relationship has been gathered and that, in the best interests of both, the couple should part. In such circumstances it is possible that the astrologer will merely be confirming what was already fairly obvious to both partners.

Too great a similarity between horoscopes may mean that the character of each partner does not sufficiently complement that of the other, with the result that competition may replace co-operation. Because of the slow motion of the outer planets, contemporaries tend to share the same sign positions of Uranus, Neptune and Pluto, while if they are born close together in time, even the same degrees may be occupied by these planets. In a general sense, these planets represent conditioning factors experienced by the whole of contemporary humanity: the impact of new ideas and new discoveries, new philosophies (both religious and political) and new attitudes, as well as group pressures and group opportunities, so that similar sign positions of the heavier planets are less likely to interfere with the development of a meaningful relationship. It is when the faster moving planets occupy the same signs that difficulties are likely to arise, as these relate to more personal factors.

Nevertheless, statistical investigations have revealed that an identity of lunar positions often occurs when the charts of compatible couples are compared.

When there is a comparatively large age gap between the marriage partners, it follows that the positions of the major planets will not be duplicated. Opportunities for contrast are therefore increased in proportion to the difference between the ages of husband and wife. When one partner is considerably older than the other there is the chance that the perspectives of the two partners may be widened, as each may tend to view the broader issues of life through different eyes. These divergences could, however, serve to emphasize any differences of temperament and make it more difficult for each to adjust harmoniously to the other. Provided enough basic harmony exists between two nativities, the positions of the major planets in different signs provide an opportunity of developing a rewarding partnership and make possible the type of interplay that could lead to an expansion of consciousness in many directions.

All chart comparisons, whether for the purpose of giving advice to partners in marriage, business, sport or the entertainment world follow the same general rules, since any type of partnership is enhanced by the measure of sympathetic understanding that exists between the partners, but with modifications according to the purpose of the partnership. A lack of harmony involving the second house may, for instance, be more crucial in a business partnership, although the second and eighth houses do have a good deal of bearing on the quality of the sex relationship. In a sporting partnership the fifth house needs special consideration as well as the aspects involving Mars and Jupiter.

Astrologers are sometimes asked by their clients whether or not they should take up residence in a certain town or city. While there are several kinds of re-location techniques that can be used to deal with this question it is often helpful to compare the client's horoscope with the chart for the foundation or the incorporation of the town or city when that is known.

The traditional Ascendant of the city of London is 17° Gemini. Many of its prominent citizens have had this degree or its opposite or its antiscion degree tenanted: Queen Elizabeth II, Pluto 13° Cancer; Prince Philip, Sun 19° Gemini, Mercury 13° Cancer; Princess Margaret, Jupiter 12° Cancer; the Queen Mother, Pluto 17° Gemini; George VI, Neptune 17° Gemini, Mercury 18° Sagittarius; Duke of Windsor, Jupiter 18° Gemini—to name but a few latter day examples.

A certain seaside town on the opposite side of England from where the writer lives has played a prominent part in his destiny. His parents were married there, he first met his wife while on holiday there, and he has spent a good deal of his leisure time there most enjoyably. Pluto in the horoscope of the town is exactly on his seventh cusp and Venus exactly trines his Moon from her own sign, Libra. There are quite a few other favorable cross-aspects.

It will very often happen that an enterprise begun under good directions will be brought to a happy and successful conclusion, while one commenced under adverse directions will result in failure and frustration. The directions of each partner measuring to the time of the formation of the partnership will therefore throw a good deal of light on to the probable outcome of that partnership and the chances of lasting and successful co-operation between them. This places an extra emphasis on the need for favorable Venusian directions at the time of marriage, and for favorable Jupiterian directions when a business partnership is first established. While it follows that good directions will not cancel out the difficulties indicated by an afflicted Venus and an afflicted seventh house in the natal chart, it is not wise to rely on the converse being true, that a good natal seventh house and a well placed and aspected Venus will entirely cancel out a difficult progression at the time a new partnership is mooted.

New contacts are often made, or old ones brought to life, when the progressed angles of one horoscope form an aspect with the luminaries or planets of the other, or if they arrive at a conjunction of the Meridian or Horizon in the other's horoscope, or if the progressed positions of the Sun, Moon, Venus or Mars in one nativity form strong aspects with the natal planets in the other. If the cross-aspects between the natal positions in the two charts do not indicate a fair degree of compatibility, a temporary contact involving progressed positions will probably denote only a passing attraction. This is especially likely when the progressed Venus in one nativity becomes involved with the natal Uranus in the other. This contact can indicate a sudden attraction leading to a temporary liaison that will disappear as soon as the contact is dissolved, unless there are indications of a more permanent association through the interplay of other bodies in the two nativities. Any relatively fast moving progressed body forming a contact with planets in another's horoscope may similarly only signify a temporary relationship unless other more permanent factors link the two nativities.

When those cross-aspects between the two nativities, which would denote a lasting attraction if they were present in the nativity, are only formed temporarily between the two by progression, the effect may be just as dramatic for a short period, especially when there is a Mars-Venus contact formed between the horoscopes of young people of the opposite sex, but they will rarely endure. It is therefore important to take both progressed horoscopes into account when estimating just how permanent a relationship is likely to be.

Before comparing the horoscopes of individuals, it is necessary to sum up first the main characteristics and principal accentuations of each nativity, not only so that an assessment can be made of the special qualities that each can bring to the partnership, but because any great dissimilarity may indicate crucial differences of temperament. Particular attention should be paid to the number of planets in each element, as too much fire, for instance, is not likely to blend well with too much water, neither is the owner of a chart with a marked accentuation of the Sun, Mars and Jupiter likely to achieve a really satisfactory partnership with the native in whose horoscope the Moon, Saturn and Neptune are prominent, unless there are strong harmonious links between the more positive groups of planets in one nativity and the more negative planets in the other.

In marriage relationships the attitude of each partner to sex and the sexual relationship is crucial. A passionate individual would obviously be ill-matched with a mate who showed a marked preference for celibacy. Some basic similarities must be present, but points of contrast are also necessary in order to provide a source of stimulus and interest for each partner, as well as giving each something to work on in order to build up and improve the relationship. There are many ways of assessing the relative amounts of harmony and disharmony when comparing horoscopes. These will be investigated in detail in the chapters that follow.

CHAPTER 4

Various Methods of Chart Comparison

Even those who know little else about astrology are usually able to say which Sun signs are compatible with their own, thanks to the widely publicised Sun sign information available to all through the medium of the daily press. When Aries, Leo and Sagittarius are linked together as compatible signs, it is because they all belong to the same element, fire. Those with a marked emphasis on one of the four elements are likely to respond favorably to others in whose horoscopes there is a preponderance of the same element, recognizing possessors of a temperament similar to their own. Merely having the Sun in the same element is no sure guarantee of compatibility, however, for while one person may have Mercury and Venus in the sign preceding the Sun, the other may have Mercury and Venus in the sign following the Sun, so that in both cases the majority of planets may not be in signs of the same element as the Sun. It is the element which contains the greatest number of bodies which is the most important in terms of compatibility.

It is possible for both Suns to be in fire signs and for one nativity to contain a majority of planets in water signs and the other to have a majority in earth signs. By determining which element holds the greatest number of planets we can arrive at a much sounder basis for our first general comparison of the two nativities. This, however, is only a beginning.

Two horoscopes which both have a preponderance of planets in the same element will hardly blend well if Mars and Saturn in one fall on the places of Saturn and Mars, respectively, in the other, so that the cross-aspects between the planets and sensitive points in the two horoscopes should always be charted. Generally speaking, a preponderance of sextiles and trines between inter-aspecting planets makes for an harmonious partnership, while squares and oppositions denote the reverse. As in genethliacal astrology, it does not always follow that "benefic" aspects are "good" and "malefic" aspects "bad" and a more detailed examination of this method of comparison will be undertaken in Chapter 7.

There are several ways in which the emphasis of a planet can be increased. Any planet which is more prominently placed than the rest may need to be given special attention in case it clashes too strongly with a planet which dominates the partner's nativity. When one planet stands alone in one hemisphere of the horoscope, that is, if it is the only planet above the horizon or below, or is the sole occupant of the eastern or western hemisphere, it is likely to represent a factor in the psychological make-up of the native which may be over-emphasized in an attempt to strike a balance with the rest of the planets in the opposite half of the chart. This over-emphasis can therefore be a crucial factor, so it is particularly necessary to see that this singleton planet is well supported by the planets in the partner's nativity. Also, if there is a singleton emphasis in the partner's horoscope as well, it will be necessary to assess whether the two singletons blend or clash with each other.

Sometimes, not one but two planets will be isolated by hemisphere. This very isolation seems to encourage some kind of combination between the two, whether or not they are technically in aspect. Where, for instance, the Moon and Uranus are both isolated by hemisphere, though not in aspect with each other, the native often tends to be rather more nervous and tense than one might expect and the general effect of a Moon-Uranus aspect seems to be present.

Planets close to the meridian and the horizon are thrown into prominence on that account and when, in both nativities, one or more planets occupy such positions it is desirable that their general natures should accord. A woman with an angular Venus and a man with an angular Mars are ideally matched as far as that particular coupling is concerned. If Saturn, instead of Venus were the angular planet in the woman's horoscope, then a potentially discordant partnership is indicated. In both cases, however, it is the total picture that must form the basis of the final judgment and not just one single item.

Two or more planets on the angles introduce a more complicated factor. If both partners have the Sun and Mars angular, the struggle to dominate each other may considerably diminish the chances of an harmonious relationship. In most cases it is probably better if the angular planets in one nativity are not the same as those which are angular in the other, though planets which are regarded as not combining comfortably, such as Mars and Saturn, Saturn and Uranus and Uranus and Neptune are probably the least conducive to harmony when competing as angular planets in different nativities.

It is helpful to compare the final dispositors in each chart, though not all planetary combinations are so arranged as to produce a final dispositor, in which case more than one planet may come into consideration. If Mars in Libra is the final dispositor in one nativity and Saturn in Cancer the final dispositor in the other, it may be necessary to ensure that there is a good number of harmonious contacts before a favorable judgment is pronounced.

In the horoscope of Steven Earl Parent (see Chapter 10) the final dispositor is Jupiter. Pluto in Leo is disposed of by the Sun in Aquarius, which is disposed of by Saturn in Libra, which is disposed of by Venus in Pisces, which is disposed of by Jupiter in Pisces. Uranus in Cancer is disposed of by the Moon in Taurus, which is disposed of by Venus in Pisces, and so by Jupiter. Mercury in Aquarius is disposed of by Saturn in Libra, which is disposed of by Venus in Pisces, and so by Jupiter. Neptune in Libra is also disposed of by Venus and finally by Jupiter. Mars in Pisces is disposed of by Jupiter. If, instead of taking Saturn to be the ruler of Aquarius, we had substituted Uranus, the final result would have been the same but if we had taken Neptune as the ruler of Pisces, instead of Jupiter, the mutual disposition between Venus and Neptune would have frustrated the attempt to find a final dispositor. A planet in its own sign does not necessarily become the final dispositor, and two planets in their own signs make it impossible for there to be a final dispositor. When there is a final dispositor there is often a greater ability on the native's part to coordinate his activities, while if the planets are divided into two or more groups each with a separate dispositor, he may tend to be at cross-purposes with himself and in extreme cases this may indicate the possibility of a split-personality. Indications given by the final dispositor therefore provide useful evidence when estimating the compatibility existing between partners.

In the Duke of Windsor's horoscope (see Chapter 10) Mars is in Aries and Venus is in Taurus. These planets dispose of Uranus and Saturn respectively, leaving the other six bodies without a final dispositor.

Another way of comparing the inter-action of horoscopes is to re-locate the planets of one horoscope in the houses of the other, according to their zodiacal longitude, in order to estimate which department of the partner's life is most likely to be affected by the psychological attitudes and event patterns of the other.

While it is obvious that a planet in 0° Cancer in one horoscope is in conjunction with a planet in the same degree in another nativity, it is possible that some students might not have considered that a planet on the fourth cusp of one horoscope might be in conjunction with a planet on the fourth cusp of another, and also that any planet in proportionately the same house position as one in the partner's horoscope could be in conjunction with it. In terms of house positions such a conjunction is a mundane conjunction. It follows that a planet on the cusp of the tenth house in one nativity will mundanely oppose a planet on the fourth cusp of another. That such mundane conjunctions and oppositions are important will be obvious when we consider that a person with Uranus in the fourth house is likely to bring a rather disconcerting and unsettling influence to bear on domestic matters and this could jar on someone with the Moon in the fourth, who would probably be extremely susceptible to the domestic atmosphere and would most appreciate a peaceful environment. The person with Uranus in the fourth might frequently be absent from the home, keep irregular hours or continually be introducing innovations that interfered with the quiet and regular routine preferred by the partner who had the Moon in the fourth.

In an early volume of the magazine "Astrology" there appeared an article by Elsie Kennison, an American astrologer, suggesting that planets in houses could be located at points in the zodiac equivalent to their house position. Thus a planet exactly on the Ascendant would be equivalent to a planet in 0° Aries, a planet on the second cusp to a planet in 0° Taurus and so on. By this system a planet mid-way between two cusps would be placed in 15 degrees of the sign equivalent to the house in which it was placed. The equivalent position of planets less conveniently placed would need to be calculated in proportion to their exact location in the house. Thus if the fourth house cusp of a horoscope is 7° Aquarius, the fifth cusp 13° Pisces, and there is a planet in the fourth house in 13° Aquarius, its house position expressed symbolically in terms of zodiacal longitude is 5° Cancer. If there are any planets close to this degree or closely aspecting it in the partner's horoscope, this will constitute a link between the two nativities in terms of the planets involved. Charles Carter christened this derived position the "domal analogue" and the calculation is made thus: Number of degrees in the fourth house (7° Aquarius to 13° Pisces)=36. Number of degrees in a sign=30. Distance of planet from fourth cusp=6°. 6x30/36=5. 4th house=4th sign=Cancer. The domal analogue of the planet is therefore 5° Cancer.

The number of degrees in each house is likely to differ according to the system of house division used. Because there are differences of opinion as to which system is most reliable there are obvious limitations in applying this type of evaluation. However, the method does provide a means of collecting evidence as to the comparative value of various systems of house division and can also be a useful tool in rectification.

I have suggested elsewhere (see *Astrology,* Vol. 40 No. 2*) that in a symbolic sense, every planet has its own zodiac, and that the elongation of all the other planets from a given planet can be expressed in terms of the number of zodiacal degrees they are distant from that planet. Thus if Venus is in 11° Capricorn and Saturn is in 12° Gemini, then Saturn is 151° distant from Venus. If we regard the position of Venus as a symbolic 0° Aries, then the position of Saturn measured as 151° from 0° Aries is 1° Virgo, which will be its position in the "Venus Zodiac." If we want to know the position of Venus in the "Saturn Zodiac" we count the degrees from Saturn to Venus (209) and again measure the distance from 0° Aries to give a symbolic 29° Libra as the relationship of Venus to Saturn. A zodiac is merely a cycle of relationship and when we relate two planets to each other in this way we are using zodiacal longitude to measure that relationship in terms of the arc along a circle.

The distance at birth between any planets establishes their basic relationship and any third factor temporarily joining in that relationship activates the two planets involved in terms of their original contact with each other, which does not have to be a recognized aspect distance.

A classical example of the repetition of an exact birth arc between two planets occurred in the case of the Archduke Franz Ferdinand of Austria, whose assassination at Sarajevo was used as a pretext for starting World War I. In the Archduke's nativity, Venus was in 9° 19' Scorpio and Pluto in 10° 30' Taurus. Pluto was therefore 181° 11' from Venus, representing a position of 1° 11' Libra in the Venus Zo-

---

*Also *Astrology 77,* Summer issue, ed.

diac. On the day he was assassinated, Venus in the heavens was in 9°45' Leo and Uranus was in 10°56' Aquarius. Uranus was exactly 181°10' of arc from Venus and therefore in almost the same 1°11' Libra in the Venus Zodiac. "A man with a drawn sword in an aggressive attitude" is the La Volasfera degree symbol for 1° Libra!

Any re-allocation of planets according to this system becomes crucial when there are planets close to the beginning degrees of the cardinal signs. This may have been one of the reasons why they have always been termed "critical" degrees. If, for instance natal Mars is in 0° Aries and natal Saturn is in 0° Cancer, Mars in terms of the Saturn Zodiac will be in 0° Capricorn, thus reinforcing the original square.

Using the Ascendant as the first point of a zodiac will give us the same results as if we had calculated the domal analogues on the basis of Equal House division. The theoretically ideal rising degree should be 0° Aries, but each individual when coming to birth chooses to identify with any of the 360 degrees. The amount of displacement between the degree chosen and 0° Aries is a personal arc of great significance. Thus there seems to be a strong case for applying this "arc of displacement" uniformly to each factor, so as to determine its relationship to the ascending degree in terms of a symbolic zodiac. This may be preferable to relying on the uneven houses of the horoscope as a framework on which to chart this particular relationship.

A zodiac based on the relationship of every body to the Moon's North Node was proposed some years ago by two European astrologers almost simultaneously and christened the Draconic Zodiac. Because the Lunar Nodes appear to have a special significance with human relationships, especially with those carrying a strong element of karma, the Nodal or Draconic Zodiac may be a particularly useful tool when investigating the potentialities of a relationship.

When comparing horoscopes it will often be found that it is important to take into account the antiscion degrees. To find the antiscion degree of any planet, reflect its zodiacal degree over the 0° Cancer-Capricorn axis, where the Sun has maximum North and South declination at the time of the summer and winter solstices. Thus a planet in 1° Capricorn has its antiscion in 29° Sagittarius, 2° Capricorn in 28° Sagittarius, 3° Capricorn in 27° Sagittarius and so on.

Planets in mutual disposition in a nativity are, on that account, considered to be linked together. A degree of compatibility is indicated if, for instance, one partner has Venus in Pisces and the other has Neptune in Libra. This kind of sympathy existing between planet and sign will often manifest itself in other ways, so that one partner may have an aspect between the Sun and Neptune, while the other partner has the Sun in Pisces. Or a woman with the Sun in aspect to Saturn and Uranus may marry a man with Saturn and Uranus angular. The sympathy between house and sign is sometimes exemplified by one partner having the Sun in the fourth house and the other partner having the Sun in Cancer and similarly with other planetary positions.

In his early studies of astrology, the writer experimented with a system of sensitive points based on the relation of each planet to the meridian when its zodiacal degree was rising or setting at the latitude of the birthplace, and to the horizon when the zodiacal degree of the planet reached the upper or lower meridian. Although the system seemed to have some merit, he did not follow it up at the the time as his main astrological interests were leading him in other directions. Recently, the same idea occurred to the English astrologer, Pamela A. Bennett, and she has developed the system in some depth, presenting a number of impressive examples in an article in the *Astrologers' Quarterly* (Associate Angles and the Daily Progressed Angles—Vol. 48, No. 4; Vol. 49, No. 1).

An example taken from the article shows how the Associate Angles are determined. If the natal longitude of the Sun is 18 Gemini and the latitude of the birthplace is 51N., the Sun is on the upper meridian at a sidereal time of 5h 7m 47s at which time the horizon is 20°45' Virgo-Pisces. When the Sun reaches the lower meridian (S.T. 17h 07m 49s), the Ascendant-Descendant axis is 0°41' Pisces-Virgo. When the Sun rises (S.T. 21h 01m 52s), the meridian is 13 Aquarius-Leo and when the Sun sets (S.T. 13h 13m 51s), the meridian axis is 20 Libra-Aries.

These Associate Angles are linked with the luminary or planet to which they relate, and when the degree occupied by one of these angles is also occupied by a planet in another person's horoscope, a link is established between the two bodies. Such a link can be a significant factor in any comparison between the two horoscopes. If the native moves away from the birthplace latitude, a new set of Associate Angles should be calculated for the new place of residence. This may, to some extent, explain why people tend to drift apart when they move away from one another's area and so change the natural links associated with each planet's rising and setting, and its appearance on the upper or lower meridian. Examples of the use of Associate Angles in synastry are given in Chapter 10.

PLANETARY PATTERNS

A comparison between the different types of planetary patterns possible in the horoscope, a concept first introduced by Dr. Marc Edmund Jones, can give some general guide as to how well two nativities are likely to blend. Seven main types are distinguished: the Bowl, Bucket, Bundle, Locomotive, See-Saw, Splash and Splay. Of these the Splay types are probably the most self-sufficient, independent and the least likely to adapt to a partner, although they might be satisfied if the partnership were run on their terms. The Locomotive pattern suggests a certain dynamic drive which might accord ill with the temperament of the Splay native. To some extent the actual shape of the pattern will provide a clue as to whether the two types will get on well together.

The Bundle is usually contained within a trine, while the Locomotive usually has an empty trine. If the Bundle consists mainly of an arc of the zodiac that is missing from a particular Locomotive pattern, the partnership could be most effective although both might tend on occasion to act without consulting the other. In all cases of pattern combinations the final judgment must depend upon whether the majority of cross-aspects is favorable or otherwise. The Splash pattern provides a dramatic contrast to the Bundle and here there may be the attraction of opposites. The Splash types can provide a variety of talents and interests that may contrast effectively with the rather limited approach of the Bundle types, who are able to turn to good account the ideas and wide experience of their partner. The Splay is apt to be similarly unyielding to the Bundle, so that adaptability could be lacking in such a partnership. The See-Saw may gain something from the Bundle type, as the more decisive outlook of the latter may help resolve some of the dilemmas the former encounters when trying to do justice to both sides of an argument. It is doubtful however, whether Bundle types will wish to spend much time assessing the merits of points of view opposite to their own and they may not be inclined to encourage the association. The Bowl types, with their desire to pour forth the fruits of their experience, may find Bundle natives too inhibited and too self-intent, although if the planets in the Bundle occupy the empty hemisphere of the Bowl pattern, the feeling that the lack they feel may be satisfied by partners with this type of Bundle pattern may attract certain Bowl types towards them. To a certain extent the above remarks also apply to the relationship between the Bundle and the Bucket types, although a great deal will depend on the cross-aspects to the "handle" of the Bucket. If these are predominantly harmonious, the two types may get on well together.

The Splash type, with a wide variety of interests, is often prepared to go more than half-way to meet others and may get on with the Splay type better than most. These natives can often fire the enthusiasm of the Locomotive type, who can take their ideas and supply the necessary drive to put them into execution. The universal interests of the Splash type may intrigue the See-Saw type and the two may get on well together although they might never actually achieve much. When the Bucket type is involved, aspects to the "handle" planet are crucial, and while the Splash type can provide a good contrast to the Bucket, any preponderance of afflictions to this planet may spoil the relationship. Inasmuch as both types are outgoing, there is a certain similarity of temperament, and Bucket types may be able to give a greater sense of direction to their partner. The self-containment of the Bowl native offers the attraction of contrast to the Splash type, with its more uninhibited approach to life on a broad front, and a good partnership can result if the cross-aspects are mainly favorable.

Splay types are very much their own people and much will depend on the willingness of other types to give them the freedom of action they require. As this pattern is the nearest approach to the concept of an "immovable object," and the Locomotive pattern is the nearest approach to the concept of an "irresistible force," an harmonious combination of the two may be difficult to bring about. The general attitude of the Splay type may be rather too impersonal and self-seeking for the Bowl type, with its greater concern for people and causes, while the Bucket type may well have the same reservations about the former. There is the added complication that both types can be rather uncompromising. See-Saw natives may be attracted to the Splay because they see this type as an anchor. On the other hand, they may suspect the definite view-points held by the latter as evidence of an inability to think all round a subject or concede that there is sometimes merit in a point of view that is not the same as their own. As with all See-Saw relationships, a crucial factor may well be whether planets in the other's horoscope build up a T-square or form trines and sextiles with the oppositions that give the See-Saw its distinctive name.

The ability of See-Saw natives to weigh the merits of opposing ideas gives them a basis for establishing meaningful relationships with others, though it may not endear them to those with a driving urge to put into practice ideas of which they are absolutely convinced. The Locomotive type, who tends to progress by zig-zagging from side to side, has something in common with the sometimes tentative approach of the See-Saw type. There is often an ability to forge a partnership when both are willing to proceed on the basis of trial and error. Bowl natives may tend to bring the See-Saw type down heavily on one side in favor of one particular point of view. As the Bowl depends for its definition on an opposition, much will depend upon how the oppositions in the two horoscopes merge with each other. Favorable aspects between the two sets of oppositions may pave the way to a rewarding partnership. In some ways the relationship with the Bucket type rests on the same factor but the uncompromising direction of effort usually indicated by the singleton planet becomes a crucial factor. If this is not helpfully integrated with the defining oppositions of the See-Saw, the relationship may not flourish.

Both the Bowl and the Locomotive types are conscious of a sense of lack. The former may attract the latter if their planets fall mostly within the empty trine of the Locomotive, who may then supply the driving force to implement the plans of their partner. The single-minded purpose of the Bucket natives may find in the Locomotive type the kind of drive they need to put their ideas into effect, but if the singleton planet does not connect favorably with the grand trine usually present in the Locomotive pattern, much of the value of the combination may be lost.

The Bowl and Bucket types have a good deal in common. If there is good support for the singleton planet in the Bucket pattern, the Bowl natives may feel that they have met a valuable ally. Much may depend however on the way in which the occupied hemispheres in the two horoscopes combine with each other. If they approximately coincide or oppose each other the attraction may be greater than otherwise, although in all Bowl-Bucket relationships there may be a special need to study the cross-aspects carefully before deciding on the degree of compatibility between the two.

It will often be found that planets in the Pre-Natal Epoch of one partner are closely configured with the natal planets of the other. If the correct Pre-Natal Epoch is known, valuable evidence is often afforded by observing this type of interplay. Not all Pre-Natal Epochs are easy to find, however, and it is best to ignore these positions if there is any doubt about their authenticity, since there is a wide variety of other factors on which a sound judgment can be based. Even when the Pre-Natal Epochs of both partners are known it is probably unnecessary to compare the two Epochs.

The foregoing paragraphs have indicated some of the principal ways in which two charts may be compared. Soon after I began to study astrology it occurred to me to devise a means by which a point in time could be found which epitomized the partnership between any given partners. This I christened the "Relationship Horoscope." Some years later I found that a method originating in Germany used mid-points to build up a composite horoscope to represent the nature of the partnership. In general broad principle, that of producing one horoscope unique to one particular partnership, the two systems agree, but in practice it will be found that the author's Relationship Horoscope is easier to handle. In one respect, it arises more naturally from the astrological relationship. *This system* will be fully explained, and examples given, in later chapters.

CHAPTER 5

Sun Sign Compatibility and other General Comparisons

The serious student of astrology soon realizes that the popular presentation of astrology in the press and over the radio bears little relationship to astrology proper. Because the Sun is the only body whose cyclic relationship with the Earth is more or less exactly repeated in each successive year, this is the only stable factor on which any mass presentation of astrology can rely. Because of this regular yearly cycle it is possible to estimate within about a degree the zodiacal longitude of the Sun on any given date during the year.

This means that everyone who knows their birthday can very easily learn what sign their Sun was in at birth, even if they do not know the actual degree, unless they are one of those "in betweens" born on the day the Sun leaves one sign for the next. Because the Sun sign is the only factor of which the majority of non-astrologers are aware, a whole system of "Sun sign" astrology has been built up. This system is only a pale reflection of real astrology but unfortunately, in the eyes of the uninitiated, it appears to be all that astrology has to offer.

One of the most publicized areas of Sun sign astrology relates to the compatibility of those born with their Suns in the same element. Thus those born with the Sun in Aries are reckoned to be compatible with those born with the Sun in Leo and the Sun in Sagittarius. While there is some truth in the fact that each element tends instinctively to understand how best to deal with its own kind, and while it is true that the Sun represents the real and essential nature of an individual, there can be many situations in which a theoretical Sun sign compatibility can be discounted. In such cases the placement of the two Suns may play a comparatively minor role in the total assessment and sometimes an over-emphasis of this factor can prove to be very misleading. If, for instance, one partner's Sun is at the very end of Aries and the other's at the very beginning of Leo, technically the two Suns will be in square aspect. This could well indicate difficulties in adapting to each other. Or it may be that the nativity with the Sun in Aries has a majority of planets in air signs, while the nativity with the Sun in Leo has a majority of planets in water signs, so that a truer comparison between the two horoscopes would be on the more representative basis of a contrast between air and water, which are not particularly compatible elements. Even if the Sun signs should be compatible and there are discordant planetary clashes between the two charts, such disharmonies may greatly outweigh any concord suggested by the compatibility of the Sun signs.

The basic idea that Sun signs of the same element are congenial to each other is a useful one in synastry, provided it is remembered that the Sun is only one of the ten bodies normally used in astrological work (to say nothing of the Ascendant, Midheaven and Lunar Nodes). The overall picture, when all these additional factors are included, may greatly modify any conclusions based on the Sun signs alone, or even those based on the general balance of the elements, when all the factors are taken into consideration, since the cross-aspects of planets from one nativity to another may produce a very different picture (see Chapter 7).

While, theoretically, solar compatibility can indicate a valuable deep level harmony, too many superficial differences, indicated by planetary disharmonies, may prevent this harmony from finding its most satisfactory expression. The Sun reaches its peak of influence from the age of twenty-two to forty. It is likely that the effects attributable to the solar position and the aspects the Sun receives will not reach their most effective expression until that period in the life.

Too great an emphasis on the same element, although it may attract at first, can ultimately produce a degree of boredom or dullness in a relationship. It is the contrast between temperaments that usually adds piquancy to a relationship, providing there is a reasonable degree of compatibility between the partners and the contrast is not so complete that neither party can successfully adapt to the other. It is not uncommon, therefore, to find the Suns of marriage partners in opposite signs, especially as, in terms of the solar houses, this will mean that each has the partner's Sun in the solar seventh house, the house of marriage and partnership.

As well as taking into account Sun sign compatibility, each planet in the horoscope can be treated on a similar basis, so that if, for instance, both partners have Mars in a water sign and Venus in an air sign, a greater degree of compatibility is likely.

The horoscope of a well-balanced individual should have a fairly equal distribution of the planets among the four elements. Most horoscopes deviate to a greater or lesser extent from this theoretically ideal situation. It has been observed that a state of perfect balance is apt to encourage inertia, consequently the horoscopes in which the planets are rather less evenly distributed among the elements lead these natives to undertake activities and gain experiences that provide them with the opportunity of enlarging their wisdom and hastening their soul growth. In assessing the balance of the elements in a horoscope, it is usual to count the number of bodies in each element. A preponderance of bodies in one element will naturally leave no doubt as to which is the most important element, but it will often be found that two elements contain an equal number of planets. Preference should then be given to the element in which the Ascendant is placed. This may not always solve the problem, since the Ascendant may be in a fire sign, while earth and air signs contain the most planets. In such cases, the majority group containing the Sun should be given the principal emphasis. If neither majority group contains the Sun, the presence of the Ascendant ruler should be used as a deciding factor, but if the issue is still unresolved, the two elements may be considered to be equally poised. It can sometimes happen that three elements are equally represented, but such cases are comparatively rare. Where there is a more or less equal emphasis on two or more elements, one may be able to associate easily with a variety of people of different temperaments, although if an element should contain only badly placed and afflicted planets the native may not mingle easily with those in whose horoscopes this element is strongly represented.

* * * * * * *

THE TRIPLICITIES

When comparing two horoscopes with a clearly defined emphasis on one particular element, certain general conclusions can be reached on that basis alone, though it should be remembered that many other factors need to be taken into consideration before a final judgment is reached. It is unlikely that any single factor will spoil a relationship. Even an apparent clash between the most emphasized elements may be greatly modified by a preponderance of other factors more conducive to mutual compatibility. Before examining the probable effects of different combinations of the four elements, it is first necessary to take into account the general characteristics likely to be present when one particular element predominates in a nativity.

The Fire Element

Those in whose nativities the fire element predominates are likely to be active, courageous and spirited, full of drive and vitality, generous and optimistic. They are capable of being "fired" by an enthusiasm that lifts the confidence, boosts the ego and increases any tendencies to exuberance and aggression. Emotions are very positively expressed and the love nature is often ardent. This type is unmistakably extrovert, usually with a marked interest in self-promotion.

The absence of any planets in an element is also revealing, especially as the native often tries to compensate for such a lack in other directions. When fire signs are not tenanted in a horoscope there is often some lack of energy, enthusiasm and the more positive kinds of optimism that encourage enterprise and initiative. As a compensation there is sometimes a tendency to live in the mind, so that the native may become a thinker rather than a doer, channeling a good deal of energy in the drawing up of wonderful plans that may never come to fruition.

The Earth Element

Those in whose nativities the earth element predominates are likely to be practical, matter of fact, solid, dependable and loyal, relying on common sense and established procedures to solve problems. There is a tendency towards a materialistic and somewhat conservative outlook. The nature tends to be painstaking and persevering. This type greatly values stability and usually makes no attempt to overturn the status quo. In marriage relationships the physical aspect is usually very important. The type generally tends toward the introvert.

When earth signs are not tenanted in a horoscope there is often a lack of the practical virtues and a neglect of material considerations. Sometimes there is a tendency for these natives to live in the clouds and to be in some way out of touch with the ordinary everyday world in which they live. Their unrealistic approach and a tendency to take things for granted may produce carelessness and irresponsibility in dealing with practical issues.

The Air Element

Those in whose nativities the air element predominates are likely to be polarized largely in the realm of the intellect. A certain detachment is usually present and even emotional problems may be subjected to a process of logical analysis. The power of the idea is all important and they may become so obsessed by some new concept or theory that they are ready to make drastic changes without first taking into account the possible emotional reactions of others. These natives are capable of much refinement and inspiration and often have high ideals, though they may find that these ideals are not always capable of being realized. Because of their ready adaptability they are usually very sociable and approachable, though sometimes there may be a lack of real depth in their relationships. Occasionally flights of fancy may encourage a tendency to daydream, while a lack of capacity for any deep emotional involvement can lead to fickleness. The type generally tends towards the extrovert.

When air signs are not tenanted in a horoscope there is often an inability to communicate effectively. Others may be at a loss to understand the motives of these natives. They often neglect to plan ahead and, acting without foresight, needlessly dissipate their energies in impulsive action which may prove abortive or lacking in wisdom. At best they may fail to think things through thoroughly, so that they only make progress through a system of trial and error.

The Water Element

Those in whose nativities the water element predominates are likely to become emotionally involved in many of the issues with which they have to deal. There is usually a very receptive and impressionable side to the nature, which makes them particularly responsive to circumstance and to their environment. This sensitivity tends to invest all their relationships with a certain fragility, since other types may not always be aware of the extent to which those with a preponderance of water signs allow their emotions to become involved. Their ready sympathies, when directed outwards, enable them to appreciate others' emotional problems, so they will usually shield and protect those for whom they care. There is a marked tendency to introspection and, in less evolved types, to a certain amount of self-pity.

When water signs are not tenanted in a horoscope there is often a lack of true feeling or sympathy for others, or a basic inability on the part of these natives to make others aware of the fact that they really care. They may distrust their emotions and so project an image of themselves that appears hard and calculating. Occasionally this lack gives rise to a cold and cynical personality even though outward appearances may be to the contrary.

Those lacking a certain element in their horoscopes are usually inclined to look for ways of compensating for such a lack, consequently they are often greatly attracted towards those in whose nativities signs of this element are strongly accentuated.

When comparing the effect of the various elements in combination with each other it has often been the practice to use analogies based on the actual effects on each other of the elements in nature. Fire, for instance, needs to be fed by earth and air in order to continue burning. Strictly speaking, fire is not an element, but its role is to transform substances. Ice, for instance, when heated, turns to water and water, heated sufficiently, turns to steam, so that three states, solid (earth), liquid (water) and vapour (air) depend upon the amount of heat (fire) present. Heat (fire) applied to some substances (earth) can liberate gases (air) and reduce substances to ash, destroying forms and preparing the way for new creative activity. It has been said that water and fire do not mix, because fire either heats up water until it becomes steam, or water damps down fire and finally extinguishes it. Yet in practice it is often necessary to create steam in order to use it as a motive force, just as it is sometimes necessary to use water to extinguish fires before large scale destruction takes place. The analogy, in fact, is only valid when related to the uncontrolled impact of one element on another.

Earth and water can form mud, but unless earth is irrigated by water little vegetation would grow. The accumulation of river mud in the form of a rivermouth delta can produce an extremely fertile area. When earth predominates in a contact with water, it can act to clog up or dam the free flow of the water. On the other hand, an excess of water in contact with some materials can eventually cause them to rot. Air dries up earth so that erosion can finally result, with the wind continually blowing away surplus dust, but unless soil is properly aerated, vegetation would not receive essential nutriment.

In nature each element needs the other and while, in psychological terms, the interplay of fire and air may be more compatible than the interplay of fire and water, the controlled and balanced interaction of all the elements is necessary in order to achieve a perfect blend. Thus the most perfectly balanced horoscopes are likely to be those in which all four elements are more or less equally represented and with each planet in aspect to a majority of the others. Unless heavy afflictions in any one element are present, such well balanced genitures may indicate that the natives are able to get on well with most of their fellows. On the other hand, it has been suggested that a degree of unbalance is likely to attract more opportunities for soul growth.

An over-accentuation of one element can produce problems in adjusting to other types. It is with this kind of over-accentuation that the following paragraphs are primarily concerned.

Air and water each contain something of the other, for there is always a certain amount of moisture in the air, while water is formed out of the combination of oxygen and hydrogen and some degree of compatibility is possible. As in other combinations it is only when one of the elements is disproportionately activated that disasters are possible as, for instance when a hurricane lashes the waves of the sea into the full fury of a storm.

Fire/Fire

When there is a partnership between two natives in whose horoscopes the fire element predominates, as with all pairings of the same element, this indicates that there will be a number of common factors in the psychological make-up of each partner. Both may see themselves to a certain extent reflected in the other. Since those with an excess of fire are rather inclined to self-promotion, there may be a clash of wills if one partner is not prepared to concede leadership to the other. (The more natural arrangement is for the male to exercise the initiative.) If each partner's capacity for enthusiasm is not similarly oriented there may be times when they are each pulling in different directions. However, when two fire partners are able to unite in achieving some common aim the possibilities for creative enterprise and thoroughly effective action are considerable. They may "spark each other off" and "get on like a house on fire," but any basic clash of temperament may result in sudden and all-destructive "flare-ups." Since both partners should have no lack of energy, they may tend to burn each other out. Wounded pride may be the underlying cause of a break-up. A fire needs to be fed, contained and conserved, the function of the air and earth signs respectively, so that fire, more than any other element perhaps, is most in need of the support and contrast of the other elements.

Fire/Earth

The link between fire and earth is perhaps best illustrated in the blacksmith's forge, where metal (earth) is rendered malleable by heat (fire) so that it can be shaped the more readily into various useful or decorative forms. Fire can destroy materials that are inflammable, while "scorched earth" may be a military necessity or a punitive measure. Too much earth can stifle fire. Once again we have a combination that depends on the right blend to produce the maximum good.

This is a combination which represents spirit working with matter.

The pioneering, high spirited and enthusiastic fire natives may find earth partners too slow and plodding. Those with the earth element strong are concerned with establishing firm foundations and sorting out the practical issues before they embark upon a project, while their fiery partners want to get started immediately, being eager to see the project take shape quickly and not entertaining too many doubts about its feasibility. Earth can supply a practical check to the Fire natives' impetuosity and prevent their enthusiasm from running away. Fire likes to " strike while the iron is hot" but Earth is apt to counter with the reply that "Rome wasn't built in a day."

Earth may criticise Fire for leaping impulsively before looking, but Fire often feels that Earth spends so much time looking that the leap may be too late. Fire may find that Earth lacks imagination; Earth may regard Fire as being too optimistic for his own good. Thus Fire types can sometimes feel stifled by Earth and may grow more and more impatient as they find themselves unable to rouse their partner's enthusiasm, while their pride may be nettled when they find their optimistic plans continually being scrutinized by their partner to see if they are financially viable and capable of practical realization. The conservatism of Earth may jar upon the pioneering instincts of Fire while Earth's desire to sift and test everything may cause Fire natives to feel resentment that their judgment should ever have been doubted.

Fire's sexual ardour may find Earth's rather introverted approach difficult to contend with, but Fire natives can appreciate the loyalty of which Earth is capable once their partner's emotional self-expression becomes less inhibited.

Although the harmonious combination of Fire and Earth may not be easy to achieve, each needs the other, for enthusiasm unchecked by common sense can lead Fire into foolhardy and dangerous action, while Earth needs vision and imagination and a touch of daring to escape the rut of the commonplace.

Fire/Air

Between Fire and Air there is considerable affinity. Fire needs the oxygen in Air to keep burning; a breeze can fan flames into greater activity. Air natives can feed ideas to their Fire partner to fan their enthusiasm, though there is a risk of such a partnership becoming too volatile. There may be a danger that this combination of enthusiasm with idealism leads the partnership into a utopian way of life that lacks contact with reality. Consequently the practical approach may be missing, or the partners may become too excitable for their own good. In order to get the best out of this combination Fire natives should try to imbue their Air partner with a greater sense of purpose and show them how to translate ideas into action, while Air natives may need to bring logic into play to cool down the Fire partner's enthusiasm when it appears to be too far divorced from common sense and reason.

Fire/Water

Fire can evaporate Water and Water can extinguish Fire. Fire natives direct their emotions outwardly and any emotional tension is likely to be thrown off in vigorous action and spirited behaviour. Water passively allows its emotions to be worked upon for long periods, suffering inwardly and tending to brood and sulk when hurt. If emotional tension continues to mount, the ultimate effect is much the same as the bursting of a dammed-up river, when the waters gush forth with suprising suddenness, perhaps doing untold damage before once again finding their natural level. Water takes the shape of any container that holds it, while heat expands and so the unsympathetic combination of Fire and Water may result in the water bursting its container and perhaps extinguishing the fire.

The self-confident drive, brash approach and sometimes reckless courage of Fire natives may daunt their sensitive, timid and susceptible Water partners, who may also feel that Fire lacks true sympathy and understanding. It is often difficult for the two to find a common meeting ground, even though the Sun is the principal significator of Fire and the Moon of Water and the two luminaries are symbolically regarded as the Cosmic Man and Wife. Fire natives may tire of finding their impetuous urge to action repeatedly baulked by the timidity and lack of spirit in their Water partner, who may be more concerned with whether a project "feels" right and whether it will cause emotional stress to anyone. As a result Water natives may question the confident assumptions and blind faith of their Fire partner, who may appear to be lacking in wisdom and social conscience;

The ardent love nature of Fire natives may tend to overwhelm the delicate susceptibilities of their Water partner.

In order to get the best out of this combination Fire may need to have more patience with the sensitivity and susceptibility of Water, and to curb any tendency to outspokenness, bearing in mind that Water has a good deal of emotional vulnerability while Water may need to realize that its instinct for self-preservation, when overdeveloped, can prevent the proper exercise of initiative. This can prove very frustrating to an enterprising and enthusiastic Fire partner.

Earth/Earth

The partnership of two Earth natives is likely to result in a mutual respect for each other's practical common sense approach, but the relationship could be rather unadventurous, lacking the spark of inspiration and the element of novelty, unless there are planetary clashes between the two horoscopes to provide some fireworks. The solid and dependable qualities of both partners favor the gradual building up of a sound relationship. An interest in the more physical aspects of marriage may provide a basis for mutual satisfaction in the early stages of the relationship, but if the partners should eventually feel a need for greater excitement and the opportunity to escape from rather humdrum routine, they may be inclined to look elsewhere for satisfaction. There may be a tendency for the partners to take each other too much for granted. The more inspirational and aesthetic interests in life may be sacrificed to the pursuit of an ambition or even lost sight of in the general struggle for existence.

Earth/Air

When Earth is matched with Air, a balance needs to be struck between practice and theory. Earth natives, immersed in the practical realities of life, may not appreciate the intellectual approach and the flights of fancy of their Air partner, while Air may not relish the slow, methodical and conservative methods of Earth. Air tends to dry up Earth, causing dust to be formed, which is probably the least attractive and useful form Earth can take. Yet Earth needs to be aerated in order that organic life can continue to flourish. Just as the human mind is often limited in its scope by the capacity of the brain, the physical vehicle through which it functions, so Air often feels frustrated by the slow reactions of Earth and the scepticism with which some of the more extravagant flights of fancy are sometimes received. Earth is apt to find Air too easily carried away by splendid theories and high-principled idealism that may not be capable of realization. Air is polarized in the intellectual sphere and too often up in the clouds, while Earth natives prefer to concentrate on more materialistic aims, keeping their feet on the ground. Air feels that Earth lacks true refinement and is too slow and heavy, while Earth has little time for social "airs and graces," and Air's preoccupation with etiquette, which is apt to be regarded as lacking in sincerity.

Air natives may not appreciate their partner's pre-occupation with the physical side of sex, while Earth may not understand the Air natives' apparent detachment, and desire for a union of minds, and the need to allow Air partners to give free rein to their romantic imagination, sensing instead some kind of "disloyalty" in such flights of fancy.

If Air does not mind being brought down to Earth fairly regularly and is prepared to deal with ideas and aspirations strictly on their practical merits, and if Earth is willing to concede that life does not consist entirely of experiences on the material plane, a useful and worthwhile partnership may result.

Earth/Water

When Earth is matched with Water, two negative elements are in combination. The partnership may suffer from a lack of motivation. Both elements tend to react rather than to take the initiative, even when expressed through their cardinal signs, so that the couple, lacking the spark of true inspiration, may need to find some vital incentive to action. Each may find the occasional moodiness of the other difficult to cope with. The stolidity of Earth natives may make them unable to understand an emotionally sensitive partner, who cannot appreciate Earth's insistence upon achieving practical results if bringing about the greatest good for the greatest number entails ignoring the emotional reactions of others.

The physical and sensual side of the sex relationship is very important to these partners, though too much sentimentality on the part of Water is likely to meet with too little response from the more prosaic Earth. The sheer earthiness of their mate may sometimes offend the delicate susceptibilities of Water natives.

As in all other combinations the best results are obtained when both partners work together to understand and adapt to the other. Earth contains and limits the rivers and the oceans, while controlled irrigation of deserts makes arid land arable. If Earth makes an effort to understand Water's emotional moods and whims, and Water concedes that other people's feelings sometimes have to be sacrificed in the cause of progress, an harmonious partnership may result.

Air/Air

When Air predominates in the horoscopes of partners the union may rightly be described as a meeting of minds. Both partners will work together best on an intellectual basis. They will probably have no difficulty in communicating with each other and exchanging ideas on a variety of subjects. They may spend more time debating the pros and cons of a situation than they do putting their plans into action. There is a danger that they will become too involved in abstract issues and theoretical problems, and so fail to devote sufficient time and energy to practical, near at hand issues.

Both parties may have a marked liking for social life. If their social engagements do not coincide there may be a danger of seeing too little of each other; consequently, in some cases, home life may be neglected. Much may depend upon the inter-action of the two Mercurys and, if they are harmoniously configured, the intellectual pleasure that each experiences in the company of the other can prove to be very rewarding. This tends to be a partnership that needs some "ballast," otherwise each partner's restlessness may only serve to increase the nervous excitability of the other.

Air/Water

Air in combination with Water implies a partnership between intellect and emotion. To the detached intellect of Air, the ready sympathies of Water do not always appear to be too sensibly bestowed, while the Air natives' apparent ability to insulate themselves from emotional issues may appear to Water to be shallow or callous. Water is inclined to translate past or even present emotional experience into prejudice. Air natives find this very difficult to understand or accept, as they usually prefer to adopt an impartial attitude, or at least to have logical reasons for their likes and dislikes. On the other hand, Water is inclined to accept people as they are, while Air adopts a more critical approach, and is often concerned to discover what motivates them. Water is apt to entertain strange and unaccountable fears which Air tends to laugh at or deride on the grounds that they are without any rational foundation. Far from removing such fears, the ultimate result may be to cause Water to develop a phobia, since nothing is more frightening than to be menaced by some apparent danger, of which others are quite happily oblivious. The Water native can sometimes be rather superstitious. Air likes nothing better than to puncture superstition with a cold blast of logic, perhaps completely unaware of the fact that superstition was the partner's way of covering up or coping with some half-hidden fear. The ultimate result may be for Water to replace the original irrational belief with some new (and possibly more absurd) superstition.

Much of Water's behaviour springs from a lively interest in the past, while Air tends to live for the moment. The Water native knows from past experience that, given a certain set of circumstances, a certain train of emotional reactions may occur, while the Air native, who rarely pays a great deal of attention to other people's emotional reactions, may be completely unaware of the reason for Water's concern.

Intellect and emotion are a most necessary blend, for intellect divorced from emotion may result in a callous attitude towards others, while emotion, without the benefit of intellect, may result in stupidity.

When Air predominates on one side and Water on the other, a good aspect between Air's Mercury and Water's Moon may greatly assist the harmonious blending of the two elements. In order to get the best out of this combination, the Air native should try not to poke fun at the illogical fancies of the Water partner, while the Water native should try to understand that sentiment unguided by reason can easily lapse into sloppy sentimentality, becoming its own worst enemy. Just as in nature, high winds can whip the waves into furious activity so, if Air criticises Water too scathingly, Water will eventually react and instead of merely having recourse to moodiness or a sulking attitude, a full scale emotional storm may result.

Water/Water

The blend of Water with Water produces a highly emotional partnership. Both partners are likely to be highly intuitive and at best each may know instinctively what to do to satisfy the needs of the other and to anticipate the other's probable reactions. There can be a tendency for each to cling to the other in a kind of mutually protective association. This can be a very home-loving and domesticated combination.

The weaknesses of such a partnership spring from the fact that a strong accentuation of the water element can bring about a rather indrawn and over-sensitive personality with a tendency to lapse into occasional moodiness which the partner will lack a sufficiently positive approach to dispel. Sometimes the water native is prone to develop certain phobias, which the partner may easily reinforce by misplaced sympathy, instead of making attempts to discourage this form of self-indulgence.

In order to get the best out of this combination it is necessary for each to make due allowance for the other's moods, or mutual resentment can result. There may be times when one of the partners stands in need of reassurance and it is then that the other should try to strike as positive a note as possible in order to lift his or her partner out of the doldrums.

THE QUADRUPLICITIES

In addition to assessing the effects of combinations of the various elements we can also compare the signs in terms of the majority positions in the Quadruplicities: that is by determining whether the majority of planets are in Cardinal, Fixed or Mutable signs. Theoretically speaking it is better for the partners' Sun signs not to belong to the same Quadruplicity, because signs of the same mode (when not in conjunction) are in square or opposition to each other.

Before examining the probable effects of different combinations of the three qualities, it is first necessary to take into account the general characteristics likely to be present when one particular quality predominates in a nativity.

The Cardinal Signs

Those with a majority of planets in Cardinal signs want to initiate action and are more concerned with the outward expression of the elements they represent. The positive signs, Aries and Libra, are apt to act more spontaneously, though Libra often allows its course of action to be dominated by a need to adjust to and find a balance in relation to other people. Cancer and Capricorn are more likely to react as a result of some outside stimulus, albeit in a positive manner, or to initiate action with some long term plan in mind. Cardinal sign natives have no liking for opposition and much prefer to receive positive encouragement. These signs are equivalent to the Hindu guna *Rajas*—Activity, the irresistible force. These natives are enterprising and ambitious, preferring to occupy prominent and responsible positions. The path-finding instinct is well-developed. The nature is likely to be rather self-assertive and independent with an ability to pioneer and institute change.

The Fixed Signs

Those with a majority of planets in Fixed signs are the builders of the zodiac. They are opposed to change and tend to obstruct innovations of which they do not approve. This opposition can be stubbornly maintained when they feel that personal pride is involved. They are likely to be determined and self-reliant, with the ability to wait patiently for their opportunities. Under stress they can exhibit great powers of endurance. They usually succeed through sheer persistence and the ability to ignore distractions as they move relentlessly towards their goal. They often see power as a means of ensuring their security. Occasionally some are tempted to behave too autocratically when they reach a position of authority, or they may attempt to assume an authority to which they are not entitled. This mode represents the Hindu guna *Tamas*—Inertia/Stability, the immovable object.

The Mutable Signs

Those with a majority of planets in Mutable signs are the intermediaries of the zodiac. They maintain a link between the forthright action of the Cardinal signs and the stoical immobility of the Fixed signs. They hold the balance between progress and innovation on the one hand and entrenched conservatism on the other. They tend to develop versatility in order to adapt to a variety of different situations. There is usually a need for someone or something to adapt to, so they are often at their best in a supporting role. Mutable signs represent the guna *Sattva*—Mindstuff/Intelligence. Just as the mind is ready to dart hither and thither with quicksilver rapidity, so they tend to become rather restless and sometimes discontented as they seek a satisfactory means of expressing their talents as intermediaries. The sympathies are usually well developed and the mind active, though sometimes indecisive.

Each quality needs to be harmoniously blended with the other two, just as the gunas, *rajas, tamas* and *sattva* need to function in perfect balance in the whole man.

Cardinal/Cardinal

A partnership between two Cardinal types may work well on an all-action basis, provided both partners can agree beforehand exactly what their aims are and whether their ambitions can best be realized by joint action. If there is any doubt about this it may be better for them to plan their activities so that there is a clearly defined sphere of action for each. In this way any tendency for the competitive nature of one partner to clash with the other will be minimized. Cardinal natives need enough elbow room to pursue their own enterprises and maintain a measure of independence which means so much to them. When there is a good degree of planetary harmony between the two horoscopes there can be a good deal of mutual admiration, each appreciating the achievements of the other. This is the most dynamic of combinations but, if strong planetary stresses are present between the two horoscopes, there could well be a tendency for the partners to get at cross-purposes. In such a situation any undue assertion of independence on either side or any attempt to force the issue could prove harmful to the association, since the Cardinal native does not like to be opposed.

Cardinal/Fixed

A partnership between a predominantly Cardinal person and one who has most emphasis on the Fixed signs can represent the irresistible force coming into contact with the immovable object, in which case a very great deal will depend upon the way in which the mutable quality is represented in both horoscopes, since a fair amount of adaptability is often needed on both sides in this situation. When the same element predominates in both nativities and, to a lesser extent, when a majority of the positive elements Fire and Air, or the negative elements Earth and Water, are grouped together in both horoscopes, the partners will be able to combine their individual talents with greater effectiveness and less friction. The Cardinal natives can provide the initiative, while their Fixed partners can supply the motive power to establish the position gained through the enterprise of their Cardinal allies. If there is a lack of basic compatibility, the Fixed signs are apt to find their Cardinal partners too rash and careless, while the Cardinal signs may regard their Fixed partners as too lazy and unenterprising, and too concerned with maintaining their position and holding on to their resources.

Cardinal/Mutable

A partnership between a predominantly Cardinal and a predominantly Mutable person will work best when both have a majority of planets in the same element or when the pairing brings two positive elements together. As Mutable natives are willing to adapt to their more active partners, the result may be a very active partnership that lacks any kind of anchor.

Fixed/Fixed

In this combination much will depend upon the basic emotional attitude of the partners. The fixed signs tend to be conservative and resistant to change. When there is a preponderantly harmonious planetary relationship between the two charts, this is an excellent combination on which to build a lasting marriage, a business or some joint enterprise on a lasting basis, though there may be a need to ensure that there is sufficient scope for adaptability to changing circumstances, as the element of flexibility is less likely to be present in this type of partnership. At best, the partners can combine effectively in activities that call for perseverance, faithfulness and fixity of purpose. Since neither partner will wish to be dominated by the other, such an association needs a marked degree of planetary harmony between the nativities of the two partners if it is to succeed. When there is a larger proportion of planetary afflictions between the two any differences between the partners may become aggravated by the inability of each to concede to the other, due to their pride becoming involved. A small rift may develop into a major disagreement through a mutually stubborn and inflexible attitude. In such circumstances the partnership may sometimes be bedeviled by intolerance and jealousy, and a battle of wills may result.

Fixed/Mutable

Unless Mutable natives are content to follow a mainly passive role unhappiness may arise with a Fixed companion, who may continually fail to satisfy their eager appetite for variety and change and who may fail to attain that degree of mental rapport with them that the Mutable natives are so anxious to cultivate.

When signs of the same element predominate, this partnership stands a better chance of success. Mutable partners may develop great admiration for their companion's strength of character. They often tend to be rather dependent, feeling that they need a stronger partner in order to achieve personal success. Sometimes the Fixed sign partner enjoys playing the major role, but unless there is a fair degree of planetary harmony between the two horoscopes, and unless there is a mutual recognition that one possesses important qualities that the other lacks, the fixed sign native may fail to be impressed by the mutable partner's versatility and may consider the latter too flighty and undependable, while the Mutable native may consider his companion too stolid, autocratic and unyielding.

Mutable/Mutable

This type of partnership is likely to flourish best on the mental level. If the majority of planetary cross-aspects are favorable, a high degree of mental rapport may be present. Both partners are likely to be of a highly adaptable type. Since natives with this proclivity usually need someone to adapt to, and someone who can supply the element of continuity that they lack, the tendency is for this type of combination to lack an anchor and to fail to act with sufficient thoroughness in circumstances which call for total commitment. Unless Saturn is strong in both nativities and harmoniously configured with a majority of the partner's planets, the partnership may lack sufficient stability. The common aim may become too indeterminate, with one partner's restlessness feeding the other's. This partnership usually flourishes most effectively through the development of shared mental interests and a mutual ability to communicate freely, though in some cases, particularly when the earth element is lacking, the partners may have a distaste for coping with practical issues, encouraging each other in mutual fantasies that lead to a marked degree of escapism.

PLANETARY HOUSE GROUPS

A third grouping of planets which can be highly informative concerns their distribution in terms of the angular, succedent and cadent houses. Before examining the probable effects of these three groups in combination it is first necessary to take into account the general characteristics likely to be present when one particular grouping predominates in a nativity.

Angular

Those with a majority of planets in angular houses usually want to make an impression on the world and to feel themselves to be at the center of everything that is happening. The impact of their personality will be immediate, whether it is attractive or repugnant. These types enter easily into relationships, perhaps because they need the reactions of others in order to become more aware of themselves. A number of planets harmoniously aspecting each other in angular houses may indicate a rather self-satisfied person, while discordant aspects linking angular planets tend to produce a more rugged type of personality, usually with a strongly accented ego and a desire to take the lead in a partnership.

Succedent

Those with a majority of planets in succedent houses are more concerned with establishing roots and building up the schemes initiated by those with a majority of angular planets. They therefore have a vested interest in stable partnerships although discordant aspects between planets in succedent houses may indicate some difficulty in establishing a stable life pattern. There is usually a great need for emotional security. When the Moon, Venus, Jupiter and Neptune are involved in these inharmonious aspects, there may be a tendency to seek the pleasures of life instead of settling down, while malefics afflicted in these houses can indicate a rather jealous nature and a strong need for a feeling of security in sexual relationships that can work out disastrously unless the partner's horoscope provides enough harmonious cross-aspects to the succedent planets.

Cadent

Natives with the majority of planets in cadent houses tend to hide their real personality and often have some difficulty in finding a really effective way of self-expression. Sometimes, as in the case of Sir Arthur Conan Doyle, who had six bodies in the twelfth house, this is compensated for in literary activities or through dedication to a life of service. There is some talent for acting as an agent or go-between, and adapting to a variety of different people and circumstances. There is often more tendency to live in the mind than with the other types, so that they may tend to withdraw into the world of the abstract. Consequently mental compatibility is more important to them and they need a partner who can draw them out and help them to realise their latent potentials.

When two partners both have a majority of angular planets, a great deal will depend upon whether these planets blend harmoniously and whether their intrinsic natures are compatible. If they clash, a smooth relationship is unlikely to be established since both partners will have a marked interest in getting things done. If they are at cross-purposes, they may try to forge ahead with their own plans at the expense of the other. The angular type may blend well with the succedent type if the cross-aspects are harmonious but usually there is less chance of an harmonious relationship with the cadent type. Of the three types, the succedent is the only one which has an equal chance of achieving a good blend with either the angular or cadent types, provided the majority of cross-aspects are not discordant. A partnership with one whose planets are mainly in succedent houses may also work out well, provided the cross-aspects promise harmony. Those with a majority of planets in angular houses, who like to concentrate on putting ideas into action, are the least likely to get on well with the cadent type, who tend to concentrate on planning and perfecting the theoretical approach.

CHAPTER 6

Benefic and Malefic Planets
Harmonious and Discordant Aspects

A famous English astrologer, having ruefully surveyed the effects of transits of Uranus, Neptune and Pluto over sensitive points in his horoscope was heard to observe: "I hope the next planet they discover will be a benefic!" Such a sentiment raises several questions. Why, for instance, do we label some planets benefic and others malefic? By what standards are we measuring?

If we are measuring from a worldly point of view then everything which is conducive to maintaining and increasing our creature comforts and to bringing us pleasure must be regarded as benefic, while everything that causes us pain and thwarts our desires must be classed as malefic. No one says: "Hooray, I've broken my leg" or laments the inheriting of a large fortune and so it is that the former type of event is nearly always found to occur when the so-called "malefic" planets are active, while the latter take place when the so-called "benefic" planets are operating.

The world's great religious teachers have always stressed that true happiness is not to be found in pursuing the pleasures of the material world. It seems that the majority of mankind's restless search for pleasure is but a pale reflection of the religious devotee's quest for a state of ecstatic bliss. Such a quest demands a life of rigid self-discipline and self-denial, qualities which do not reflect the essential nature of the traditional benefics, Venus and Jupiter. Yet Love and Wisdom are both essential to the quest, which demands for its ultimate fulfillment, an harmonious response to all the planetary rays.

The terms "benefic" and "malefic" may suggest that they are the agents of the twin forces of good and evil. If so, the forces of evil seem to have a huge advantage, since the extra-Saturnian planets appear to indicate as many troubles as the traditional malefics! It is probably truer to say that the forces represented by the planets are neutral and that whether they operate for good or evil in a particular nativity depends upon the evolutionary status of that particular native. It has been said that we suffer from the defects of our virtues and our individual response to planets may at times invoke both their more desirable and less desirable qualities and this two-way operation of the planetary forces accounts for the fact that various authorities have equated the Sun, Moon and the planets as far as Saturn, both to the Seven Great Virtues and the Seven Deadly Sins.

Additionally, man incarnates on earth in order to learn certain lessons; by struggling against adversity, soul growth is speeded up and gains in spiritual stature. Thus any planet which signifies difficulties, opposition and afflictions of various kinds can assist the native's soul growth and by this reckoning must be productive of "good."

It is easy to see how Venus and Jupiter came to be classified as benefics. An excess of self-love and self-indulgence usually harms no one except the one who indulges in it, though admittedly an excess of the benefits apparently conferred by the benefics can occasionally have disastrous results. I well remember an incident in an early Eddie Cantor film, "The Kid from Spain," in which he was captured by a fierce Mexican bandit, whose idea of benevolence was to offer him a choice of ways to die, perhaps by the knife or by the gun. Eddie thanked him for his generosity but said: "If it's all the same to you, I'd rather die of eating strawberries!" Excesses can lead to trouble just as deprivations can.

The energy of Mars, used selfishly, can easily manifest as aggression and even cruelty, while the misuse of Saturnian energies can result in a cold and callous self-interest and the over-zealous imposition of discipline on others, all activities calculated to produce unpleasant experiences for others. In the light of this type of low-level response to their stimulus it is easy to see how these two planets became "branded" as malefics. Yet the higher qualities of Mars, courage and a desire to champion the cause of the weak, and of Saturn, dependability, perseverance, self-discipline and a never ending quest for self-perfection, make a mockery of the term "malefic."

There is no better illustration of the benefic/malefic potentiality invested in a single planet than in the various effects of Neptune to be discerned in individual nativities. The ecstatic realization of heart's desire and the drugs that provide a short cut to ecstasy both belong to the domain of Neptune—boundlessness—the absorption in Nirvana of the Buddhist—Universal Love. Neptune can bring one's heart's desire, thus appearing to act as a benefic. But if one desires the wrong thing through immaturity or an exaggerated self-interest, then the realization of envisioned goals can become a disastrously shattering experience, so that the gifts of Neptune are ultimately regarded as totally undesirable. Neptune has been labelled the planet of illusion by those who judge by worldly standards, when in actual fact its function is to destroy illusion by presenting man with the results of yearnings after false gods and becoming seduced by illusory concepts of happiness. Thus Neptune can be regarded as benefic or malefic, according to men's expectations, and so it is with the other planets.

Some of those who recognize that there is a more desirable goal beyond the pleasures of this world fail to understand that this goal is only reached through unceasing effort and iron self-discipline and seek short cuts through the use of drugs, which, although capable of opening doors of consciousness hitherto undreamed of, can have side effects which ultimately destroy the user.

Just as we speak of benefic and malefic planets, so the aspects are divided into two principal categories. The energies denoted by the good aspects, the trine, sextile and semi-sextile, are easier to handle because they appear to produce satisfactory results with less effort than the more powerful energies of the square and opposition (and to a lesser degree the semi-square, sesquiquadrate and quincunx) which are often indicative of obstacles, opposition and delays, though these are not necessarily catastrophic. As with the malefic planets, it is often the so-called bad aspects which provide the conditions most conducive to soul growth, setbacks to be overcome, pain and suffering to be surmounted. Such obstacles to progress, by setting up resistance, serve as the basis for a kind of spiritual isometrics, by which spiritual "muscle" may be developed and strengthened.

Ptolemy's division of the aspects into "harmonious" and "discordant" is one again based on a sound mechanical assessment of the problems inherent in combining planets in signs of different elements. The trine is usually formed between planets in the same element and the sextile between planets in compatible elements, either both positive or both negative. It therefore follows that a trine between a planet at the very end of Cancer and one at the very beginning of Sagittarius is less likely to operate entirely harmoniously, since water and fire do not easily mix. Similarly, a square between a planet at the end of Cancer and one at the beginning of Scorpio is not likely to operate so adversely as one between planets not in the same element.

The present writer prefers to retain the long established practice of referring to aspects as harmonious and discordant in the belief that most students are aware that this does not imply any prejudgment of an aspect's operation for good or evil in a particular horoscope but merely refers to the fact that the achievement of a smooth combination between the two planetary forces involved may require a greater degree of effort from the native, when the aspect is discordant, to achieve the best results. If the greater power of the so-called discordant aspects can be controlled, correspondingly more productive results may eventually be obtained. If this power cannot be controlled, a state of crisis may be precipitated, just as a man who is not strong enough to handle a pneumatic drill properly may do damage with it, while in capable hands it can prove to be a most effective tool.

While there has been no attempt to refer to benefic and malefic planets by other terms, there have been several attempts to find an alternative way of referring to harmonious and discordant aspects, and the pairings of static and dynamic, active and passive spring to mind as couplings which suggest a slightly different view of the working out of aspects. Other couplings, such as easy and difficult, helpful and adverse and favorable and unfavorable, merely reiterate the underlying idea contained in the terms "harmonious" and "discordant" and readers will no doubt notice that the author occasionally makes use of these alternatives for the sake of variety.

It is worth re-emphasizing that the so-called favorable aspects do not of themselves promise an harmonious combination of the qualities signified by the planets in aspect to each other. Not only does much depend upon the intrinsic nature of each planet but also upon whether those planets are well placed by sign and well aspected by other planets. Mars, for instance does not combine easily with Saturn, even when in trine aspect, while a square between the Sun and Jupiter can indicate much success. However even a trine between the Sun and Jupiter can be spoilt if either body is in its detriment or fall, while a technically adverse aspect between two planets may be much improved if either or both planets are dignified by sign.

The above observations hold good also in the comparison of horoscopes, and a trine between one person's Venus in Scorpio and another's Saturn in Cancer could signifiy a rather less happy association than if both planets formed a conjunction in Libra.

There is a further point to be considered in this context. If our horoscope contains, for instance, a Mars-Saturn square, suggesting some difficulty in combining the forces signified by the two planets, an aspect from another's Saturn to our Mars, or from Mars to our Saturn, will serve to remind us of our difficulties. The other person will, so to speak, personify our own psychological problem and since we tend to attract others according to our own planetary make-up, there is a good chance that a number of our own harmonious and discordant planetary complexes will frequently become "personified" in this way. As a result we shall probably look benevolently upon those who stimulate our best aspects, and entertain considerable reservations about those who make us uncomfortably aware of the disharmonies in our own nativity.

It is through the dual working of the benefic and malefic possibilities associated with the planets and of the harmonious and discordant possibilities associated with the aspects that we can find the most satisfactory answer to the old chestnut: "If God is a God of Love, why does he permit pain and suffering to exist?" The evolutionary plan of the universe is so constituted that each individual has the possibility of achieving the status of a Divine Being, a possibility which can only be realized after many incarnations of unremitting effort and sustained aspiration. Only by being free to respond in our own way to the planetary forces playing through our solar system, represented by the Sun, Moon and planets, can we ultimately fit ourselves to become a perfect channel for the expression of those planetary forces.

The amount of pain and suffering in any individual life can be a measure of that individual's failure to respond in the best possible way to the rays of a particular planet or planets, a failure which may stretch back over a number of lifetimes. If, for instance, we fail to use properly the power represented by Mars and allow our energies to control us instead of us holding them in check, we may fail to exercise proper control over our temper, become unduly aggressive or unreasonably reckless and so precipitate situations which result in our being given a short, sharp and painful lesson, a lesson which may be repeated over and over again if we do not learn to improve our handling of the Martian energies. If we do not respond as we should to the power represented by Saturn and allow ourselves to become dominated by a cold and restricting self-interest and allow our worldly ambitions to blind us to all other considerations, we may find that in the long term we are denied the love and affection that we have omitted to bestow on others and are isolated in some way from the world in which we live. The lessons of Saturn are stern, but dictated by strict and logical justice. In similar fashion, our failure to respond adequately to the other planetary forces can involve us in a variety of unpleasant experiences.

The repercussions of wrong living may not make themselves felt in one lifetime. Indeed, most of us are much too fragile to bear the accumulated burden of all our previous misdeeds during the course of any one incarnation. Thus Dr. Davidson in his lectures on Medical Astrology, cited the case of a woman with consumptive tendencies, shown by a much afflicted Neptune, who had built this predisposition into her system through a lifetime of fasting and midnight vigils in spartan surroundings in a previous existence as a nun. Not for nothing did the Buddha counsel the wisdom of the Middle Way!

Thus by the way in which we respond to the play of the planetary forces, do we become our own judge and jury. It is we who precipitate our own suffering and the unpleasant effects resulting from our own mishandling of the forces at our disposal are the inevitable results of immutable law. The alternative to this process of learning by trial and error is for man to remain ever in the robot stage, a state of existence not far removed from permanent annihilation!

The foregoing is, of course, an over-simplification of the picture, since our own evolution is bound up with the evolution of the wider units to which we belong, of the family into which we are born, of the nation of which we are a part, and, indeed, of the whole human race. Thus it is that the story of the most perfect Being who ever incarnated on Earth tells of the ultimate sacrifice on the Cross, not only for the purpose of paying off any remaining debts of his own to the past, but with the object of freeing the whole human race from the crushing burden of their own accumulated karma.

CHAPTER 7

Interaction between Nativities
Part One

As a matter of convenience the masculine pronoun is used in this chapter (except where feminine planets are involved) though the readings will apply equally well when the sexes are reversed.

Interplanetary Cross-Aspects

Of all the factors in chart comparison, the interplay of the planets and angles in one nativity with the same factors in the other is the most important. When the elements or the qualities do not appear to blend very harmoniously, a number of strong, favorable planetary inter-aspects may alter the total picture very considerably, while if the elements and qualities blend harmoniously, much of the apparent rapport may not materialize if the cross-aspects between the planets in the two nativities are discordant.

The same rules apply to the judgment of cross-aspects in chart comparison as in the judgment of planetary aspects in the natal chart. Sextiles and trines promise an harmonious relationship, while squares pose difficulties. Conjunctions and oppositions are variable, according to the nature of the planets involved. Any planet debilitated by sign can to some extent spoil the harmony inherent in the trine and sextile, while a planet dignified by sign can greatly minimize the friction usually indicated by the square and opposition. Mars, Saturn, Uranus, Neptune and Pluto, even when combined with each other by favorable aspect may produce tensions that require careful handling and much will depend on their strength and the way they are integrated into the general pattern of each nativity.

As in individual nativities, the so-called inharmonious aspects can play an important part in assisting the soul growth of each partner, but it is worth bearing in mind that a partnership requires that two people (or perhaps more if a business partnership is involved) work together in harmony and there can be plenty of opportunity to find testing experiences in the outside world without the partners themselves clashing in such a way as to create difficulties for each other. If the general indications in the native's chart indicate the kind of temperament that finds difficulty in adjusting to others, he is likely to attract a partner who will make him uncomfortably aware of such a difficulty. There may also be karmic reasons why two people should mate or go into partnership and if the meeting is truly one of destiny it will often seem that no amount of apparent incompatibility is going to keep them from establishing a relationship. However, the most harmonious relationships usually result when there are a large number of favorable contacts between the two nativities, though some discordant aspects may prevent the partnership becoming too unadventurous and can serve a useful purpose should either of the parties thrive on an occasional diet of excitement.

The opposition plays a special role where partnership is concerned, because the cusp of the seventh house of partnerships is in opposition to the Ascendant. Since we tend to seek complementary qualities in a mate, an opposition between the same planet or luminary in each nativity can prove a source of strength to a partnership unless another planet in either nativity stands in square to the two poles of the opposition. Conjunctions are also important and again, much will depend on aspects received by the planets in conjunction. An affinity suggested by each partner having planets in the same sign may be considerably diminished in practice if the planets in that sign are inimical to each other. When there are several planets in a sign, the total impact of the stellium needs to be taken into account.

Sometimes one partner's horoscope will supply some factor which actually improves the working of the other, as when for instance one partner's Jupiter is placed in trine and sextile respectively to two planets forming a difficult opposition in the nativity of the other, where no such helpful factor is present. On the other hand, if a difficult configuration between two or more planets in one nativity is stimulated by a conjunction or opposition from a planet or luminary in the partner's horoscope, the one with the difficult configuration becomes very uncomfortably aware of the stresses it represents. On this account the latter may resent that particular quality in the former which causes the development of such feelings of tension.

A similar kind of situation arises when one of the partners has a much afflicted planet in the horoscope and the other has that same planet close to an angle, especially if it is rising. An individual tends to express himself principally in terms of the rising planet or planets. Therefore when one partner has a rising planet much afflicted in the other's horoscope, the former will continually "remind" the latter of the tension or difficulty denoted by the afflicted planet, tending to make the latter feel ill at ease in the former's presence.

Significant cross-aspects between most of the major planets are not likely in the case of contemporaries but if there is a large age gap between the two parties in the relationship any clashes between the outer planets can be significant.

A favorable aspect between the rulers of each partner's seventh house is a useful indicator of harmony, but more crucial still are the cross-aspects to any planets in the seventh house. Minor aspects, such as the semi-sextile, semi-square, sesquiquadrate and quincunx should not be ignored. The quincunx often has some karmic significance and may perhaps relate to a service one partner "owes" the other. There is often a challenge to effect some kind of self-transformation implicit in the quincunx. Stresses denoted by such a cross-aspect between "difficult" planets may be resolved through a determined effort on the part of one or both partners to examine themselves as objectively as possible, working on any faults of character of which they might become aware with a view to their ultimate eradication.

Any reference to minor aspects naturally brings up the question of allowable orbs. While it may be prudent to take into account possible stresses in situations where one partner has Saturn in a sign and the other has Mars in the same sign, irrespective of the distance they are apart, it is a good general rule not to allow more than about two or three degrees of orb for the conjunction, sextile, square, trine and opposition adding perhaps a degree or two more if the luminaries are involved. All other aspects should be within about a degree and a half of exactitude. The smaller the orb, the more significant and the more crucial the contact is likely to be.

Sometimes it will be found that a planet in one nativity falls on the mid-point between two planets in another's nativity. When this occurs the effect is to bring about an increased awareness in the latter of the two planets concerned and if these are not linked by a recognized aspect, the partner's planet acts as a catalyst, with the result that he experiences the impact of both planets in the other's nativity, which will appear to act as if they were actually linked together by aspect. If, for instance, Mars is in 24 Leo in one horoscope and Saturn is in 12 Scorpio, while Venus in the partner's horoscope is in 3 Aries or Libra, or in exact square to these degrees and so squaring the mid-point, the combination of Mars and Saturn may operate very much to the disadvantage of the partner with Venus involved, as a result of a Mars-Saturn type of reaction from the other in relation to all the things signified by Venus in the nativity in question.

THE PLANETS

Before we consider the probable effects of one planet in combination with another, it is first necessary to take into account the significance of the luminaries and the planets that have a special bearing on personal relationships.

The Sun represents our integrity and inner motivating force, our aims in life, the ideals that spur us on to achievement, and our ability to integrate the various forces with which we have to deal. It epitomizes the masculine approach to life and signifies in a man's horoscope his inner attitude to his role as a man, and in a woman's horoscope, her concept of ideal manhood.

The Moon represents the feelings, the instinctive behavior patterns and the way we respond to other people. It epitomizes the feminine approach to life and signifies in a man's horoscope his concept of ideal womanhood. In a woman's horoscope, it is her feminine appeal and her attitude to her role as a woman, particularly as a mother. It relates to the amount of magnetic attraction that natives of either sex can project.

Mercury represents the mind in action and the general manner in which we deal with and analyze ideas, and communicate with others. To some extent it shows our versatility and powers of mobility and adaptability.

Venus represents the capacity for creating and maintaining harmony, and is therefore highly important in all relationships. It is related to our sense of values indicating what we like to receive and what we expect to receive from others. It represents the feminine and pliant side of the nature. In a man's chart, it shows the type of woman he is likely to attract and his concept of ideal womanhood at the physical level. In a woman's chart it shows how she is likely to play her feminine role.

Mars represents the energies at our command and the way they are deployed in action (which can be either constructive or destructive). It shows how much initiative we are likely to possess, the nature of our desires and how we set about satisfying them. It is the masculine, aggressive side of the nature, acting to disturb the equilibrium that Venus seeks to bring about, in order to create new situations. In a man's chart it shows how he is likely to play his masculine role. In a woman's chart it represents the type of man she is likely to attract and her concept of ideal manhood at the physical level.

Jupiter represents the capacity to extend a benevolent understanding to others, giving them a feeling of encouragement and well-being. It denotes the capacity for enthusiasm, for expansion on all levels, for multiplying resources and generally preserving that which is considered to be of social and moral value.

Saturn represents the capacity for self-discipline; the amount of perseverance and endurance we are capable of in attempts to realize our practical ambitions. It signifies a sense of integrity and devotion to duty, though service may sometimes (out of a sense of obligation) be rendered more in the letter than in the spirit, or with an air of martyrdom that leaves no doubt that we are making considerable sacrifices in order to oblige. Saturn builds slowly and thoroughly, though perhaps with too little imagination and over-much respect for tradition. Saturn's lack of warmth, exuberance and seeming lack of sympathy can slowly cool, though not necessarily terminate, a partnership. It is the planet of old age and its greatest effect may not manifest until the later years of life.

Uranus represents the capacity for inventive ingenuity and the ability to plan imaginatively for the future, cutting out dead wood and any outdated legacies from the past. It encourages the accentuation of a personal uniqueness that can add a dynamic new dimension to the personality, though there can be a tendency to erratic, unpredictable and sometimes dictatorial behaviour, that can test the strength of the bonds of any partnership.

Neptune represents the capacity for transcending the normal range of perceptions and sense impressions. Unless our feet are firmly on the ground it is possible to get drawn away from our center of gravity by visions of strange new worlds (which are not really new, but may have remained mysteriously unattainable through lack of the proper means to contact them). We may become unsure of our own exact standpoint, with the result that others tend to lack confidence in our reliability.

Neptune's ultra-sensitive perceptions sometimes give the native the tendency to invest even the commonplace with some strange glamour, and this, together with a capacity for idealism and aesthetic susceptibilities, can make him a fascinating companion. The planet can also encourage the growth of an all-embracing compassion that can also make allowances for many of the partner's shortcomings, though on the negative side this can occasionally deteriorate into over-sentimentality, while a capacity to deceive, whether intentional or not, or some degree of self-deception, can produce unfortunate complications in a relationship.

Pluto can denote a capacity for compulsive attachments that can arise through the powerful fascination engendered by previous lives spent together. It supplies a challenge to discover new depths of meaning in relation to the things signified by any planet with which it is in aspect and it can therefore prove to be a very vital, if disturbing, link between two nativities, acting to bring about a complete reassessment of attitude in relation to certain factors of each partner's psychology.

Sun/Sun

This contact is the one which is most familiar to the layman since most purveyors of popular astrology in newspaper columns rely almost entirely on the theoretical compatibility of Sun signs, with rarely a thought as to whether there is a recognized aspect distance between the two Suns. A trine between the Sun in Taurus and the Sun in Capricorn may denote a good measure of harmony if both luminaries are in the thirtieth degree of their respective signs but if one Sun is in the first degree of Taurus and the other in the thirtieth degree of Capricorn, the square aspect between them may noticeably diminish the harmony.

A favorable aspect between the Suns in two horoscopes indicates that the individuals concerned can harmonize their aims in life and their basic approach to living without undue friction. A mutual respect for each other's worth as an individual and a pleasing compatibility of temperament should form a solid foundation for a lasting relationship.

The conjunction does not necessarily mean a firm partnership, especially if one or both Suns are afflicted at birth. Even if they are free from affliction, sometimes one partner may find little exhilaration in the company of the other.

The opposition aspect between marriage partners may prove very felicitous if the Suns are well aspected at birth and each may particularly appreciate in the other the qualities that compliment his own. In some cases the partners seem to be "made for each other"—love at first sight! If either Sun is much afflicted at birth, differences of temperament may prove a barrier to a proper understanding, and even open enmity or a "power" struggle can result.

When the Suns are in adverse aspect to each other or either is in Aquarius or Libra, the contact may not work out favorably. There may be a clash of wills, with each insisting upon his rights. When the Suns are in square, each partner should be prepared to surrender some sovereignty in order to help the relationship to work more smoothly. The differing talents and abilities which each brings to the partnership should be appreciated as a contribution towards increasing the resources available to both. Each may flourish more harmoniously if allowed to deploy his special talents in his own field of operation and in his own way, so that the partners do not get at cross-purposes. Each may then learn from the other and the relationship grows in value accordingly.

The quincunx can pose difficult problems although this relationship can be highly educational. One partner may have to nurse the other or shoulder some of the other's burdens. Circumstances may arise in the relationship which challenge one or both partners to transform some of their long established attitudes and habits.

Statistical studies comparing the horoscopes of married couples suggest that the sextile aspect occurs very frequently in harmonious marriages and that the square is most often present in discordant partnerships.

Sun/Moon

This is the classic compatibility combination, with the masculine and positive Sun joined to his natural mate, the feminine, receptive and passive Moon. The forces represented by the luminaries complement each other, just as Night complements Day.

In a man's horoscope, the Moon represents the type of feminine ideal that he carries in his subconscious mind, as opposed to Venus, which represents among other things the more voluptuous aspects of femininity, particularly in relation to physical appeal. The Moon's attributes are more readily sensed at a psychic level. In the same way, the Sun in a woman's horoscope relates to her concept of the ideal man, as distinguished from Mars, which represents a more physical approach to the male sex.

In an ideal marriage, true harmony should exist on all levels and good aspects between the partners' luminaries and between the partners' Venus and Mars ought to be present. In passing, it is worth noting that Mars and Venus rule Aries and Taurus respectively, the first two signs, and the first masculine and feminine sector of the zodiac. In these two signs the luminaries are dignified, for the Sun is exalted in Aries and the Moon in Taurus.

Because the Sun is the masculine luminary and the Moon the feminine, it is often assumed that true compatibility between the sexes requires that the male Sun be in favorable aspect to the female Moon, but when this combination is reversed it is no less potent, since a favorable aspect from the female partner's Sun to the male's Moon indicates that the woman is able to illuminate the man's concept of his ideal woman. Thus aspected, the male Moon is also able to reflect back to her the woman's concept of the ideal man.

In the marriage relationship the man's Sun can bring significance and illumination to the woman's Moon, encouraging her to take pleasure in playing the role of wife, while the woman's Moon can magnetically draw out the solar qualities that fit her partner to play the husband's role.

In all types of relationship, the Moon can adapt to and sustain the Sun's quest for independent self-expression and an acknowledgement of his worth as an individual. The Moon instinctively understands the Sun's basic motives and responds accordingly. The Sun is likely to play the leading role in the relationship, with the Moon adapting to Sun's wishes.

The conjunction is a particularly powerful contact between the horoscopes of opposite sexes and usually signifies a high degree of compatibility unless either luminary is much afflicted at birth, when antipathy may result. Between those of the same sex there is usually a great deal of sympathy so that a particularly happy friendship can develop.

When the luminaries are in adverse aspect or either is debilitated, the Moon's sensitivity tends to place it on the receiving end of any discords that may arise. This may accentuate any tendencies to moodiness, so that the solar partner feels aggrieved and his pride is hurt at the suggestion that any conduct of his could have brought about such a discord. Solar egotism may fail to take account of the delicate and fragile susceptibilities of the Moon. The square is a particularly unaccommodating aspect and the Sun's capacity for self-esteem and belief in the rightness of his cause may prove an insurmountable obstacle to sympathetic acceptance of the partner's changes of mood and feeling, so that the Moon may despair of ever getting her partner to show her the amount of consideration she feels to be her due. She may be more concerned with life at the personal and emotional level, and not be able to appreciate the broader considerations that motivate her solar partner.

While the conjunction and sextile are often present between the nativities of marriage partners, the adverse aspects do not on their own necessarily indicate the type of incompatibility that leads to a breakdown of the relationship. To some extent they involve an element of fascination even when stress is present at the same time.

Sun/Mercury

The role of Mercury in facilitating communication is obviously helpful in any relationship, as a useful mental rapport can easily be established when the two bodies are in favorable aspect. In such cases, the Sun provides a willing listener, encouraging Mercury to communicate and put over ideas, so that Mercury feels he has a partner who really understands him. The Sun may provide Mercury with opportunities for literary endeavour or suggest areas of study that may prove fruitful. Mercury is likely to find a helpful collaborator in the Sun, provided he listens to the Sun's ideas with attention and due deference.

When either body is debilitated or there is an adverse aspect between them the results are hardly likely to be disastrous, although the Sun may find Mercury frivolous or his ideas unworthy of serious attention, while Mercury may feel that the Sun is unable to appreciate the spirit in which his ideas are conceived and communicated.

Usually the Sun will influence Mercury and in a favorable combination, Mercury can prove to be an efficient interpreter of and a helpful agent for his solar partner's ideas, while the unfavorable aspects may result in his advocacy of the partner's cause doing more harm than good.

Sun/Venus

This is a highly satisfactory contact for any type of partnership and one frequently found between the horoscopes of marriage partners. It promises a congenial relationship unless either body is much afflicted at birth, although if there is an adverse aspect between them or either is debilitated the Sun may find that he does not share the tastes and leisure interests of his partner, who may seem to him to be too self-indulgent. Generally speaking, the Sun and Venus have no trouble in keeping on friendly terms and unless there are strong impediments elsewhere, the Sun's warmth can draw a good deal of affection from Venus, who will recognize in the solar partner someone who is well worth making a special effort to please, while the Sun, unless unutterably complacent, will feel flattered by the warmth of affection that he is able to inspire.

The high degree of harmony that can exist under the good aspects can produce the kind of marriage partnership where the couple are regarded as being "made for each other," while in other types of relationship, mutual affection and esteem can combine to cement a friendship or produce an unusually harmonious link and an extra capacity for co-operation between casual acquaintances.

The adverse aspects rarely signify major difficulties though disharmonies may occur as a result of Venus using her persuasive powers for her own advantage, or leading the solar partner on, only to withhold favors at the last minute. Hurt feelings and emotional disappointments can result from the Sun's wounded pride, while Venus may sometimes feel that her partner is too dictatorial. Occasionally the adverse aspects signify situations where the partners are temporarily separated, with the result that they find that "absence makes the heart grow fonder."

The arrival of the Sun by progression at the conjunction of Venus, when this planet is aspected by another person's Sun may signal the beginning of a highly significant relationship between them.

Sun/Mars

This is a contact frequently found between the horoscopes of marriage partners. Occurring in other areas of human relationship it usually means that the two people concerned will take notice of each other, since the combined influence of the two bodies is likely to create some degree of warmth, if not actually heat.

In a romantic association, the desire nature represented by Mars, is stimulated by some basic inner quality of the solar partner's being. When it is the woman's Mars that is involved, her ideal of virile masculinity is illuminated by the presence of her solar partner, who seems more desirable on that account, and so if her Mars is strong, she may be tempted to make the running. When it is the man's Mars that is involved, the aspect from his partner's Sun will encourage him to identify himself more thoroughly with his own concept of manliness. Such solar aspects to the Mars of either sex act to stimulate the desire nature.

In other fields, Mars can arouse the sometimes dormant energies of the Sun and give impetus and direction to his constructive efforts, while the Sun's benevolent interest can give Mars added confidence and the encouragement to sustain his efforts, when they might otherwise have flagged.

A good deal of energy can be generated by this combination. If the bodies are in adverse aspect or either is debilitated, this energy may be difficult to handle smoothly as the Sun's pride may clash with the wilfulness of Mars, resulting in a struggle for supremacy. According to the aspects the luminary and planet receive at birth, the possible effects range from petty irritation and a tendency to argue at the least provocation, to downright and open hostility and, in some cases, to violence. If the partners are continually in contact with each other they may feel that life together is rather like living on top of a volcano. When opposite sexes are involved, the relationship may function more smoothly when the man's Mars is in aspect to the woman's Sun. When, in a marriage partnership, the situation is reversed, the sexual relationship may prove very difficult to handle, each partner tending to grate on the other. This combination, even the square, does not preclude children, while the favorable aspects (especially the trine) are almost a guarantee that the union will be fruitful.

When benefic aspects unite the two bodies, an enthusiastic co-operation between partners can lead to significant achievements. A mutual interest in physical activities involving friendly rivalry may be conducive to a congenial companionship. Such a contact promotes good teamwork in business relationships, where Mars can supply the drive to put into effect the grand strategy conceived by his solar associate, especially if both bodies are well supported in the two nativities.

The effect of the conjunction very much depends on the aspects to each body at birth. If there is a majority of good supporting aspects, it is a useful combination between the horoscopes of marriage partners, though in other walks of life an element of rivalry may be present.

Sun/Jupiter

This is another aspect frequently found between the horoscopes of marriage partners. In all types of partnership it promotes a degree of good fellowship, a generosity of spirit and much mutual respect, appreciation and encouragement. This combination can enhance and strengthen any partnership, and may even sustain a relationship in which there are also present a number of difficult cross-aspects, because each recognizes the good intentions of the other and will on that account wish to put forth his best efforts on the partner's behalf and be more tolerant towards his shortcomings.

Jupiter may know exactly how to enhance the Sun's self-esteem, though if there is an adverse aspect between the two bodies or either is debilitated, Jupiter may use this factor to his own advantage, employing flattery in order to deceive or the Sun may be led astray by Jupiter's over-confidence. As a result, a lack of good faith may develop on either side.

The Sun is likely to show favoritism to Jupiter and, if he is in a position to do so, may be the means of gaining him advancement, improving his financial position or increasing his material welfare. Each will be likely to take pleasure in the company of the other. Between the horoscopes of marriage partners this contact is often a guarantee of a fruitful marriage.

In a business relationship, the favorable aspects and the conjunction, if both bodies are well aspected at birth, make possible a happy and profitable collaboration.

Sun/Saturn

Saturn rules Aquarius, the seventh house sign of the Sun, and so this pairing has a crucial bearing on the marriage relationship, Saturn making the Sun aware of his responsibilities to his partner. Marriage is a sacrament and an initiation, providing the possibility of learning valuable lessons in co-operation and Saturn can be the teacher who provides the opportunity for learning such lessons. The exaltation of Saturn in Libra and the Sun's fall there suggest that the discipline of working in partnership with Saturn can provide the Sun with most valuable experience.

However, there are probably very few people who enter into marriage with the idea of submitting themselves to a new form of discipline, most of them being more concerned with the pleasure they take in each other's company and the mutual support arising from the partnership. The influence of Saturn in relation to the marriage partnership is nevertheless discernible on several levels. The Church has always emphasized the sanctity of marriage and the necessity for it to be established as a permanent relationship, while at a considerably lower level, the connection of Saturn with the need for security has made the institution of marriage seem attractive to those who may lack significant independence of spirit to contemplate with equanimity the task of facing the world alone.

When the two bodies are combined by favorable aspect, the Sun can provide the warmth and reassurance that Saturn needs, while Saturn can contribute a stabilizing influence and exert some kind of control over the more flamboyant extravagances of his solar partner.

The Sun's natural integrity, Saturn's strong sense of duty and a mutual determination to fulfill their responsibilities can combine to forge a link that guarantees the continuity and durability of the partnership, even if there are strongly adverse cross-aspects in other sectors of the two horoscopes. In such cases, and also when the bodies are in conjunction or adverse aspect or either is debilitated, the link may be maintained more in the spirit of "better the devil you know than the devil you don't!" In a situation like this each partner may seek psychological consolation in playing the role of martyr, telling himself that he is nobly doing his duty in the face of great difficulties and provocation.

The Sun is likely to be the positive and Saturn the negative influence in this relationship. When the two bodies are in affliction the Sun's naturally joyous nature and sense of independent initiative may meet with setbacks from Saturn's pessimistic, over-cautious, ponderous approach and lack of a forward-looking attitude. Sometimes Saturn's general inertia, obstinacy and even downright meanness can cast a heavy cloud over the relationship, leaving the Sun with a sense of restriction and frustration. In some cases, Saturn's heavy hand and constant readiness to criticize may have the kind of soul-destroying effect that leads the Sun to rue the day he ever entered into such an unlikely partnership that constantly drains his vitality and makes no allowances for his need for creative self-expression.

When conflicts occur, the solar partner may know just how to play on Saturn's weaknesses and inferiority complexes, especially when Saturn occupies a negative sign and this is likely to increase any subconscious fears of the solar partner that may be harbored. As a result, Saturn may adopt a policy of clinging ever more closely to his partner, instead of making the best of a bad job and severing the relationship.

In all walks of life the conjunction often produces a long term relationship, though the Sun may be conscious that he has to carry Saturn's burdens and provide the main source of animation to the association. Saturn's guarded responses and seeming lack of enthusiasm may test the Sun's patience, while Saturn's refusal to take positive action until he feels absolutely safe and convinced of the rightness of his action may considerably cramp the Sun's style. If, in spite of reassurances from the Sun, Saturn's efforts fail, the blame will probably be put on the partner.

When the two bodies are in opposition, Saturn is theoretically in a position to counter the Sun's every move, supplying the necessary inertia to halt any initiative taken by his partner. Saturn's lack of emotional buoyancy can prove a sore handicap to his more exuberant partner, though if both bodies are favorably aspected at birth an effective compromise may eventually be reached.

The square usually poses more difficult problems, so that the Sun finds it more difficult to cope with Saturn's obstructive tactics, usually dictated by an excessive caution, which takes fright at the Sun's policy of bold commitment, demanding guarantees and safety clauses that would effectively balk the whole project. Such behaviour may result in a sequence of lost opportunities that sicken the solar partner, whose Saturnian confrere may never have realized that such opportunities existed in the first place. This continual frustration of his plans may lead the Sun to keep the partner in ignorance of his intentions until it is too late to intervene. In this type of situation, Saturn's subsequent recriminations may prove more disturbing than the stubborn opposition that might otherwise have been encountered.

Very much will depend upon the condition of the Sun in one nativity and Saturn in the other as to whether the role of Saturn is regarded by the partner as that of a reliable anchor, a steadying hand on the tiller or a millstone around his neck that prevents him from achieving some spectacular success.

In many cases both partners may recognize this as a particularly karmic relationship, in which Saturn has much to teach the Sun, increasing his patience and grasp of practical issues, while the Sun can show Saturn the advantages of a wider vision based on Faith and benevolent goodwill. One partner, usually the Sun, may owe a service to the other and Saturn, who is usually as punctilious in collecting his dues as he is in fulfilling his obligations, may point out to the Sun where his duty lies, so that the partnership, however insecure the foundation may appear to be, may endure at least until one partner has learned all the lessons that the relationship has to teach him and the karmic debt has been repaid.

If they fail to solve their major problems satisfactorily or to reach an effective working arrangement, the net result could be for them to build up new karmic debts to each other that would create the necessity for some equally arduous association in the future.

Under such a cross-aspect, partners joined together by the marriage "bond" may come to realize that the term is not merely a figure of speech and those who are unwilling to accept that marriage is a relationship for better or worse may feel very ill-used by such an arrangement.

Sun/Uranus

The high-powered dynamism generated by this combination is the almost exact antithesis of the Sun-Saturn combination. Here tensions, excitement and mental stimulus take the place of boredom and frustration, though a well balanced integration of the two combinations working together is probably the ideal situation.

Both luminary and planet signify a capacity for independence but while the Sun tends more to orthodoxy and established rituals of procedure, Uranus, unfettered by tradition, is always seeking to cut out an original path, often guided by a transcendent vision of some highly desirable utopia, more characteristic of a future golden age of enlightenment. Uranus, together with Saturn, rules Aquarius, the natural seventh house sign from Leo, the abode of the Sun. This pairing represents the challenge by the partner to expand the individuality in some new and nonconformist direction, unfolding new facets of being in the process. And so the Sun is likely to find his Uranian friend a novel and intriguing companion who is able to show him fresh fields to conquer.

Uranus will probably keep the Sun continually on his toes, but unfortunately the constant challenge to adjust and explore can sometimes stretch the Sun's capacity in this direction to the limit, wearing him out in the process, so that the relationship is often not an easy one.

This combination works best if both partners agree to allow each other plenty of freedom, respecting each other's right to an independent existence at least in some areas. Uranus in particular should be given room to experiment. If either body is in the seventh house the partnership may have a particularly fragile basis but if the bodies are in adverse aspect or either is debilitated, a degree of tension that tests the strength and pliability of the link between them is likely, whatever the natal house positions. Unless other strong links are operative, some sudden clash of wills may result in a quarrel which ends the relationship. Any incompatibility of temperament is apt to assume an importance far beyond that which it deserves and explosive situations may develop too frequently for comfort.

If both parties are prepared to take in their stride any differences of opinion that may arise, and the solar partner can adopt an indulgent attitude towards his opposite number's eccentricities and occasionally erratic behaviour, and if Uranus is prepared neither to coerce nor to ignore the Sun, thus challenging his sovereignty or wounding his pride, a satisfactory working relationship may result. The conjunction spells death to a static relationship, while the square and opposition add a further element of excitability to an already electric combination. The tendency towards disintegration may be kept in check if a good proportion of mutual favorable aspects to each partner's Saturn are present.

Occurring between the horoscopes of relatives, friends or associates, the contact may signify a mainly intermittent relationship that is frequently interrupted by the lengthy periods of absence of one party or the other.

Sun/Neptune

The Sun's desire to include everyone within his orb of influence can unsettle Neptune, whose loyalties are universal and who consequently wishes to avoid any commitment that is too definite. When Neptune feels that he is likely to be tied down, he may adopt evasive tactics that the Sun finds difficult to understand. Yet a common bond of idealism can encourage a subtle feeling of camaraderie and Neptune's capacity for capturing inspirations from the higher planes may intrigue and elevate his solar partner, who can encourage him to yet further endeavour along these lines. This contact is likely to operate most specifically on the emotional plane and a subtle feeling of rapport can result from favorable aspects between the two bodies.

Neptune may stimulate the Sun's imagination and open up glamorous new insights that prove a source of great fascination, and he may see in his partner a personification of his ideal while the Sun may give a feeling of greater direction and purpose to Neptune's yearning for a sense of greater wholeness, encouraging self-transcendence in some way. The combination is therefore conducive to the expansion of the partner's aesthetic and cultural interests and at best it can produce an atmosphere of mutual sympathy that inspires Neptune's confidence and the Sun's benevolence.

If they are in adverse aspect or either is debilitated, a vague uncertainty about each other's intentions may cause a feeling of uneasiness, and sometimes distrust, to arise in the relationship so that the Sun will never feel quite sure where he stands with his Neptunian partner, while Neptune may think the Sun is too demanding, and feel uncomfortable on that account. Neptune's capacity to weave creative fantasies may cause the Sun to have grave doubts about Neptune's general reliability and lack of really solid qualities and any attempt on his part to demand guarantees of good faith may embarrass Neptune, causing a state of nervous discomfiture that makes the situation even more difficult to deal with. Issues that seem clear cut to the Sun may appear to Neptune to have many subtle implications that his more uncomplicated partner has failed to observe.

The square is a particularly unsettling combination, while the conjunction and opposition may operate more beneficially if both bodies are well aspected at birth. With the conjunction some kind of psychic rapport may exist, together with a mutual interest in aesthetic pursuits. When the opposition is present, each partner may have to come to terms with the fact that a need exists to build up confidence in the other, with Neptune curbing a tendency to over-exaggerate, and the Sun accepting the fact that the partner's imaginative gifts do not always lead him to confuse fantasy with reality, but they may be the means of bringing about a spiritual insight, that can eventually elevate the partnership to new levels of understanding.

At best, the Sun/Neptune combination can produce a delicate sense of well-being in each other's company and encourage the pursuit of common ideals. Sometimes this contact occurs in a platonic friendship. At worst, there may be some grave element of deception present, with Neptune covering up the details of an unsavory past or attempting to take advantage of the Sun's magnanimity by boosting his self-esteem or abusing his confidence.

Unless there are good Saturnian aspects to the Sun in one nativity and to Neptune in the other, this is not a particularly encouraging combination for a business collaboration. Neptune's highly imaginative schemes for spectacular financial coups may need to be subjected to the closest scrutiny and rigorous practical tests before they are given final approval.

Sun/Pluto

The Sun and Pluto represent opposite ends of the psychological spectrum, for while the Sun works openly to achieve its ends, Pluto usually works under cover. A favorable combination between the two can result in a considerable strengthening of forces, since Pluto can reinforce the Sun's belief in himself, while the Sun can provide Pluto with an effective outlet for his subconscious drives and encourage him to mobilize widespread support for the partnership or to subject it to a thorough-going re-organization. The contact often indicates a relationship brought about by destiny. Between opposite sexes, a good deal of physical attraction is often present.

A recognition of some deep-level bond between them may encourage the formation of a firm friendship, but if the two bodies are in adverse aspect or either is debilitated, it may be that both parties sense the existence of some deep-seated and basic lack of compatibility, which prevents the development of a rewarding association. This contact may then signify a type of rivalry and a struggle for supremacy, with Pluto seeking to undermine the Sun's position and block his plans for progress. Pluto may be able to recognize and exploit those elements in the solar character that are most vulnerable, especially when pride and passion are involved. Having become aware of the Sun's principal defects of character, Pluto may tempt him to over-reach himself, placing him in situations where he realizes he must conquer his weaknesses or admit defeat. The Sun may in turn test Pluto's capacity to stand alone and openly declare his aims and he may also try to exploit any element of jealousy present in Pluto's make-up. Sometimes Pluto will react by remaining aloof, so that a really close collaboration becomes almost impossible to achieve.

* * * * * * *

Moon/Moon

The Moon represents the native's feelings and instinctive responses and when there is a conjunction between the Moons in partners' horoscopes there is an identity of feeling and a sense of rapport between them. Each partner's instinctive reactions and habit patterns tend to coincide, which helps to build up a feeling of mutual confidence and trust. It has been observed that the conjunction frequently occurs between the horoscopes of married couples. Mutual tastes and interests provide a good basis for a permanent relationship and the chances of domestic harmony are good unless planets in either partner's nativity are in unfavorable aspect to the conjunction.

Both partners can easily become accustomed to the idea of having each other around and a good deal of emotional interdependence can develop as a result. An easy adjustment to each other's patterns of feeling and response encourages that sense of well-being in each other's company which can form the basis of a lifelong relationship.

To a lesser extent, a favorable aspect between the two Moons indicates a sympathetic appreciation between two individuals, who can work harmoniously together in terms of a mutually compatible response to everyday situations. The unfavorable aspects suggest conflicting habit patterns and a failure to appreciate each other's instinctive reactions to a problem situation. There may be an instinctive dislike of some of the partner's personality traits. The opposition can provide piquantly contrasting habit patterns, unless squares or conjunctions from malefics afflict either Moon. The quincunx can indicate some fundamental lack of unity between the feelings and instincts of each partner which is difficult to counteract.

Moon/Mercury

This is not a particularly important aspect in romantic partnerships but it has more significance in pupil-teacher relationships; the Moon can provide a focus of interest for Mercury's intellectual activity, presenting facts in an imaginative way so as to invest them with a greater appeal. As both bodies are somewhat variable by nature, very much will depend, in all types of relationship, upon the condition of Mercury by sign and aspect and unless the Moon is in a fixed sign the contact may relate only to the more superficial aspects of a relationship.

Mercury may attempt to rationalize the Moon's feelings and may sometimes appear to the sensitive Moon as too detached and, in some cases, when Mercury is afflicted at birth, scathing in his treatment of the Moon's seemingly irrational moods. When the planets are favorably combined, Mercury may be able to explain the Moon's moods satisfactorily to himself and in the course of arriving at such an understanding he may find that the lunar qualities of the partner become more endearing. The Moon may be fascinated by Mercury's intellectual qualities, so that Mercury can put over his ideas to a receptive audience.

When the bodies are in adverse aspect to each other or either is debilitated, Mercury may appear to the Moon to be too aloof, too ready to pick holes in her way of doing things, and unable to comprehend her feelings. The Moon may object to Mercury's plans because she feels instinctively that they are not going to be conducive to mutual happiness. When the two bodies are in square, Mercury may fidget and fuss in an attempt to soothe the Moon, often only making matters worse.

Mercury's ability to adapt at an intellectual level may be matched by the Moon's ability to respond instinctively. The conjunction, when unafflicted, makes for ease of communication and the sharing of common interests, while the adverse aspects can indicate a tendency for each partner to be at cross-purposes with the other.

Moon/Venus

This is a contact frequently found between the horoscopes of marriage partners and is one of the best contacts to have in any kind of relationship unless either body is much afflicted at birth. When there is a favorable aspect between the Moon and Venus, both partners are likely to take much pleasure in each other's company. There may be shared cultural pursuits and the same tastes in entertainment. Venus has the knack of making the Moon feel at ease, bestowing affection, and making allowances for her moods. Such treatment usually evokes an affectionate response from the lunar partner, with the result that both are able to contribute to the establishment of a really harmonious atmosphere, especially in a marriage relationship, where a particularly loving bond may be present.

If the bodies are in adverse aspect or either is debilitated, Venus may indulge the Moon too much or disharmony can result from a too casual approach to matters involving the affections, with Venus turning on the charm in order to take advantage of a temporary relationship or the Moon appearing to respond for the sake of a flirtation or to gain some short term benefit, particularly if the aspect joining the two bodies is a square.

Unless either body is strongly afflicted at birth the discords signified by adverse aspects may be of a minor nature amounting to no more than occasional hurt feelings, possibly through one of the partners failing to get his own way. However, this can be a particularly tantalizing combination when Uranus is also involved, when an apparently perfect union may be prevented or broken up, causing emotional distress to both, or it may signify a relationship where the partners are frequently separated from each other, either through the obligations of duty or as a result of an alternating enchantment and disenchantment with each other.

Moon/Mars

This is an important contact relating to the sexual side of the marriage relationship. Mars is exalted in Capricorn, the Moon's seventh house sign, while the Moon is exalted in Taurus, Scorpio's seventh house sign (Scorpio being the negative sign of Mars). The interplay of these two bodies can produce a stimulating relationship.

The man's Mars can challenge the woman's Moon to express its female qualities to the full, while the receptive Moon can invite the man's Mars to display its masculine qualities. If the position is reversed and the woman's Mars is in aspect to the man's Moon, his concept of the ideal woman he desires will be stimulated by this contact. Magnetism, ruled by the Moon, is a force which operates through the metal iron, ruled by Mars, so it is hardly surprising that this is a contact which denotes the possibility of much physical attraction.

If the Mars partner happens to suffer from any sexual repressions, an attempt may be made to arouse a more spirited response from the mate by investing his advances with a strong element of challenge and there may be some need to avoid behaviour or language which might affront the delicate susceptibilities of the lunar mate. Under provocation, the Moon may sometimes be driven to adopt a temporarily aggressive attitude in sheer self-defense.

It is well to remember that such a contact between individuals who have no emotional interest in each other can sometimes prove a source of irritation, and while this somewhat "high potency" vibration can be an asset in sexual relationships, it does not always promise mutual consideration in everyday activities, especially as Mars may be tempted by the Moon's pliant attitude to over-assert himself and drive the Moon too hard.

When the two bodies are in conjunction, Mars may try to dominate the relationship (and will often succeed in so doing). When they are linked by opposition a rather nervy atmosphere can develop, especially if either body is afflicted at birth. Some facets of the Martian partner's personality may jar on the Moon, and Mars may show a lack of consideration and tolerance that irritates his lunar partner.

Under favorable conditions, Mars can supply a useful stimulus to the Moon's powers of imagination.

Moon/Jupiter

An aspect between these two bodies favors an easy-going relationship and is a most helpful factor in smoothing over any differences of temperament that may be denoted by inharmonious cross-aspects. Jupiter's aspirations, general moral standards and expressions of goodwill will instinctively appeal to his lunar partner, who is likely to hold him in high esteem. The Moon will therefore make a special effort to accommodate her Jupiterian partner, whose expansive attitude and respect for the conventional proprieties make her feel thoroughly at home.

The contact makes for a good social relationship between all types of individuals, unless either body is much afflicted at birth, when the Moon may not always subscribe to Jupiter's good opinion of himself or she may impose on Jupiter's generosity while Jupiter may arouse false hopes in his lunar friend, making promises for the sole purpose of soothing, or over-estimating the help he might be able to give.

Free from affliction, the conjunction is a pleasing contact, though there is a possibility that Jupiter will over-indulge his lunar partner, who is happy to give Jupiter opportunities to display generosity. The opposition, if both bodies are well supported at birth, can act as a complementary factor with reciprocal benefits to both partners.

No great difficulties should result from this combination unless afflictions to either body at birth are severe.

Moon/Saturn

Although Saturn rules Capricorn, the Moon's seventh house sign, it is exalted in Libra, in square to Cancer and while a contact between the two bodies often signifies a long-term link, by itself it does not tend to produce a particularly joyous type of partnership, since Saturn may hesitate to break any legal bond between the partners out of a sense of duty, while the Moon may grow so accustomed to having Saturn around that she may develop a "better the devil you know" type of philosophy about the relationship. Saturn may feel that he needs the Moon as a means of demonstrating his constancy and sense of duty, while the Moon may cling to Saturn as a father figure and get into the habit of becoming dependent upon him.

These may not be the best or the most exciting reasons for embarking upon and sustaining a partnership, but it is likely that other links will have played a stronger part in bringing the two together.

When the two bodies are linked by an harmonious aspect, the Moon will appreciate Saturn's attitude of responsibility and willing acceptance of the hard work necessary to build a firm foundation to the partnership. Unless there are cross-aspects to the partner's Moon from other planets, Saturn's seeming lack of enthusiastic emotional response may cause the lunar partner to long for a more exciting, less matter-of-fact mate. Saturn may have a lesson to teach the Moon, according to the sign Saturn occupies, and may provide an example of dedication to duty that the Moon will eventually come to appreciate. Saturn may be a in a position to render some long term service to his partner, taking on extra responsibilities because of her failing health or as a result of some other handicap.

In marriage this can be a testing combination if either partner feels that he is bearing too heavy a share of the duties and responsibilities inherent in the relationship. Those who are not ready to accept willingly the "bonds" of marriage may find their responsibilities irksome in the extreme.

When the bodies are in adverse aspect to each other or either is debilitated, there may still be a strong link between the partners, but the Moon may find Saturn too cold and austere, making no allowances for or misunderstanding her moods, so that she may retreat more and more into her shell for fear of being rebuffed. Saturn's lack of imagination and sometimes narrow-mindedness can prove a source of frustration to the Moon, who feels she cannot "get through" to her partner. The Moon may resent Saturn's attempts to lay down the law and dictate procedures to be followed, and may react by sulking or even rebelling, if the natal Moon should be afflicted. In some cases a state of total frustration may be reached and because neither partner may be prepared to consider the possibility of changing the status quo, however embittered each may become, a stage may be reached where each assumes the air of a martyr, stoically trying to do what he or she regards as their duty in the face of almost insuperable difficulties.

The Moon may feel she can never commit any indiscretions or behave uninhibitedly for fear of displeasing her critical Saturnian partner, who will deplore the unreliability of his partner's moods. The lunar partner will always be the one who suffers most.

When this cross-aspect is present between the charts of two people who are meeting for the first time and there are few helpfully favorable cross-aspects between other planets, a feeling of antipathy may prevent any friendship developing, or eventually result in the break-up of the association.

In an emotional partnership that has already developed, Saturn may need to show more consideration for his partner's feelings, finding some way of taking himself less seriously and bringing a lighter and less critical atmosphere to the relationship while the Moon may find the association more rewarding when she learns to appreciate her partner's self-discipline and dedication to duty, even if he does sometimes make heavy-going of it.

Moon/Uranus

This is a somewhat crucial combination in that it can signify a good deal of magnetic attraction though at the same time tension can develop. The Moon may be fascinated by what seems to be very unusual or particularly dynamic qualities in the partner, while Uranus may react in no uncertain fashion to the lunar partner's feminine appeal. If it is the man whose Moon is so aspected he may find that his Uranian partner seems to add a new dimension to his concept of the ideal woman. This is a contact that usually provides a continuing variety of stimulating experience although it is well to remember that a diet of constant excitement usually begins to pall after a while, so that this cross-aspect alone is not a guarantee of a particularly lengthy relationship, though a good deal of fascination may initially be present.

When these bodies are in adverse aspect or either is debilitated, the erratic behaviour and general unpredictability of Uranus may jar on his lunar partner in such a way as to jangle her nerves and upset her feelings so that in some cases she becomes distraught over the lack of understanding shown and because of total inability on the part of Uranus to perceive that he may be behaving in such a manner as to cause the Moon distress.

Sometimes this cross-aspect is present between the horoscopes of friends who do not meet very often, so that the element of novelty is preserved. Casual contacts, encountered in everyday life, may easily prove to be a source of irritation when this interchange is present.

Moon/Neptune

A delicate and sensitive empathy can exist between two people when these bodies are related by conjunction or beneficial aspect. Neptune can exert an ethereal fascination over the susceptible Moon and the contact can be particularly helpful to a lunar partner with strong aesthetic susceptibilities, for Neptune's idealistic approach to life can fire the Moon's imagination and open up a new world of beauty and alluring fantasy. There is however, a danger that the Moon will become carried away by the fascination of the mysteries hinted at by Neptune so that she may become confused and enmeshed in a web of fanciful and illusory ideas, failing to appreciate that what seems real and significant to Neptune may be related only to the perceptions made possible by dealing with the more prosaic details of everyday life.

While this contact makes possible a strong sympathetic link between partners, it does not always produce a passionate involvement and is frequently a factor in platonic friendships.

When there is an adverse aspect between the bodies or either is debilitated, a subtle lack of emotional rapport may result, so that although there may be a desire to please, neither partner is quite sure how to go about it. Neptune may get completely out of his depth in trying to fathom the moods of his lunar partner, while the Moon may misunderstand Neptune's intentions. The Moon may feel instinctively that Neptune is unreliable and too much at the mercy of his emotional susceptibilities. The difficult aspects, however, need not play havoc with a partnership, for the Moon and Neptune both share the qualities of receptivity and plasticity, while Neptune's capacity for compassion may respond more positively when the inharmonious aspects are present.

Moon/Pluto

Pluto can have an hypnotic effect on the Moon, who will instinctively recognize in her Plutonian partner some deep quality of being that either attracts or repels, according to whether or not the two bodies are in harmonious aspect. If either body is debilitated even the good aspects may not be productive of harmony. In some cases a karmic emotional bond may have drawn the two together. The male partner whose Moon is involved may recognize his image of the ideal woman compellingly personified in his Plutonian partner, while the woman whose Moon is thus aspected will find her womanly instincts intensified by the contact with Pluto in her partner's nativity.

Because Pluto moves very slowly, large numbers of people will have approximately the same degree occupied by Pluto, so that this contact may depend to a large extent for its effectiveness on the involvement of Pluto at birth with some of the other faster moving planets, which will act to differentiate the quality of the contact existing between a number of contemporaries. When the two bodies are in conjunction, the Moon, unless much afflicted at birth, may be sympathetically disposed towards the outlook and philosophy of the whole generation sharing this position of Pluto. Pluto may instinctively understand the moods and feelings of the Moon, so that a deep level understanding can be developed. If the Plutonian partner should ever wish to take advantage of the ability to influence the Moon's moods, he will probably know exactly how to find the most vulnerable spot in her defenses and consequently can, in other circumstances, become a very unwelcome enemy.

Mercury/Mercury

This contact is the main index of compatibility at the mental level. When the two are conjoined or in good aspect to each other and relatively unafflicted by other cross-aspects, there will be a good measure of mental empathy, facilitating an harmonious interchange of ideas so that conversation about subjects of mutual interest will bring pleasure to both partners. The sharing of common interests or an appreciation of each other's mental attitude will encourage free communication and when the conjunction is present each may be able to anticipate the other's thoughts. The conjunction, and to a slightly lesser degree, a close favorable aspect can denote a very harmonious student/teacher relationship.

A difficult aspect between the two Mercurys signifies that there is a basic difference of approach to mental problems, with the result that the thought patterns of one partner may differ radically from those of the other. There can be an element of challenge inherent in this combination leading to spirited arguments or even disagreements over fundamental intellectual issues. In some cases each may tend to be too critical of the other.

The opposition can result in a blend of opposite views taking place and such diametrically opposed opinions may stimulate each partner's mental development although this will be more difficult to achieve if Mercury is in a fixed sign, when some tendency to dogmatic thinking may be present, or if it is stationary or retrograde, when the native will be less likely to listen sympathetically to ideas contrary to his own.

Mercury/Venus

This is a pleasant link, signifying that Mercury's ideas will be well received by Venus. Venus can encourage Mercury and give him extra confidence to communicate his ideas and may even help him to propagate them.

When the two planets are in adverse aspect, Venus may be too uncritical and fail to challenge any logical inconsistencies in Mercury's thinking or in some cases, even mislead him into believing that his erroneous conclusions are the result of brilliant deduction. Sometimes Venus may be too involved in her own self-indulgent schemes to pay more than superficial attention to Mercury's plans. Mercury may feel moved to criticize any tendencies to laziness in his partner or an excessive preoccupation with pleasurable pursuits.

Mercury/Mars

Mars supplies an element of challenge to Mercury's ideas, keeping him alert and on his toes when the aspect is a favorable one or perhaps arguing too forcefully and critically with him when the aspect is unfavorable, as a result making Mercury liable to some degree of nervous tension.

This is a contact which needs careful handling, for while the favorable aspects can promote a healthy exchange of ideas, with Mercury spurred on by the constructive criticism of Mars, there is a temptation for Mars to adopt a provocatively aggressive mental attitude. In self-defense, Mercury may resort to a dazzling display of verbal gymnastics that are too clever by half.

A great deal may depend upon the strength of Mercury and his ability to profit from Martian criticism, which can help to improve and quicken his mental reactions. Thus, in a professional partnership, the combination of the two talents can lead to the successful planning and carrying out of business operations.

If Mars is strong, and Mercury is weak by sign and aspect, there may be a tendency for Mars to take a perverse delight in picking holes in Mercury's arguments or to make his presence felt by nagging his partner, especially if Mars is conscious of any intellectual inferiority. Mercury is then apt to get "needled" by Mars and will either express himself more forcibly than usual or develop nervous tension.

If Mercury is strongly placed and able to enjoy stimulating intellectual exchanges, he may appreciate the challenging attitude of Mars but the adverse aspects, or even favorable aspects from a debilitated Mars, can denote a divergence of mental interests and thought processes that will finally lead to discord, if the disagreements are on too fundamental a level.

Mercury/Jupiter

This is a very helpful contact for mental harmony, though if either body is debilitated or the aspect between them is adverse, there may be problems. Jupiter can draw on his experience to develop Mercury's thinking, helping him to expand his knowledge, giving him the benefit of his wisdom and sometimes helping him to gain new philosophical insights. Jupiter can support and encourage Mercury, so that it is not surprising to find that this aspect is often present in parent-child relationships. When the child's Mercury contacts a parent's Jupiter, this may denote that the child's education is likely to be a source of expense. Any restlessness the child displays may call for wise handling on the part of the parent and, in the early years, mutual participation in games and pastimes may greatly assist the relationship. The Jupiter parent can often deal most successfully with his Mercury child's worries.

This is also a contact frequently met with in business partnerships, where Mercury contributes the ideas and Jupiter supplies the necessary capital and encouragement.

When there is an adverse aspect or Jupiter is debilitated, Mercury's ideas and abilities may be exploited by Jupiter, who may be out to capitalize as much as possible on the relationship.

Generally speaking, Mercury's ideas are received by Jupiter with a broad tolerance, which can result in the establishment of an harmonious mental atmosphere conducive to creative thinking. Mercury can help Jupiter to formulate ideas more crisply although if he is thrown off guard by Jupiter's over-optimistic support, errors of judgment may be made or Mercury may become over-complacent. Under the helpful influence of the Jupiterian partner, Mercury is often willing to adjust his ideas, to adapt for the good of the partnership and to devote much thought to making it run smoothly.

Mercury/Saturn

Saturn acts to steady Mercury and deepen his thinking, drawing attention to the more serious side of life, checking Mercury's ideas in the light of his own experience, and generally providing solid, practical advice. If Saturn is prominently placed and badly aspected, he may act to dampen Mercury's spontaneity by questioning the judgment and pointing out errors, or Saturn's own fears may cause him to raise objections to Mercury's plans. If the aspect is an unfavorable one, Mercury may find that it is hard work trying to convince Saturn, who sometimes appears to be rather slow on the uptake. The conjunction is sometimes difficult and Saturn may check and double check Mercury's statements, a procedure very likely to sap Mercury's confidence. When there is a good relationship between the two planets, Mercury can often provide extra facts or a new way of looking at things for Saturn to ponder over.

Mercury/Uranus

Uranus can stimulate Mercury to direct ideas into new channels and take up new studies. Mercury may be intrigued by the novel way of looking at things that Uranus can bring to the relationship. It is possible that Uranus may succeed in causing Mercury to change some hitherto strongly held opinions, though this is less likely if Mercury is in a fixed sign (especially Taurus) or in aspect to Saturn.

The conjunction may have a particularly stimulating effect on mental interchanges, with the possibility of mind-reading or thought transference, but if Uranus is debilitated or much afflicted, its effect on the partner's Mercury, especially when in adverse aspect, may prove over-stimulating, so that Mercury is carried away on a novel train of thought that may eventually lead him nowhere and waste his time in the process, or there may be arguments because Uranus fails to do what Mercury expects of him. In some cases disputes may lead to mutual loss of temper.

Mercury/Neptune

Mercury's logical thinking does not always blend easily with Neptune's sensitivity and imagination, so that the partners may misunderstand each other. When the contacts are favorable and Neptune is strong by sign and well aspected, he can intuitively sense what Mercury is thinking. Adverse aspects may make it difficult for Neptune to appreciate Mercury's logic and for Mercury to take a sympathetic view of Neptune's readiness to indulge in flights of poetic imagination, or to become involved with issues that appear to be far removed from practical considerations. Sometimes this may lead to situations where Mercury feels that Neptune has been less than frank, while Mercury may have failed to appreciate the finer nuances of meaning that Neptune was trying to convey or have taken some allegorical illustration as literal truth. Working together at their best, both planets may co-operate to enhance an intuitive understanding of each other's viewpoint and a mutual interest in artistic or perhaps mystic pursuits with Neptune contributing a certain refinement of thinking, otherwise there is a tendency for misconceptions to abound due to Neptune's apparent lack of clarity or Mercury's insistence on concentrating upon the letter rather than the spirit of Neptune's intellectual contributions. Sometimes the conjunction may denote a high degree of mental rapport, but if it is afflicted by other planets, misunderstandings may be frequent.

Neptune may sometimes respond emotionally to the more persuasive of Mercury's arguments while occasionally some of Neptune's more inspiring flights of fancy may fire Mercury's imagination.

Mercury/Pluto

In order to convince Pluto, Mercury has to strike a chord in Pluto's subconscious mind. In the course of any exchanges, Mercury may find that some of his ideas have become transformed during the discussion, for Pluto is anxious to examine Mercury's ideas in depth and may supply the necessary pressure to make Mercury add a new dimension to his thinking. Such examinations may give Mercury a sense of oppression and possibly a feeling of being brainwashed. In some cases Pluto may seem to have a blind spot as far as picking up Mercury's ideas is concerned. If Pluto should be representing a group, Mercury may find him a difficult proposition to handle, as he may not feel at liberty to change the ideas that he has been asked to communicate.

Venus/Venus

When Venus in one horoscope is in favorable aspect to Venus in another, a congenial link is formed which encourages the development of a happy companionship and an affectionate consideration for each other's needs. The likes and dislikes of the partners will rarely clash, although the condition of each natal Venus needs to be taken into account. The conjunction, unless either Venus is afflicted, is a particularly happy contact, denoting tastes in common and inviting shared confidences, but it is not an infallible guarantee of a lasting marriage. The writer has on his files the horoscopes of a married couple, both of whom were born with Venus in Taurus within a few degrees of each other in the respective seventh houses. When discords arose (indicated by other cross-aspects), each left it to the partner (seventh house) to take the initiative in re-establishing harmony, and as Venus in Taurus is one of the least likely indicators of positive action (the placid bull has to be goaded) the discords were left to multiply, finally resulting in divorce.

The warm mutual regard and shared attitude to relationships is apt to diminish to some extent when the two Venuses are in adverse aspect or if either is debilitated. Outside pressures or a too possessive attitude on the part of one or both partners may produce a cloying relationship, or they may be at cross-purposes when trying to please each other and become somewhat petulant at any lack of appreciation. There may be a lack of agreement over leisure activities and the partners' tastes may differ widely, though when a majority of helpful cross-aspects between other planets are present, no very adverse effects are usually experienced.

Because Venus rules the natural seventh house, an opposition aspect can sometimes work out well, though less so when Venus is debilitated.

Venus/Mars

This contact is the primary indicator of compatibility at the physical level. A tacit acknowledgement of this occurs in the use of the symbols of Mars and Venus in zoology to distinguish between the masculine and feminine sex at the animal level.

In the marriage partnership, the contact between these two planets indicates a ready response to each other's animal magnetism. It is therefore understandable that the good aspects between the planetary pair do not necessarily cement a marriage partnership, or even bring one about, unless other indications of compatibility on a less physical level are also present.

Nevertheless, the physical element in marriage is usually quite important, particularly in view of the declaration in the marriage sacrament that one of the purposes of marriage is the procreation of children.

The interpretation of Venus-Mars aspects perhaps calls for more consideration of each person's age and circumstances than most other pairings. For instance, if the two planets are in aspect between the horoscopes of a very young child and her grandfather, the contact may signify no more than an ability to gain mutual pleasure in games requiring some degree of physical effort, or one may be able to suggest activities that will amuse and stimulate the other. A Mars-Venus contact does not necessarily denote a pronounced emotional or physical stimulus but when the cross-aspect is present the natives should be able to work smoothly together in each other's company.

Mars represents the desire nature and Venus the desired, so that in a romantic relationship, Mars is apt to take the initiative and Venus to invite that initiative. For this reason it has been suggested that it is desirable for the male Mars to be in aspect with the female Venus, rather than the reverse. Ideally, perhaps, the Mars and Venus of one partner should be linked respectively with the Venus and Mars of the other, but there is no real ground for questioning the desirability of the male Venus to be in aspect with the female Mars, rather than the reverse. Quite apart from the fact that all men do not require an equal degree of passivity in their partner and that not all women are content with a merely passive role, the fact that Venus in a male horoscope represents the man's feminine ideal, while Mars in the female horoscope represents the woman's masculine ideal, suggests that it is better for these ideals to be aligned in harmony rather than to be unrelated to each other. When Mars in a female horoscope aspects Venus in a male horoscope, this provides a stimulus and perhaps a challenge to his concept of the ideal woman, while the male Venus will pleasantly make the woman aware of her ideal concept of manhood. Such a reversal of Mars and Venus need not imply a lack of masculine qualities in the man or a lack of femininity in the woman.

Mars is able to excite the passionate devotion of Venus and much mutual affection may develop out of what was initially a purely physical attraction. Venus can provide the loving response that Mars desires and can do much to bring a feeling of harmonious well-being to the partnership so that a feeling of belonging to each other often develops together with the ability to understand intuitively the best way to please each other.

Apart from the romantic angle, the two planets can work well together in a business partnership, with Mars providing the initiative and drive and Venus supplying the finesse and polish.

Because Venus and Mars rule opposite signs of the zodiac, the opposition need not necessarily denote disharmony. In fact, when Venus is in Aries and Mars is in Libra, or when Venus is in Scorpio and Mars is in Taurus, the mutual reception between them may considerably strengthen the bond. Otherwise, if either planet is debilitated or there is an adverse aspect between them, it may not be easy for partners to adjust to each other on the physical or emotional level. Venus may find Mars too rough or aggressive. Mars may tire of finding his advances unsatisfactorily received by Venus or he may make himself a nuisance to Venus in sundry ways, sometimes acting provocatively, perhaps as a result of his own repressed desires, or his enthusiasm may eventually wear itself out.

The physical attraction may be no less when adverse aspects are present but there can be problems in expressing it to the satisfaction of both parties. Mars may tend to force the pace too much while Venus may become too highly selective about bestowing her favors. If Mars feels he is not getting the attention and appreciation he deserves he may soon seek consolation elsewhere. The relationship may therefore be subject to some stress and one or both of the partners may become jealous. The amount of feeling on each side may be uneven and sometimes one partner may be antipathetic to the other.

Those who only wish to indulge in a casual love affair may enjoy the challenge and excitement generated by the discordant aspects.

In relationships unconnected with romance and marriage, Mars may usefully stimulate a lazy Venus to action, while Venus can show a precipitate Mars how to act with more finesse and perhaps less alacrity.

Venus/Jupiter

This is a most felicitous contact and one frequently found between the horoscopes of marriage partners, when each may vie in lavishing gifts on the other. Venus will attract Jupiter's goodwill, while Jupiter will bring out the affection that Venus seeks an opportunity to bestow. When Jupiter in the man's horoscope aspects Venus in the woman's, he will be able to bring out all her latent ability to play her most attractive feminine role. When Jupiter in the woman's horoscope is in aspect to the man's Venus, she may appear to him as a larger than life personification of his ideal mate.

This combination encourages a high level of co-operation between the two partners based on the mutual esteem in which each holds the other. The contact promises a happy social relationship between friends and in the marriage relationship the support which each is willing to give to the other can do much to cancel out any disharmonies indicated by adverse cross-aspects between other planets. Jupiter will appreciate the artistic talents and social graces of Venus, while if Venus sets a special value on an optimistic and philosophical outlook in her partner, Jupiter is assured of an affectionate ally.

The sporting attitude of Jupiter and the fun-loving propensities of Venus combine to give a shared interest in pleasurable and light-hearted leisure time activities.

When the planets are in adverse aspect or either is debilitated, quite a few of the above benefits may be present but there may be too much emphasis on extravagance or self-indulgence and if Jupiter is the stronger planet, Venus may be led into excesses, while if Venus is better placed she may attempt to become too possessive or resent her partner's success if it means he devotes less attention to her. In some cases, Venus may become too self-involved to appreciate Jupiter's many virtues.

Venus/Saturn

If the Venusian partner places a high value on integrity and dependability, she will appreciate her Saturnian mate. This contact tends to favor the long term build-up of an affectionate link between two partners but of itself it is hardly a combination promising ecstasy.

The good aspects encourage loyalty but often Venus has to supply most of the affection, while Saturn, even if equally affectionate, may have difficulty in demonstrating his affection outwardly or may lack gentleness in expressing it, though he is likely to have a sober regard for the sterling merits of his partner.

Ptolemy speaks well of the conjunction as a combination promising happiness and constancy but it has been observed that on occasion, Saturn's apparent coldness can evoke in Venus such a feeling of restriction and of not being appreciated that the partnership may never flourish. Saturn may be tempted to demand too much from his partner.

It may sometimes happen, especially with the conjunction, that Venus has a great deal to learn from Saturn and when Venus is attracted to an older person, his greater experience may be the means of steadying the emotional responses of Venus and helping her to develop a sound all-round sense of values. Sometimes Venus will develop an affection for a Saturn person who for some reason does not return her love or whom she subsequently finds is inaccessible to her.

When the planets are in adverse aspect or either is debilitated, Saturn may in some way be the means of denying pleasures to the Venusian partner. The opposition can even prevent a friendship forming, but if other contacts bring two people together, a relationship may exist in which Saturn is prepared to sacrifice love for the sake of financial gain and to take everything Venus is prepared to give without making any noticeable return. Saturn's lack of consideration or constant neglect may eventually dampen the gaiety of Venus and exhaust the Venusian capacity for giving affection, while Saturn may consider it his duty to adhere to certain rigid principles of behaviour that make no concession to his partner's special need for love and attention.

Saturn may try to discourage any excessive show of feeling from the partner, who consequently feels denied a natural outlet for her emotions. Venus is always the one who suffers more, though Saturn may feel ill-used by the less responsible or even frivolous attitude of his partner, who does not appreciate all the hard work being done to provide a firm foundation for the relationship.

Saturn may have to carry a good deal of the responsibility in such a partnership and while a good aspect between the two planets can signify a ready acceptance by Saturn of the burdens he may have to carry, the adverse aspects can bring about a situation where Saturn can begin to wonder whether it is all worth while and Venus feels discouraged by what seems to be undeserved criticism from her partner, perhaps associating him with outside circumstances that may cramp her style and limit her freedom.

Venus/Uranus

This contact frequently occurs between the horsocopes of marriage partners though it is not of itself an ingredient which makes for permanency in the relationship. In a nativity the contact represents the capacity for ecstasy. Occurring between two people of opposite sexes it can signify a sexually stimulating relationship. Just as moments of ecstasy cannot be indefinitely prolonged, and such moments probably derive a great deal of their desirability because of their exciting contrast with more prosaic experiences, so the Venus-Uranus contact is not one of the most stabilizing factors in a relationship. It tends to represent everything the Venus-Saturn partnership is not, so that life can become very interesting indeed when these two planets are working in combination.

Uranus, according to Rodney Collin, rules the sex glands, which appears to confirm the exaltation of Uranus in Scorpio. Scorpio bears a seventh house relationship to Taurus, the negative sign of Venus, so the planetary contact can be a crucial one in sex relationships.

Uranus can exert an electric fascination over Venus, who finds Uranus "extra special" and is intrigued by his originality of approach, independent way of doing things and ability to bring her new creative insights while Uranus is particularly susceptible to the charm and attractiveness of Venus, who appears so desirable that he must possess her at all costs. Sometimes Venus may not appear to realize at first the extent of the attraction she holds for Uranus, and so she is able to view the association with greater detachment and exercise the greater control over the relationship. Uranus can become infatuated with Venus, thus the romantic possibilities of this combination are considerable, although they do not necessarily make for a long term relationship, especially if both partners are not sufficiently mature at the time of their meeting. They may find it difficult to live on a permanent diet of excitement! The result is that one of the partners, usually Uranus, may abruptly lose interest, especially when the physical charms of Venus grow less attractive through familiarity or merely with the passing of time and it is worth paying attention to directions and transits as they affect the position of the two planets, in order to estimate when any danger periods may occur.

The conjunction is a particularly compelling aspect, denoting a great deal of mutual fascination and a lively interest in each other, though it is possible for tension to develop through the feeling that the relationship is "too good to last."

Apart from the romantic possibilities, which will not be present between all individuals, the contact promises to enrich the social life of each, and their cultural and creative activities. It is the type of contact that may occur, for instance, between Uranus in the horoscope of a composer, long since dead, and Venus in the horoscope of a person to whom his music has a vivid appeal, or between an actor's horoscope and those of his most ardent fans.

When there is an adverse aspect between the planets or either is debilitated, an abrupt ending to the partnership is more likely, although while the fascination lasts, it may be more intense, so that the final break may prove to be a highly emotional experience.

This contact is perhaps best handled by really mature individuals, though this is no guarantee that it might not produce an attack of "midsummer madness" even in ripe old age!

The philosophy most typical of the Venus-Uranus combination is: "Better to have loved and lost than never to have loved at all."

Venus/Neptune

Purity of affection is the ideal keynote of this combination and for ordinary mortals this ideal is difficult to realize. When love is confused with physical attraction and mutual self-indulgence, the combination is apt to produce something less than the state of perfection for which both partners may yearn.

This contact can indicate much tenderness of feeling on both sides, but unless both partners are very clear-sighted, Neptune may hold an element of glamour for Venus that is more illusory than real, with the result that Venus may eventually realize that the ideal relationship that once seemed in prospect is not likely to materialize. At the highest level, Venus can inspire in Neptune a considerable degree of compassionate understanding and perhaps self-sacrifice, while Neptune may succeed in many subtle ways in drawing out the Venusian partner's capacity for affection.

When the planets are in adverse aspect or either is debilitated, some lack of understanding on the emotional level may develop. Neptune either misinterprets the affectionate reponses of Venus or becomes nervously embarrassed by them and takes some kind of evasive action at the last moment so that Venus never feels secure or completely satisfied.

Neptune may be the means of giving Venus a new and more visionary insight into the worlds of art and music and this contact may be present between the horoscopes of some artists or composers long since dead and those to whom their creations have a special appeal.

Venus/Pluto

Pluto's capacity to intensify other planetary vibrations is particularly important in personal relationships and especially when Venus, the planet representing an individual's capacity to create harmony is concerned. When the planets are well placed and favorably combined, there is often a mutual recognition of some deep emotional tie which seems so well established and is accepted so unquestioningly that it is not difficult to imagine that it could have resulted from happy experiences together in previous incarnations. When occurring between members of the opposite sex, the contact is likely to increase their sexual awareness of each other.

If the planets are in adverse aspect or either is debilitated, this awareness can be embarrassingly increased and Pluto's advances may become uncomfortably pressing to Venus, who always likes to act in a way pleasing to others if it can be accomplished without too much loss of comfort and composure. The conjunction and opposition may produce situations in which the partners seem to be irresistibly drawn together for better or worse, according to the natal aspects to each planet. In some cases, Pluto may attempt to block any intimate overtures from Venus, preferring to remain aloof or to terminate a relationship that threatens to produce an emotional involvement although sometimes the situation may be reversed, with Pluto pressing unwanted attentions upon Venus.

Mars/Mars

When Mars in one horoscope forms a good aspect to Mars in another horoscope, the persons concerned should be able to work harmoniously together. Much will depend on the natal condition of Mars in each horoscope, since the planet represents the energies available to the native and the way he is likely to apply them. If a joint effort is required, the effectiveness of the collaboration will depend upon how well each Mars is integrated with the totality of the planets in the other's horoscope. Energy has to find an outlet and when one Mars is at cross-purposes with the other, irritation and perhaps enmity can result. Nevertheless, if a favorable aspect joins the two, a compatibility of aim may assist smooth co-operation. Friendship may be encouraged by a mutual interest in physical fitness and sport.

Between opposite sexes the contact is apt to provide a mutual stimulation of the desire nature so that strong and passionate sex attraction can often result, especially through the conjunction or trine.

When either Mars is debilitated or there is an adverse aspect between them, a good deal of friction and even a tempestuous relationship can result. There may be a clash of wills with both wishing to assert themselves in opposite ways at the same time or each may alternatively irritate the other. As soon as one takes the initiative, the other may launch a counter initiative, each trying to outdo the other, so that the final result may be the exhaustion of both.

When collaboration is necessary in such cases, a master plan may need to be carefully worked out in advance or a third party, in whom both have confidence, invited to act as a referee in any disputes. Even so, it may be difficult for them to bring any major operation to a completely successful conclusion.

Mars/Jupiter

Mars is able to spark Jupiter's enthusiasm. This is a useful contact for members of teams engaged in athletic and sporting contests and those engaged in coaching them.

Jupiter can support the endeavours of Mars with wise advice and sometimes financial aid, though there may be a tendency for Mars to take advantage of Jupiter's generosity, especially as Jupiter tends to be rather easy-going. Jupiter can guide the energies of Mars wisely but much will depend on the natal condition of both planets, since the combination can be rather inflammatory and unbalancing.

If there should be an adverse aspect between the planets or either is debilitated, Mars may rouse Jupiter's enthusiasm and Jupiter may challenge the enterprise of Mars, to produce a situation where

Jupiter becomes too optimistic or careless, while Mars grows too rash and takes undue risks. Each may overstimulate the other and when such a contact is present between the horoscopes of immature individuals left to complete a job without proper supervision, they may spend so much time in strenuous by-play that the work is neglected.

When the two planets are harmoniously blended, Mars can be stimulated by his Jupiter partner to reach new heights of achievement, while Mars may bring financial benefit to Jupiter by his energetic promotion of schemes for their mutual gain.

Mars/Saturn

No combination of planets has achieved a worse reputation in astrology. The reason for this could be that laborious effort has never been particularly congenial to mankind. Mars represents energy, Saturn represents mass or substance, particularly in relation to the resistance it represents when contrasted with energy. Energy, before it can be used for constructive purposes, needs to be channeled and controlled, while substance needs to be shaped and transported if any worthwhile construction is to be attempted. The need to control and discipline the use of energy is shown by the exaltation of Mars in Capricorn, while the use of a lever and fulcrum to simplify the moving of large masses is shown by the exaltation of Saturn in Libra. This exaltation of Saturn in the seventh house sign measured from Aries suggests that any tendency to adopt an inflexible position in partnership needs to be energetically worked upon by Mars, while the self-assertive tendencies of the first house (Mars) need to be disciplined in order not to upset the stability of a partnership.

It has been observed that the Mars-Saturn conjunction does not prevent marriage and does not even deny a fruitful union, for Saturn may stabilize and direct the energies of Mars, while Mars ensures that Saturn does not neglect responsibilities. Each can, in fact, keep the other on his toes. When there is a good deal of mutual understanding and goodwill shown elsewhere in the contacts between the two horoscopes, partners should be able to co-operate to bring the best out of this rather "edgy" and sometimes intolerant combination. Saturn tends to indicate a lack of the qualities of the sign in which it is placed and is sometimes lacking in sufficient confidence to express these qualities openly, feeling in some way inadequate. Mars, on the other hand, usually emphasizes with confidence the qualities of the sign in which he is placed, so that when both planets are in the same sign, Saturn may be reassured by the confidence of Mars and as result fortify his feeling of insecurity and vulnerability. In return, Saturn can sometimes help Mars to tone down his tendency to express these qualities in too uninhibited a fashion.

When the two planets are in conflict, especially if either is debilitated by sign, there is likely to be a fight to a finish, as a result of which the vanquished may be left with a permanent sense of frustration or, should the battle be unresolved, a constant war of attrition may finally destroy any remaining vestiges of goodwill between the antagonists. When frustrated, Mars can resort to vigorous or violent action to cut loose from anything that is holding him back, while Saturn may take a special delight in suddenly applying the brake to Mars in order to demonstrate his power. The desire of Mars to push ahead and make speedy progress may not blend very effectively with the slow, deliberate and cautious approach of Saturn, especially when he is given to procrastination as well. Mars feels out of his element when unduly slowed down, while Saturn suspects that too much haste may invite mistakes.

Saturn's role may be to teach Mars how to be more patient and to look before he leaps while Mars can show Saturn the value of initiative and daring. Saturn may consider the enterprises of his Martian ally to be ill-considered and under-prepared, while Mars may consider that his Saturnian partner should do the tidying up, rectifying any omissions or mistakes committed as a result of Mars being in too much of a hurry. The best working arrangement may be for Saturn to draw up the plans and for Mars to put them into execution.

This is a difficult combination to cope with when present between the horoscopes of those who are in everyday contact. It may signify anything from a sado-masochistic relationship to a relatively satisfactory collaboration in which Saturn is content to adopt the role of guide and mentor to his impetuous partner, leaving Mars to take care of any main action that may be necessary for the effective continuation of the partnership. A great deal will depend on other contacts between the two horoscopes as to whether the partners can successfully handle the occasionally difficult situations that may arise as a result of this rather brittle planetary combination.

Mars/Uranus

This is a high tension combination that may prove a fascinating stimulus to partners who thrive on excitement, but if they should prefer a quiet life the difficult aspects can prove particularly disruptive.

Uranus can provide a dynamic stimulus to the drive of Mars, suggesting new areas for the exercise of initiative, while Mars can supply the energy to encourage the inventive genius of Uranus to flourish.

As Mars represents the desire nature and Uranus has rule over the sex glands, this combination can indicate a powerful physical attraction. The female Uranus can challenge the male Mars to demonstrate his manly qualities, while the male Uranus can add a new dimension to the ideal concept of manhood signified by the female Mars.

Uranus can motivate Mars and show him how to deploy his energies more effectively, but there may often be an element of tension present. If there is an adverse aspect between the planets or either is debilitated, situations can develop which involve anything from minor irritations to an explosive situation where both partners lose their tempers, with neither wishing to give way to the other. Violent quarrels may occasionally result, although in the case of a married couple, these may only temporarily interrupt the sexual relationship. Whether such disputes will be regarded as an interesting variation on the usual routine, or whether they cause a mutual hatred slowly to build up, will very much depend on the number of harmonious contacts between the two nativities.

If two people with this adverse cross-aspect are in everyday contact with each other, irritations can multiply and it could be helpful for them to have an occasional break from each other's company or at least ensure that they are not alone together too often. They should also allow each other as much freedom as possible.

The square is a particularly difficult aspect and Mars may feel that Uranus is too erratic and unpredictable for comfort. In order to understand his partner better he may continually probe and test the reactions of Uranus, who is not only apt to resent such conduct but may eventually remove himself to an environment where his actions do not continually have to be explained and justified.

The conjunction and opposition pose difficult problems. When the conjunction is present, both may feel they are suffering from a lack of room in which to maneuver and as a result they constantly seem to be treading on each other's toes. Feeling a need to indulge in a trial of strength from time to time, they may deliberately needle each other, provoking a fight in order to discharge some of the tension that has been building up between them. An agreement to differ can save a lot of wasted energy but if battles do occur, both partners may need time to recover their composure if the relationship is to survive successfully.

When the planets are in opposition, both partners have room for maneuver, so a good deal of fencing may take place, each trying to establish his position at the expense of the other. Mars usually favors the direct approach, while Uranus usually does his best to throw his opponent off guard, relying on the element of surprise. Should each choose to play a waiting game, a situation of stalemate may result. Uranus may ignore the hostile threats or activities of Mars, continuing to pursue his own course as if no one had any right to question it. Such behaviour may only serve to infuriate his partner the more.

The adverse aspects call for a good deal of careful handling if unpleasant friction is to be avoided. Every attempt should be made to talk over problems amicably rather than for one partner to attempt to force a solution on the other. Uranus should remember that Mars needs to take the initiative at times, while Mars must allow Uranus sufficient freedom of action. When such efforts to accommodate each other's needs fail, or are not even attempted, the relationship may well break down irretrievably.

Mars/Neptune

Occurring in a nativity, this combination tends toward an excess of emotion that leads the native to exaggerate his moods and attitudes. When this contact occurs between nativities, Neptune may introduce some new dimension of feeling and sensitivity to the desire nature of Mars, who finds his Neptunian partner mysteriously desirable.

The contact is basically a difficult one inasmuch as Mars favors the direct approach and the clear cut objective, while Neptune's methods are often devious and the aims are tinged with an idealism and universality that is not conducive to the kind of short, sharp campaign that his partner prefers. Mars is therefore likely to feel puzzled or annoyed by Neptune's lack of certainty or seeming lack of clarity and drive, while Neptune cannot understand why Mars must always make an issue of things or fail to take into account the feelings of others when pursuing his own interests.

When the planets combine favorably, Neptune may be able to help Mars appreciate the tactical virtues of the less obvious maneuver and teach him the value of gentleness and compassion, while Mars can help Neptune to give direction to and use greater drive in reaching his ideals. Occasionally, by the positive certainty of his approach, Mars can sow doubts in his partner's mind when he was already determined upon some different course of action. When the battle-weary Mars is licking his wounds, Neptune can provide a source of sympathetic understanding and support although there may be times when Neptune worries over some imaginary disaster that may beset his partner.

When the planets are in adverse aspect or either is debilitated, a relationship between those of opposite sexes may take on rather sensual overtones. Neptune may draw Mars on and play on his passions while at the same time remaining provocatively inaccessible or simulating an affection that is not there. A very great deal may depend upon the evolutionary status of the couple concerned, as this combination can provide possibilities of high aesthetic inspiration and endeavour at one end of the scale, and of sensuality and depravity at the other.

With the conjunction particularly, a physical relationship with particularly strong emotional overtones may exist, but cases have been noted where one or both of the partners has no real love for the other. A conjunction of the male Neptune with female Mars sometimes occurs in cases of seduction and rape.

The opposition brings to a head the problem of reconciling the directness of Mars with the devious approach of Neptune. The Mars-Neptune combat, symbolic of the changeover from the Age of Aries to the Age of Pisces, when the Roman Empire flourished, was presented in striking visual form by the combat in the Roman arena between the Secutor (a gladiator who was fully armed) and the Retiarius (armed only with a net and trident). The all-enveloping net was often triumphant over the limited, if forceful, attack of the swordsman. With the opposition, Neptune may fail to appreciate what Mars is driving at and what his wider aims are, while Mars will want to pin Neptune down to specific issues and clear away the aura of mystery with which Neptune loves to cloak his activities. Mars must try to allow for Neptune's sensitive feelings, while Neptune must remember that the conscious awareness of Mars is usually focused on the problems of practical everyday living and not in the more ethereal realms.

The square emphasizes the basic differences of the two planets in such a way as to increase the difficulty of achieving a really harmonious combination. Here, Neptune's reply to the insensivity and insistence of Mars may be to resort to deceit and subterfuge, perhaps simulating emotions not felt, pretending acquiescence in order to prevent Mars from acting in a hostile manner. Mars, on the other hand, may take Neptune's counterfeit responses as genuine if they are what he has naturally been expecting to receive as a tribute to his own clear-cut and attractive personality. The whole emotional atmosphere of the relationship may turn sour because the partners have no real insight into each other's emotional needs and spiritual aspirations.

While an initial fascination may arise as a result of this contact, the long term effect may be one of mounting frustration and eventual disillusionment, as Mars begins to realize that what he first identified as "glamour" was merely the result of Neptune's refusal to approach any issue in a straightforward way while Neptune may be affronted by the everlastingly brash approach of Mars, who fails in quite outrageous manner to appreciate Neptune's most cherished ideals and cannot seem to avoid trampling on his sensitive nature.

Mars/Pluto

This is a particularly compulsive aspect as Mars may draw to the surface Pluto's repressed physical desires which can in turn arouse a responsive chord in Mars. The female Pluto may be irresistibly drawn by the masculine qualities she sees in her male Mars partner, while the Pluto man may be particularly attracted by the energy, drive and initiative symbolised by Mars in his female partner's horoscope. Mars may feel an irresistible urge to probe the hidden psychological depths of his Plutonian partner.

A great deal may depend upon the aspects to Pluto at birth, as there is a marked tendency for Pluto to bring out the Martian capacity for action. This combination can be helpful and constructive when both planets are well aspected natally, while it can be dangerously destructive if both are severely afflicted. Under these conditions, Pluto's power to draw out Mars may be focused in a deliberately provocative manner, with the intention of forcing Mars to over-reach (and so destroy) himself. Pluto's action may be the result of strong subconscious urges and when there is a conjunction or an adverse aspect between the planets or either is debilitated, Mars may play on these urges for his own advantage.

A sense of rivalry may develop between the partners. If this gets out of hand, Mars may adopt a policy of all-out aggression with no holds barred. In some cases a weakly placed or aspected Pluto may consciously or unconsciously invite sadistic treatment from the partner. When this contact is present between two nativities, its effects are hardly likely to be negligible and the ability of each partner to react in a positive and constructive fashion to the stimulus provided by the other may depend a great deal upon the way in which the planets are integrated in the respective nativities.

Jupiter/Jupiter

A good aspect between two Jupiters indicates that both partners can agree on matters involving philosophy, ethics and general moral standards. There is usually a common recognition of the factors that will be most beneficial to the partnership and so this can be a useful contact between the horoscopes of business partners. Each is likely to have a healthy respect for the other and work for the other's benefit. This contact encourages mutual consideration and a willingness to appreciate the partner's good points.

If one or both Jupiters are debilitated, there may be a difference of outlook on philosophy or religion or they may have different moral standards. Such differences may occasionally be the cause of disagreements. Any tendencies towards over-expansiveness in one partner may remain unchecked by, or even be encouraged by, the other, with the result that extravagances may be recklessly multiplied.

Normally, this is a helpful contact whatever type of partnership is involved, making for mutual tolerance and a broad-minded acceptance of the partner's way of life.

Jupiter/Saturn

This is a complementary pairing though it does not automatically promise benefits. Much depends on whether either planet is debilitated and upon the nature of the aspect between them. Jupiter's plans for expansion and improvement can be given clearer definition and more practical form by a well placed Saturn, who can apply the benefit of his experience to render such plans more effective.

The two planets working harmoniously together can ensure a solid financial basis to any partnership, with Saturn checking any unwise expenditure on Jupiter's part, while Jupiter can encourage Saturn not to hold back when more expansive action might produce better results. Jupiter may more often be the giver and Saturn the receiver and if either planet is debilitated or they are joined by adverse aspect, Saturn may, on the material level, cause Jupiter to suffer financially or in kind, perhaps borrowing money and delaying repayment or, on the psychological level, Jupiter may find his buoyancy somewhat restricted by Saturn. When the planets are in adverse aspect, there may be a lack of mutual appreciation.

When Jupiter makes errors of judgment, Saturn may intervene with a steadying hand. If Jupiter should embark upon philosophical studies, Saturn may suggest ways of applying them in everyday life. When Jupiter devises a money-making scheme, Saturn can ensure that it is organized on the soundest possible basis. Jupiter's impulse to foster growth in every direction is helpfully channeled by Saturn into the most practically rewarding enterprises.

When the two planets are in square to each other, it may be difficult for the partners to agree upon a common goal and they may fail to appreciate each other sufficiently. A certain amount of give and take can help to improve the relationship and much will depend upon the general pattern of the interplay between the two horoscopes.

Jupiter/Uranus

When these two planets are favorably combined, Jupiter will encourage any originality and inventive ability that his partner displays and will be tolerantly disposed towards any manifestations of Uranian independence that may occur. In a business relationship Uranus may supply the creative originality and Jupiter the capital to finance his partner's inventions and novel ideas.

The occult or metaphysical interests of Uranus will receive sympathetic support from Jupiter, who may appreciate the unorthodox approach of his partner. The conjunction may be something of an unknown quantity unless one partner's Saturn is in good aspect to it, otherwise the excitability of Uranus may cause Jupiter to gamble needlessly or act imprudently, taking unnecessary risks in the process. When either body is debilitated or there is an adverse aspect between them, Uranus may resort to erratic action to break up Jupiter's irritating air of complacency, provoking him into behaving unwisely. In some cases, the opposition may pose problems through the partners not being able to see eye to eye over financial problems. On the other hand, when the planets are favorably configured, Uranus may be the sudden recipient of Jupiter's bounty.

Jupiter/Neptune

A sympathetic rapport exists between these two planets and when one partner's Jupiter is in favorable aspect to the other's Neptune it is possible for them to develop an intuitive understanding of each other's spiritual aspirations and sense of moral values. Jupiter can foster and encourage Neptune's inspiration and idealism, while Neptune's compassionate nature can help to find suitably charitable outlets for Jupiter's philanthropic impulses, adding a subtle new dimension to his philosophical understanding.

The conjunction is particularly felicitous unless adversely aspected from other sectors of either chart. Each will sympathetically appreciate the aspirations of the other and Neptune can bring a feeling of rich fulfillment to Jupiter, which can extend to the material plane, bringing financial benefits.

When the two planets are in unfavorable aspect or either is debilitated, Neptune may mislead Jupiter, not always deliberately, so that Jupiter feels his confidence has been misplaced. A mutual lack of trust may develop and in some cases Neptune may succeed in taking advantage of his generosity, perhaps playing on his sympathies with hard luck stories or defrauding him of financial or other resources. Jupiter may not appreciate Neptune's broader interpretation of moral issues and may doubt his sincerity of purpose.

Both planets are expansive in action and can lead to exaggeration of various kinds when they are combined in a nativity. This tendency to exaggeration, operating in the realm of human relationships, may encourage Jupiter to "show off" in front of Neptune, and Neptune to play act before Jupiter.

Jupiter/Pluto

Pluto can make Jupiter more aware of his generous impulses and philanthropic urges and help him to realize some of the deep level potentials underlying his understanding of philosophical concepts, with the result that some kind of transformation takes place in Jupiter's awareness. Jupiter can increase Pluto's optimism and give him a greater understanding of philosophical values, assisting him at the same time to achieve his ambitions more smoothly and persuasively and helping him to find himself a position of power and influence. Through his inside knowledge Pluto may be able to help Jupiter financially.

When the two are in unfavorable aspect or either is debilitated, Pluto may obstinately refuse to accept Jupiter's philosophy of life and moral standards, while Jupiter may find Pluto too single-mindedly set on his own course of action and completely unwilling to make concessions.

Saturn/Saturn

When the two partner's Saturns are in favorable aspect, they will each appreciate the other's sense of responsibility and each will feel he can rely upon the integrity of the other. One partner's capacity for self-discipline will not operate to the discomfiture of the other and each should be able to pursue his practical aims and ambitions without clashing with the other. This contact is a stabilizing factor in marriage, business and friendship, introducing an element of solidarity, reliability and dependability that makes for permanence in the relationship. The partners should be able to collaborate successfully in making plans for financial security and retirement. The experience of one partner will complement and reinforce the experience of the other, while each may be able to teach the other valuable lessons, the process being much less painful than when the two Saturns are in adverse aspect.

When they are linked by an adverse aspect or either is debilitated, the partners may not see eye to eye over the division of responsibility, particularly when the two Saturns are in square. Any area of life in which one partner feels inferior may lead him to overcompensate at the other's expense. Such situations are apt to lead to a struggle for supremacy and, while each partner may have justice on his side according to his own way of thinking, the methods by which each tries to achieve his results can differ so fundamentally that it becomes difficult for the two to find any real basis on which they can work together in harmony. An agreement to allocate to each his own separate areas of responsibility, in which he will operate according to his own ideas and methods, may be the best way of dealing with the situation. There may also be need to avoid a clash between the ambitions of each partner and in some cases each may be better off following his own independent career.

The adverse aspects tend to test each partner's sense of security and to probe his inferiority complexes, producing a rather edgy atmosphere. In parent-child relationships this contact may be particularly difficult, while it tends to have a dampening effect on friendships.

When the opposition is in force, and this can only happen when there is a difference in ages of about fifteen, forty-five or seventy-five years, each may seem to the other to be too self-contained to be particularly forthcoming, while each may be tempted to question any assumption of authority on the part of the other. The opposition may workout largely in terms of the pair of houses in the two horoscopes across which the two Saturns fall and if one partner has Saturn in the seventh house this may be a particularly testing relationship.

The conjunction is something of a mixed blessing and can represent shared responsibilities, cares and experiences, each partner learning from the other. In some cases a bond may be formed because they feel themselves to be partners in adversity. Friends with this conjunction may become too dependent on each other for their own good. It is not a particularly good augury for a relationship between doctor and patient or between business adviser and client.

Adverse aspects between the two Saturns need not work out in psychological terms but may indicate circumstantial difficulties. One partner may have to cope with the sickness or infirmity of the other, or a parent may have to rear a child that is mentally or physically handicapped. Whatever the circumstances may be, they will be likely to test the partners' capacity for patient endurance and willingness to accept heavy responsibility, probably the result of karmic duty owed to each other. When psychological differences do arise they may result from the fact that Saturn indicates those activities and interests in life that the native is likely to take seriously. If one partner is not prepared to respect the most serious commitments of the other, this may eventually lead to discord.

Saturn/Uranus

Saturn rules the old order and Uranus the new. This basic difference does not promise an easy combination of the virtues they represent. A too conservative attitude can narrow the mind and lead to missed opportunities, while a too forward-looking and too experimental approach may encourage mistakes through neglecting the lessons of history, or through failing to take the necessary precautions. Each planet, therefore can be helped by the modifying influence of the other.

When the two planets are in adverse aspect in a nativity there may be much psychological tension. The same factor in synastry can be the indicator of discord so that both partners may have difficult problems to solve before they can feel truly at ease in each other's company.

When there is a favorable aspect between the planets, Uranus can demonstrate to Saturn the advantages of an original approach in dealing with long-standing problems while Saturn can show Uranus how to discipline his erratic tendencies and tone down his eccentricities so that they become more acceptable to the orthodox element in society, and how to organize his inventiveness and to apply his originality and ingenuity in the most effective and practical way.

There is a tendency for Saturn to feel ill at ease in the presence of the independence and lack of conformity displayed by Uranus. When either planet is debilitated or they are linked by adverse aspect, there is a notable lack of sympathy between the partners. Saturn may regard the more extravagant behaviour of Uranus with distaste and disapproval, seeking to curb his eccentricities and disregard for convention, attempting to inculcate in his partner a sense of self-discipline and respect for established custom that he feels is lacking.

Such a course may provoke Uranus into even more extravagant behaviour, with the object of shocking his partner's outdated sense of propriety. Uranus may succeed in helping Saturn to adopt a more modern, original life style.

When the planets are in conjunction there is an implied struggle for power between the old and the new. Uranus is sometimes apt to maneuver Saturn into a trial of strength, seeing just how far he can assert his independence and break down Saturn's stubborn opposition to a line of action that appears to be outrageously unorthodox. The opposition can result in a useful containment by Saturn of the more eccentric proclivities of Uranus, but unless Uranus is prepared to accept that new departures are only acceptable when they are capable of being reasonably integrated with established practice, and unless Saturn realizes that new ideas are the life blood of progress and that to stand still in life is to invite eventual deterioration and decay, the partners may find that discords in the relationship will inevitably develop. These can lead to a mutual distaste that may eventually spoil the union unless a number of other more harmonious factors are present. With this type of contact a go-stop-go kind of situation can exist, where both partners, although despising certain traits in the other, also find much to admire. Saturn's cautious delaying tactics may clash with the confident spontaneous approach of Uranus, to produce a situation where each feels that the other is throwing him off-balance. As a result, Saturn loses confidence in his sense of timing and Uranus feels that his talent for on the spot improvisation is being wasted.

When the adverse aspects are present between nativities of those meeting for the first time, they may quickly become aware of a sense of mutual irritation which can prevent a lasting association from developing.

Saturn/Neptune

This is another difficult combination. At best, Saturn can show Neptune how to give his ideals, inspirations and dreams practical expression, and how to contain and put to effective use his flights of fancy while Neptune can introduce Saturn to a less prosaic and more idealistic way of looking at things.

Saturn represents the capacity to develop a hard-headed, practical approach to life. Neptune indicates the potentiality of modifying a purely pragmatic outlook by a wider and more compassionate understanding of the oneness of all life. Saturn may distrust the apparent lack of definition inherent in Neptune's attitude, feeling that most problems can be expressed in terms of black and white; Neptune is aware of the myriads of subtle shades in between. While Neptune may long wistfully for the ideal solution to a problem, Saturn will uncompromisingly opt for a practical commonsense solution that may leave the partner aghast at his lack of feeling, sympathy and the apparent absence of any awareness of the more spiritual sides of life. In some cases, Saturn's materialism may prove a source of keen disappointment to Neptune.

When the two planets are harmoniously configured, Saturn can help Neptune to adopt a more practical approach, while Neptune can show Saturn that life need not be ruled entirely by the force of tradition and the dictates of necessity. Saturn may have a hard time trying to make Neptune realize that he should take responsibility, especially as the issues that seem important to Saturn may appear of very little consequence to Neptune.

Any attempt on the part of Saturn to exert unwelcome pressure on his partner may result in Neptune seeking to gain his ends by subterfuge. What Saturn may have regarded as a binding promise may not have been intended as such by Neptune, whose way of expressing his thoughts could have been misinterpreted by Saturn, who is often apt to interpret literally what Neptune's more poetic language was only intended to convey figuratively.

It follows that when the planets are in adverse aspect or debilitated, some difficult problems may have to be solved before the partnership can flourish. Saturn may have doubts about Neptune's integrity, while Neptune may find Saturn's insensitivity and self-centeredness a source of great disappointment. There could be some failure to reconcile material and spiritual values and any attempt by Saturn to force the issue or to lay down the law may cause more trouble than it is worth. In some cases, visions of profiting financially through the partner may prove to have been only pipe dreams while if the Saturn partner is unscrupulous he may be tempted to play on the gullibility of Neptune for his own financial ends. Any financial agreement between the partners should in any case be as watertight as possible.

Some kind of accommodation between the material ambitions of Saturn and the spiritual aspirations of Neptune may be possible when the planets are in opposition, but the square may leave each partner with a sense of frustration and even dismay at the seemingly impossible task of reconciling their widely different aims and viewpoints. For Saturn, Neptune sometimes represents the threat of the unknown, while to Neptune, Saturn's lack of finer susceptibilities is completely incomprehensible and an obstacle to be overcome by any subtlety that suggests itself.

The conjunction is apt to face the partners with the decision as to who shall take responsibility in the area represented by the sign and houses in which the conjunction takes place, though much may depend on any aspects to the conjunction from either partner's planets. Since any attempt by Saturn to force Neptune to take responsibility is likely to meet with little success, he had far better resign himself to what he may regard as Neptune's chronic irresponsibility and take charge of things himself. Neptune can, in fact, teach Saturn to practise a measure of resignation, as well as a degree of reverence for the more spiritual aspects of life, while Saturn can help Neptune to make a more matter-of-fact assessment of everyday problems, especially as Saturn sometimes feels it incumbent upon himself to take Neptune in hand to teach him to be more efficient.

Saturn/Pluto

This is a difficult combination in the natal horoscope and the best results are gained in partnership when each partner has a healthy respect for the other's qualities. When the planets are in good aspect Saturn can appreciate Pluto's all-consuming dedication and Pluto can admire Saturn's dependability, application and ambition. In a business relationship such a combination can help the partners to place their enterprise on a firm foundation.

When these planets are in adverse aspect or either is debilitated, Pluto may play upon Saturn's fears, undermine his sense of responsibility or perhaps destroy what he is carefully trying to build up. Saturn may try to restrict Pluto's freedom of action and in some cases this may be like trying to permanently prevent a volcano from erupting. As a result, Pluto may adopt a more aloof attitude and work under cover to achieve his ends. Unless very strong elements of compatibility are present in other sectors of the two horoscopes, the clash between Saturn and Pluto, particularly when they are in square aspect, can lead to envy, mutual distrust and in some cases to deep-seated antagonism.

The conjunction is a crucial aspect which may have a particularly karmic significance, with Saturn being aware of some strong compulsion to render service to his Plutonian partner.

Uranus/Uranus

While close contemporaries will have a conjunction with their partner's Uranus, there must be at least fourteen years' difference in age before the sextile can occur, while the square requires about twenty-one years' difference and the trine, twenty-eight. These two latter aspects can therefore sometimes feature in parent-child relationships.

With the conjunction, much will depend upon the mutual aspects to this point, but if the planets are favorably aspected, the partners should see eye to eye over any new departures they may plan and the new ideas they encounter. This can be rather a nervy contact and each partner should show due respect for the other's rights and due concern for his freedom of action if discord is to be avoided. To a large extent, this conjunction may refer to the impact on the partners of events in the outside world. When the faster moving bodies are involved with Uranus, however, special care may be needed to avoid autocratic or erratic behaviour that could arouse obstinate opposition in the partner and cause him to assert his independence in no uncertain manner.

A sextile or trine between the two may indicate that the older partner's experience can stimulate the younger in ways that show him how to explore new avenues of thinking, enhancing his creative originality in the process. This is a useful contact between friends who share some particular hobby, as each may contribute a viewpoint which opens up new vistas for the other. Mutual benefit may accrue from a business relationship when this aspect is present, where the "senior" Uranus is the employer of the "younger." The older person will appreciate the outlook and aims of the younger and may be the means of giving him the necessary freedom to put his plans into operation. This is a useful contact between the horoscopes of agent and client, the former being able to present the latter with new opportunities for development.

The square aspect may make it difficult for a parent to understand his child's desire for freedom of action and may be the prime reason for that difference of outlook that has come to be referred to as the "generation gap." The square signifies that the two individuals' urges towards dynamic self-expression are at their point of greatest conflict. This is the kind of aspect that may be present when the parent feels that he has the right to dictate the pattern of behaviour he expects from his offspring, who then resents what he considers to be an unjustified limitation of his freedom and deliberately sets out to find ways of demonstrating his independence. Such relationships obviously require careful handling on both sides. Offspring may need to appreciate that independence without a sense of responsibility and self-discipline can sometimes prove disastrous, while the parent must recognize that a sense of responsibility and self-discipline can best be encouraged to flourish by giving the child a certain amount of freedom in which to gain experience.

The square is potentially an explosive aspect and the best results may be achieved when both parties are prepared to concede that each generation has its own approach to moral, intellectual and spiritual matters, and each its own role to play in the cycle of human progress. Any attempt by the older generation to turn back the clock is completely alien to the spirit of Uranus and can only result in friction or revolt.

The opposition implies about a forty-two year gap between the individuals concerned and can be present in grandparent-grandchild relationships or between student and teacher or employer and employee. Any unorthodox behaviour on the part of the younger person may cause a feeling of irritation in the elder, especially if he is inclined to adopt an indulgent attitude towards the foibles of youth. The complementary nature of the opposition can be mentally stimulating in some relationships, but only when the Uranian vibration is well integrated in the individual nativities.

Uranus/Neptune

The opposition between these two planets occurred just prior to World War I, when Europe was thrown into the melting-pot, and the danger of cut-throat national rivalry was made plain for all to see, but as a consequence a whole new range of exciting possibilities gave rise to hope of great new opportunities for developing the quality of human life. At its closest exactitude the opposition produced a high proportion of the outstanding musicians whose genius first established jazz as a recognised art form in the 1920s and 1930s. The two planets symbolize opposite poles of high-level awareness, Uranus representing a positive, dynamic mobilization of the intuitive faculties; Neptune a negative, receptive and ultra-sensitive state of consciousness.

A tendency to discount aspects between the major planets in synastry has resulted in less attention being paid to this area, but all contacts have some significance and, while the conjunction and adverse aspects between these planets may produce a vague kind of dissonance between partners that is difficult to account for, it can be none the less real. Uranus may play upon the imagination of Neptune to produce a level of emotional intensity which is difficult to control but which may in some cases inspire Neptune to reach a new level of artistic creativity and enhance his spiritual awareness. On the other hand, Uranus may merely increase Neptune's capacity for being deluded or his inability to formulate ideas with crystal clear precision. For his part, Neptune may be able to add vision and compassion to the utopian outlook of Uranus or subtly play on his partner's capacity for excitement, which can either increase his innate intuitive capacity, make him more restless and erratic, or leave him feeling totally frustrated at the unpredictability of his partner.

When either body is debilitated or when the planets are in adverse aspect, the partnership may be vaguely unsatisfactory, being plagued by some subtle, nebulous discontent that is difficult to identify and even more difficult to cure. This contact is one which is best handled by those whose self-development is well advanced.

Uranus/Pluto

When the planets are in favorable aspect, Pluto can assist Uranus to assert his individuality more effectively, and to express his originality more dramatically, mobilising support to help him achieve his objectives and spurring him on to greater efforts. Uranus can show Pluto new ways of reaching his goals. If both should have interests that are out of the ordinary, their collaboration can produce exciting results.

This can be a very useful contact when both partners are ambitious and enterprising and so it is particularly helpful to a business partnership, though when either planet is debilitated or the aspect between them is adverse, the element of self-will on each side may be abruptly brought into play, with Uranus acting more openly and often erratically in order to get his own way while Pluto may operate undercover and mobilize powerful opposition against his partner. Pluto may object to the erratic or unpredictable behaviour of Uranus, while Uranus may feel ill at ease over some of the less obvious traits of Pluto's character that appear to dominate his feeling and thinking.

The element of change may become a crucial issue in such a partnership and an agreement upon the drastic elimination of those factors that are mutually irritating may be essential if the partnership is to survive. Occasionally situations may arise when neither party will wish to compromise and, if neither is willing to yield a point, a final break in the relationship may be inevitable.

Neptune/Neptune

The only significant aspect that can occur between members of the same generation is the conjunction and mutual aspects to this point may well decide whether the compassionate impulses and spiritual aspirations of each are likely to prove a source of harmony or discord. Neptune will indicate how each partner responds to the emotional atmosphere and envisioned goals of his own generation. Each partner may feed the other's dreams and foster his illusions according to the aspects to the conjunction from other sectors of the partners' charts. A conjunction between well-aspected Neptunes can bring a strong sense of sympathetic rapport between partners and is an excellent aspect between the horoscopes of a politician and his supporters (this is also true of the sextile) or between an actor and his public or his fellow workers. If one partner has Neptune adversely aspected in the nativity, the other may experience some subtle disappointment through a real or imagined quality of being that the partner displays or appears to display.

A similar sense of rapport is possible when individuals have their Neptunes in trine, which will be the case when their age difference is about sixty-one years. Most probably the younger will be in his childhood or perhaps just have reached his majority. The elder will then have the power to fire the imagination of the younger and provide a vision which stimulates the later's subsequent achievement.

The square implies an age difference of some forty-one years and suggests some failure to understand each other's subtler emotional moods. What each regards as his heart's desire may seem irreconcilable and such a contact may sometimes be present between the nativities of friends of the opposite sex when the elder is heard to lament: "If only I were young again!"

If such a contact exists between doctor and patient, misunderstandings may lead to a wrong diagnosis of symptoms, while in other types of professional relationship (such as lawyer and client) where one renders a professional service to the other, it may be necessary to ensure that each knows precisely what is expected of him and that there is a clear understanding about the fees involved.

A feature of synastry that is probably purely of academic interest lies in the influence that someone long since dead may still have on the living through the legacy of his music, art, philosophy or the inspirational quality of his life. When the works of such an individual have such a vivid appeal for another, this may well be shown by an opposition between the two Neptunes which, at the earliest reckoning, can only take place after an interval of about eighty-two years. This type of link, especially involving the benefic aspects, can also occur between the horoscope of a town or city and the nativities of those of its inhabitants who are aware of a considerable sense of rapport with their environment when living there, or who are held in great esteem by their fellow citizens.

Neptune/Pluto

In a nativity this contact sometimes indicates a hypersensitive type of awareness. When the conjunction occurs, those individuals are born who are particularly alert to the amosphere of their times. While only a very small percentage will have the opportunity to become actors on the world stage at the highest level, it is not without significance that a very great proportion of the prominent military and political figures who contributed to and participated in World War II were born at the time when this conjunction was in orbs.

When Neptune in one horoscope is in aspect to Pluto in another, Pluto may play upon Neptune's phobias and fantasies increasing any neurotic or escapist tendencies present. Pluto may probe Neptune's weaknesses compelling some kind of transformation. Neptune may react by becoming more elusive and mysterious in an attempt to baffle his partner causing him to abandon his unwelcome activities. If the partners are engaged in welfare work or activities of an artistic nature and are capable of acting with a mature integrity, a useful collaboration may occur when the planets are in favorable aspect, but when either body is debilitated or the aspect is unfavorable, a deep-seated mistrust of each other's motives may gnaw at the roots of any relationship.

Pluto/Pluto

Owing to the time taken by Pluto to make one circuit of the zodiac the only significant aspects between living persons are the conjunction, the sextile and perhaps the square. In certain areas of the zodiac, Pluto moves much faster than in others, covering ninety degrees in less that forty years while at its slowest it takes some ninety years to cover the same arc. Trines and oppositions, except in rare cases, can only be present between the horoscopes of an individual's ancestors and his own. Such contacts may be observed with the horoscopes of those historical characters whose lives have had some kind of definitive influence on a person's philosophy or overall development.

Any aspect between Plutos in two nativities is likely to work out mainly in subliminal areas of consciousness where compelling feelings of attraction or repulsion may be generated. Much will depend on the way in which each Pluto is aspected in the individual nativities as to whether the relationship will produce harmony or discord, especially in relation to those areas of experience signified by the houses occupied in each nativity.

Contemporaries involved in some form of group activity may discover a close identity in their Pluto placements.

The interplay of the luminaries and planets with the horizon and meridian of the horoscope is also highly significant but such considerations relate more to the houses concerned and are dealt with in the next chapter.

CHAPTER 8

Interaction Between Nativities
Part Two

House Interchanges

When a planet in one person's horoscope falls close to the Midheaven or Ascendant in another's horoscope, the importance of such a contact is fairly self-evident. The mere presence of one person's planets in the houses of another's horoscope may not seem quite so significant, yet this type of re-domification can give quite a few pointers as to the way in which a relationship between them may develop.

It is a good plan when comparing nativities to set up each person's horoscope and place the other's planets in an outside ring round the chart, in much the same way as one might insert the positions of transiting planets around the periphery of a horoscope. In fact the effect of another person's planets in the various houses of a partner's nativity is very much like that of a transit, representing some outside influence being brought to bear on the affairs of that house. The important difference is that such an influence is a "personified" transit, and can exist for as long as the relationship with that person lasts, but only in terms of that particular relationship and particularly when that person is present. If the relationship is a close one and the affairs of that house are connected in the native's mind with an awareness of the other's approval or disapproval, particularly in a parent-child relationship, even the physical absence of the person concerned may bring no great modification of the effect of that influence.

When a planet in one nativity falls exactly on the cusp of a house in the partner's nativity, it is likely to have its maximum effect on the affairs of that house, or perhaps more accurately, its influence upon the native's psychological attitude to the matters governed by that house is likely to be at its greatest. Some students assume that the cusp of a house forms a sharp and absolute dividing line between the two houses, but in the writer's opinion this is a mistaken assumption. The cusp of a house represents the peak of influence in relation to that house; the crest of the wave, as it were. If, for instance, the fifth house cusp is 7° Capricorn and Mars is in 4° Capricorn it would be shown in the horoscope as being physically in the fourth house. This is purely a diagrammatic device. In terms of practical interpretation it means that the planet has hardly begun to influence the fourth house and is in fact close to the crest of influence of the fifth house. This peak does, however, fall away sharply into the "valley" of the preceding house. When a planet is more than about five degrees in advance of a cusp, it will then be just beginning to exert some slight influence over the affairs of the house in which it is placed. In the judgment of solar revolutions a planet is considered to be angular, and of special importance on that account, when it is within ten degrees of the horizon or meridian, on whichever side it may fall.

When considering house positions, the controversial question of house division arises. While the writer is happy to use the Placidean system, those who prefer Campanus, Koch, Regiomontanus or other systems will no doubt check the readings that follow in terms of their own favorite system of house division before deciding which gives the better results. The fact that different house systems often produce a difference in the zodiacal longitude of intermediate house cusps is another reason why the cusp should not be regarded as a rigid dividing line between houses, however "tidy" the arrangement may appear to be.

THE HOUSES

In order to appreciate the effect of one person's planets placed in the houses of another's horoscope it is necessary to understand the significance of each of the twelve houses.

The First House represents the way in which we like to present ourselves to the world. It is the persona, the mask we put on and feel most at home with. It usually indicates the characteristics we are most easily identified by.

The Second House represents possessions of all kinds, whether spiritual, intellectual, emotional or physical, the things people gather around themselves and make their own in order to have a sense of greater security on all levels of being. It indicates those things people value, their psychological attitude towards possessions, and is related to their earning capacity.

The Third House represents the capacity to communicate, the way in which information is gathered, the ability to forge links with the immediate environment, and to establish connections on a relatively local basis. It is therefore related to the capacity for receiving education and traveling around in order to gather impressions, and maintain local contacts. It represents neighbors, also "neighbors" in the family, brothers, and sisters, and the psychological attitude to them.

The Fourth House represents roots, beginnings, home, the family (as a unit) and the parents in particular. It indicates our instinctive reactions, built up over a series of lives, and the kind of environment into which we can retreat as a haven from outward pressures and so re-charge our energies. It shows the direction in which our instincts may subconsciously lead us.

The Fifth House represents the fruits of our activities at the instinctive level, our natural creative ability, which is really the ability to reflect and act as a channel for the Creative Power of the Divine Will. It shows how we are likely to handle power on all levels, and the nature of the things we create, particularly children.

The Sixth House represents our capacity for service, our ability to relate our creative powers to those around us in such a way as to harness our talents to the needs of the community. It represents our attitude to playing a subordinate role, and our efficiency in applying techniques of all kinds. It is therefore linked to the way in which we are able to deal with and use materials, including the physical materials of the body, so that the question of physical fitness or the lack of it, also relates to the sixth house.

The Seventh House represents our capacity to relate to other people on a basis of equality, seeking in them complementary qualities so that each may reinforce the other. More specifically, it signifies the ability to co-operate in partnership with others, or to test our strength against them in a spirit of rivalry, which may be friendly, or the reverse, according to the condition of the seventh house and the impact of another's planets on this house. In its most particularized form the seventh house represents the marriage partner. In its most generalized form it indicates how the native views the world outside, the "not-self" contrasted with the self of the first house.

The Eighth House represents our capacity to draw on our inner resources and to reinforce them by drawing upon the resources of the world at large. It shows the capacity for creating new power out of our inner resources by transforming them through a process of dedicated endeavor and rigorous self-examination. Transformation spells death to outworn habits and attitudes, and physical death itself is the ultimate example of this process on the material level. Death normally releases consciousness from material bondage, just as transformations accomplished during the lifetime on other levels can release the consciousness from emotional, mental and spiritual bondage, thus tapping new reservoirs of power. On a more mundane level the eighth house represents the partner's resources and our psychological attitude towards the partner's resources.

The Ninth House represents our capacity to relate to and establish connections with a wider frame of reference on all levels, through travel, study and contact with knowledge related to philosophy, religion and all types of higher learning designed to provide an over-all view of life and to assist man's understanding of his relationship to the Cosmos: in short, everything that enables us to gain a greater insight into the meaning of life. It also relates specifically to those who are able to provide us with such illumination.

The Tenth House represents the way in which we seek to establish a place of influence in the world, not necessarily in relation to our employment but in the broader context of our career and the kind of reputation we are able to build for ourselves as a result of our achievements on all levels. It denotes our conscious aim in life and our whole attitude towards achievement. It indicates how we are likely to behave in a position of power, influence, and the type of person to whom we may have to give allegiance. It shows the type of person whom we may look up to as an example, a hero-figure who may fire our imagination, and usually indicates the parent who had the most influential voice in shaping our career.

The Eleventh House represents our capacity for engaging in creative group enterprises and working for a common ideal. It signifies our ability to mobilize support for such enterprises among those of similar enthusiasms. It signifies the results that accrue from our achievements, any reputation we may have gained, and those who are attracted to us on that account, and whom we shall be likely to number among our friends.

The Twelfth House represents our capacity to bring together and merge into a significant, integrated whole, the fruits of whatever wisdom we may have distilled from our various experiences and the talents we have been able to develop, so that our whole life has a meaning, not only in terms of our own self-development but in relation to our place in the community, and our own acceptance of our role in the Divine Plan. A failure to adjust satisfactorily to the world at the social and moral level may result in our neglecting to pay due regard to the rules and the needs of the community in which we live. A failure to adjust at the mental, emotional or physical level may produce disturbances of the psyche or physical illness. The experiences related to this sector of the horoscope are usually calculated to increase our compassion for our fellows.

> The readings that follow as a matter of convenience, are expressed in terms of the man's luminary or planet falling in the various houses of his female partner's horoscope, except where specifically stated otherwise. In general the effects will be similar whether a comparison is being made between two people of the same sex or when the position is reversed with the woman's planets falling in the house of her male partner.

These readings do not take into account the fact that one person's planet falling in a house of the partner's horoscope may at the same time form a conjunction with a planet in that house or closely aspect a planet in another house. By referring to the appropriate planetary combination in the previous chapter it should be possible to get a fair idea of how the reading should be modified. A great deal will also depend on the natal condition of the planet that is being relocated in the partner's horoscope. Sometimes more than one planet will fall in the same house of the partner's horoscope in which case further modification will be necessary. To include all possible combinations would require an enormous volume. In any case the cultivation of individual judgment can only develop through a gradual emancipation from a reliance upon stock readings. It follows that contemporaries will usually have a conjunction between the slowest moving major planets, re-emphasizing their original positions in each horoscope. Several planets belonging to one of the partners falling in a single house of the other's horoscope will increase his involvement with the affairs denoted by that house.

THE SUN IN THE HOUSES

When one person's Sun falls in a certain house of another's horoscope, it has the effect of encouraging that other person to participate wholeheartedly in those matters connected with the house in question. The person whose Sun is involved is able to exert a stabilizing and vivifying influence in this area of the other's life.

Sun in the First House

When the man's Sun falls on the woman's Ascendant or, to a slightly lesser degree, in her first house, or when it throws a major aspect to her ascending degree, there is a similarity between the man's essential self, his inner being, and the way the partner is seeking to project herself outwardly. Her psychological orientation will therefore encourage him to be his own essential self more effectively. She will appreciate his worth as an individual and have a higher regard for him, to the extent that she sees her own external characteristics and outward method of approach demonstrated in mature fashion by her partner, as if they belonged to the very essence of his being. This situation creates the possibility of much mutual attraction, with the woman demonstrating admiration for the man, who is happy to receive this appreciation. She may recognize and acknowledge his ability to lead, allowing him to fulfill his natural function and so putting him in a good humor with himself. If the Sun is not in conjunction with the ascending degree but throws a benefic aspect to it from some other sector of his partner's horoscope, a strong link can exist. In cases where the Sun is in adverse aspect, the Sun's authority may not be passively accepted, and a struggle for supremacy could develop. There can be strong elements of contrast, both psychological and physical and if the Sun is afflicted he may try to dominate his partner or impress her through his airs and graces, or try to blind her with science. The quincunx can be an indication of antipathy.

The warmth and affection of the Sun can encourage and bring out the best in his partner, giving added confidence and providing her with a source of personal sustainment and with an example that she would wish to emulate. The Sun may expect due acknowledgment of his role as patron and mentor in supplying moral and perhaps more tangible support. This could be a small price to pay for the goodwill and encouragement which he is prepared to offer freely to his partner.

When a parent's Sun falls in this area, he may try to bring his child up as a carbon copy of himself.

This solar position can be an important link, bringing much benefit, or the reverse, according to its condition at birth and the cross-aspects to it from the partner's horoscope. The Sun can provide inspiration or may monopolize attention but the relationship will never be half-hearted!

Sun in the Second House

When the man's Sun falls in the second house of his female partner, her psychological orientation will encourage him to project his essential self into that sector of her life that relates to the way in which she accumulates and manipulates her resources. Her partner's Sun can therefore bring her opportunities of a highly beneficial nature, helping her to improve her financial status and possibly even supplying the financial backing for her to do so. Her partner may offer her sound advice and provide the necessary know-how for her to build up her resources and attain a measure of financial security.

Sometimes the man's Sun in this sector of his partner's horoscope can indicate that he makes too great a claim on her resources. He may expect her to be financially self-sufficient and encourage her to become financially completely independent. He usually expects an acknowledgment of his generosity when he brings her gifts, and possibly some return in kind, and may require appreciation of any services rendered, in which case he is likely to expect to receive something befitting his station in life.

The Sun is usually a loyal supporter and advocate of his partner, when placed in this house. Sometimes this position of the Sun can denote a considerable physical attraction.

Sun in the Third House

When the man's Sun falls in the third house of his partner's horoscope, her psychological orientation will encourage him to project his essential self into that sector of her life connected with the way in which she relates to her environment and gathers information of a practical nature. She will appreciate the mental stimulus her partner is able to give her. He will usually listen attentively to her conversation, encouraging her to state her point of view and assisting her to develop her ideas on a broad basis, giving them a greater meaning and significance in the process. As a result, a lively companionship can develop, particularly on the mental level.

The Sun can sometimes help to ease his partner's traveling problems but at the mental level he may well expect her to make some effort to solve her own problems, first supplying the know-how, then leaving her to put it into practice.

Brotherly association on a free and easy basis is favored by this position. When opposite sexes are involved, the relationship may approximate more to that of brother and sister than husband and wife.

Sun in the Fourth House

When the man's Sun falls in the fourth house of his partner's horoscope, and more particularly when it falls in conjunction with her Lower Meridian, he will tend to adopt the role of parent towards her so that she will instinctively accept his guidance and leadership. He may help to bring her out and encourage her to develop her abilities and she may allow his influence to become apparent in the home environment, which will then reflect certain facets of his personality that impress her.

Sometimes the Sun's influence in this sector will have a very subtle effect, so that she unconsciously desires to emulate his example, unless there are unfavorable cross-aspects involving the Sun. With the Sun in this position in another's horoscope, there is a tendency for the relationship to be formed either very early or late in life. Such a link can be very important, however, as the one whose fourth house is involved is always aware of the standards of the solar partner.

Sun in the Fifth House

When the man's Sun falls in the fifth house of his female partner's horoscope a stimulus towards more creative activities is provided, either by inspiring her to emulate his example or by giving enthusiastic support to her projects and enterprises and generally taking an interest in hobbies. He is usually able to evoke a warm emotional response, so that she feels uplifted by the solar presence. As a result, in some cases, she may be particularly indulgent about any shortcomings in his behaviour. This is a good position for friendship and the person whose Sun is involved will have the capacity to bring joy into the other's life and will take pleasure in her affectionate responses.

Sun in the Sixth House

When the man's Sun falls in the sixth house of his female partner's horoscope, he may be in a position to offer her some kind of service. She may rest assured that she can rely on his aid, although he may occasionally call upon her to return the compliment, especially as he is likely to value her services.

His wholehearted support may encourage her to make sure that she is functioning as efficiently as she possibly can, otherwise she may find that he will be ready to suggest ways that will improve her system and make it more reliable.

In a doctor-patient relationship, this is a good house position for the doctor's Sun, provided it is well aspected in the nativity and the cross-aspects to it do not clash unduly.

This position is more likely to occur with casual relationships rather than in the case of long term friendships and the whole association may be somewhat transitory, depending upon what is convenient to both parties. The relationship may arise through the necessity of the two concerned having to earn their living in the same establishment. It can signify an employer-employee relationship, in which the person whose Sun is involved will expect a worthwhile recompense for his services.

When the Sun is re-located in the sixth house of another person there is often no emotional involvement, though any reticence over this is unlikely to originate with the Sun.

Sun in the Seventh House

When the man's Sun falls in the seventh house of his female partner's horoscope, and particularly when it is in conjunction with the western horizon, this can signify that he is the ideal person to work in partnership with her. He can help her to strengthen her weak points, which he may be able to recognize without difficulty. If strong afflictions should be involved, an element of rivalry may well be evident in the relationship and he might be tempted to exploit his knowledge of her vulnerable areas and thus throw her completely off balance.

At best he can be a desirable partner and a valuable ally who is able to augment her circle and organize considerable support for her. Under affliction he may allow his independence to over-ride any desire to co-operate and, at worst, he could prove to be a formidable opponent.

It could be in his partner's interests to co-operate as fully as possible with him and to try to reason out with him any causes of disharmony which exist in the relationship.

In a lawyer-client relationship, this is a good position for the lawyer's Sun, provided it is reasonably free from affliction natally and from the client's horoscope.

Sun in the Eighth House

The eighth house is a somewhat crucial area and when the man's Sun falls in this sector of his female partner's horoscope, this can produce a relationship in which she is made uncomfortably aware of some defect of her character that can only be satisfactorily rectified by some kind of transcendent change in herself. He may, by constructive criticism, assist her to conduct a sufficiently objective appraisal of herself and he may be able to indicate some new way in which she can face up to her problems so that she is able to tap resources of which she was previously unaware.

He may be capable of making demands upon her that bring out a response she did not realize she had it in her power to make. If the Sun is afflicted in his nativity or clashes with her own planets, a most uncomfortable situation may arise, a great deal depending upon the degree of self-esteem she possesses and her powers of self-protection, since a deficiency in these areas can invite his disapproval or more unpleasant forms of criticism. The Sun always tends to take his partner at her own evaluation of herself. If she is able to show that she is mature enough to be tolerant of criticism, she may be able to disarm her would-be critic, whose appreciation may grow in proportion to the extent to which she is able to take herself in hand and stand on her own.

She may owe some karmic debt to her male partner and the discharge of such an obligation will be facilitated or made more unpleasant according to the Sun's natal condition and the cross-aspects to it from her nativity. Valuable lessons may be learned as a result of such experiences, even if they appear to be unsatisfactory and unproductive at the time.

When the contact is a favorable one, he may supply financial aid and give sound advice on buying and selling, or he may be a source of much moral support to his partner. She should be wary of lending money to him or of becoming involved in complicated financial arrangements if his Sun is much afflicted at birth or there are a number of difficult cross-aspects to the Sun from her own chart. Such configurations may well be present if the couple are married and subsequently divorce, and the financial settlement becomes a matter of much unpleasantness.

This solar position can signify sexual attraction or repulsion, according to the circumstances of the relationship and the aspects received by the Sun.

When there is mutual respect, a lasting relationship can be built on the basis of the Sun's re-location in this house.

Sun in the Ninth House

When the man's Sun falls in the ninth house of his female partner's horoscope he may be a source of inspiration to her in her search for a vital and transcendent philosophy of life. Through the way in which he allows his life to be guided by his beliefs, he may cause her to become interested in the teachings to which he subscribes, whether they be religious or philosophical. This is essentially the signature of a "guru" relationship, with the Sun acting as mentor. He is apt to expect his partner to make a special effort to understand the ideas he is trying to put over, especially insofar as their real spirit is concerned. If the Sun receives difficult cross-aspects from his partner's nativity, misunderstandings may result unless the couple each make a special effort to ensure that the message has been properly received. There could be fundamental differences of opinion, since the Sun will not only be likely to uphold his own ideas firmly but will also tend to evoke a spirited response from his partner.

He will be happy to publicize his partner's achievements and assist in making them known to a wider audience. The contact between the two may first arise through travel. In some way, he may be able to suggest improvements in his partner's travel arrangements, and provide transport for her, or he may be the means of putting her in touch with foreign countries, helping her literally to expand her horizons as well as in the more metaphorical sense.

Sun in the Tenth House

When the man's Sun falls in the tenth house of his female partner's horoscope, and more particularly when it falls in conjunction with her Midheaven, he may be in a position to enhance her reputation. He may be responsible for supervising her work and so be in a position either to recommend her for advancement or to prevent her progress. There is some tendency for those whose Sun is placed in the tenth house of another person's horoscope to act as a parent towards them, feeling the need to accept some kind of responsibility for their behaviour.

Sometimes the man will feel that he needs his partner's support or her acknowledgment of his abilities in order to increase his self-esteem. He may, by his outstanding example, inspire her to emulate him and he will usually be happy to extend his patronage if the cross-aspects are favorable. In such cases, his helping hand may put her in touch with influential contacts who can assist her progress and make her path easier in a number of ways.

Should he make a point of being unco-operative, it would be worth her while to find out the reason as it might be due to some shortcoming on her part that acts as a barrier to future progress. He might not only be in a position to point out this weakness but give practical advice as to how it might be eradicated.

Sun in the Eleventh House

When the man's Sun falls in the eleventh house of his female partner's horoscope, he may be able to provide her with the kind of inspiration that leads her to formulate her ideals more clearly and, in some cases, he may assist her to realize these ideals. This sector of the horoscope relates to friendship and group enterprises and when the cross-aspects are favorable there is every chance of a rewarding friendship developing, with the one whose house is tenanted being drawn towards the one whose Sun is involved. The latter may occupy some leading position in a group to which the other belongs. When the man's Sun occupies this house of his partner's horoscope he may regard it as his privilege as a friend to offer a word of advice on the way she conducts her affairs. Because he takes it upon himself to to speak in a spirit of friendly criticism, his remarks may be all the more valuable on that account, especially as he will normally be prepared, as a friend, to accept her exactly as she is.

Sun in the Twelfth House

When the man's Sun falls in the twelfth house of his female partner's horoscope he may be able to encourage her to develop a wide variety of interests that will assist her to gain a greater understanding of life as a whole. He may introduce a new total perspective of life to her, though much will depend upon the condition of the Sun in his nativity and the cross-aspects to it from hers. If the majority of aspects are favorable, he may be able to imbue her with an uplifting belief in Providence, that everything happens for the best and that a yielding attitude in the spirit of "Thy Will be done" eventually brings greater happiness, and is the most effective way of avoiding "self-undoing." If the majority of the aspects are adverse, he may be a source of confusion in her life. He may encourage her to undertake a course of action which runs counter to her own physical or moral good and perhaps counter to the interests of the community.

At best he can become an unobtrusive supporter who can pull strings on her behalf and quietly organize backing for her from unexpected sources. Sometimes no sacrifice can be too great. At worst, he may have a special talent for consistently thwarting her plans, intriguing against her and subtly undermining her position, knowing just how to exploit her Achilles' heel to his own advantage.

He may have the capacity to divine some of her best kept secrets or she may instinctively feel him to be a person in whom she can confide. Those who may habitually receive such confidences, such as a clergyman or doctor, often have their Suns in the twelfth house of the horoscopes of those who choose them as their confidants. This may indicate that they are specially equipped to offer service to such people when they are at a low ebb, either physically or psychologically, and their support and help is likely to be sought when an emergency arises.

When the Sun is assailed by difficult cross-aspects, there is a possibility of misunderstandings arising due to undercurrents that are difficult to locate and negotiate, or there may even be some hidden enmity which gnaws at the roots of the relationship.

When the man's Sun is in this position it is sometimes possible for his partner to learn vicariously by analysing his mistakes, although it may be difficult for her to treat the relationship in a sufficiently objective way, because of his faculty of being able to make her subconsciously aware of her own psychological maladjustments.

THE MOON IN THE HOUSES

The Moon signifies the way in which the native's personality responds to other people, his instinctive reactions and the amount of feeling he is able to bring to a relationship.

Moon in the First House

When the man's Moon is on the Ascendant of his female partner's horoscope and to a slightly lesser degree when it is in her first house, a sensitive link between the two is likely to exist. A close conjunction between the Moon in one horoscope and the rising degree in another is often found between the horoscopes of marriage partners. This signifies the type of relationship where each feels that it is good to be in the other's company. What the man instinctively feels a need for appears in tangible form in the presence of his partner. The man will feel at home with his partner's familiar type of behaviour, instinctively recognizing those facets in her everyday approach to life that correspond to his own patterns of temperament. Unless the Moon is much afflicted, or is in adverse aspect to the ascending degree from some other sector of his partner's horoscope, he will feel at home with her and she will appreciate the sympathetic response she is able to evoke in him. She is often willing to make any necessary adjustments to render the relationship even more congenial.

Sometimes she will be able to implant the germ of an idea in her partner's mind. In the fullness of time this may develop into some really worthwhile project which he can put into operation for their mutual benefit. His lunar impulse to protect and cherish is likely to be projected in her direction. Unless she is able to accept and appreciate this interest as a gesture of friendly concern, he may tend to react by becoming moody and withdrawn. He may be able to stimulate her imagination, with fascinating results if the cross-aspects are favorable; otherwise if the cross-aspects indicate some kind of tension, there may be some morbid or unhealthy element in the responses that he elicits. For his part, he may tend to worrry unduly over her problems.

This contact usually makes for a pleasing relationship unless the Moon is much afflicted. The lunar sensitivity will enable the man to understand his partner's psychology, with the result that he will know how to capture her interest and evoke a sympathetic response from her. His partner's friendliness can originally spring from an instinctive recognition of his sympathetic regard for her, and so call out even more strongly his interest and concern, at the same time arousing his impulse to confide in her.

This contact can signify marked physical attraction when the relationship is between opposite sexes of the appropriate age.

The purpose of such a contact may be to arouse in the partner whose Moon is involved a sympathetic awareness of and consideration for the other's feelings, and to alert him to the need to adapt his approach according to the other person's particular psychological orientation.

Moon in the Second House

When the man's Moon falls in the second house of his female partner's horoscope, which is the house where the Moon is considered to be naturally exalted, he may recognize in her a naturally stabilizing influence, and take an interest in helping her to make the most of her resources. He may have an instinctive flair for giving her the right advice as to where she should invest her savings and how best she can multiply her assets and conserve her resources. He may also be anxious to contribute in other ways toward her well-being and make a practical demonstration of his interest by giving her presents, generally making her the recipient of his generosity. In some cases the motive behind such generosity may be that he gains pleasure through bringing her gifts.

His partner should always be careful to make him aware of her gratefulness for his generosity, because his feelings will usually be very much involved in any services he may be able to render. If the Moon is involved in adverse cross-aspects, he may worry unduly about his partner's financial problems and so become more of a hindrance than a help, cramping her style and even suggesting, perhaps unjustly, that she is not sufficiently appreciative of his help and generosity.

The purpose of this link may be to arouse in the partner whose second house is involved a true sense of gratitude for the kind thought on the part of the one who bestows gifts.

Moon in the Third House

When the man's Moon falls in the third house of his female partner's horoscope, he may be fascinated by the way in which her mind works and the way in which she tackles her mental problems. Her ideas may stimulate his mental reactions with favorable or unsettling results, according to the nature of the cross-aspects involving the Moon. When these cross-aspects suggest some lack of harmony, an emotional factor may intrude which prevents accurate comprehension of the ideas each may wish to communicate.

When the cross-aspects are helpful, a useful mental rapport can be established.

He may be instrumental in sowing in her mind the seeds of a new idea which flourishes in due course and he may help her to contact sources of useful information which augment and complement her own ideas. Should the Moon be afflicted at birth and the cross-aspects be unfavorable, there may be a tendency for him to set his partner off on a false trail of thought or he may even fail completely to have any sympathy for her ideas. In other cases, the man whose Moon is involved can, so to speak, hold a mirror up to his partner and point out some of the flaws in her thinking, helping her as a result to communicate more effectively with others. Such transactions may not always proceed smoothly, hence the more strenuous cross-aspects may be in evidence in such cases.

Sometimes the man may absorb his partner's ideas and later on repeat them to her as his own. On a more positive level, his memory may often assist her to add useful facts to her own store of information.

In some way, he may be the cause of his partner undertaking periodical short journeys. When the Moon is well aspected, this is a good position for a neighbour's or close relative's Moon to be located.

The purpose of this link may be to arouse in the person whose third house is involved an appreciation of the need to pay more attention to the way in which he communicates his ideas to others, selecting the method most calculated to capture their imagination and arouse their sympathetic interest. This can be a helpful factor in teacher-pupil relationships, when the teacher's Moon falls in the pupil's third house.

Moon in the Fourth House

When the man's Moon falls in the fourth house of his female partner's horoscope, and more particularly when it is in conjunction with the fourth cusp, of which the Moon is the natural ruler, she will find that she instinctively feels "at home" with him as a result of a kind of natural affinity and he will be able to make her feel that she is "one of the family." He will probably be able to anticipate what her instinctive reactions to a certain situation are likely to be.

He may be able to make helpful suggestions that facilitate her domestic chores, perhaps helping with house decoration or improving her cooking arrangements or generally suggesting beneficial changes in her domestic environment. He may tend to assume a somewhat motherly role, going out of his way to protect her, sometimes to such an extent that he appears to monopolize her. Much will depend upon the sign occupied by the Moon and the aspects it receives. This is a link frequently found between the horoscopes of marriage partners (and between one of the partners and his in-laws). The one whose Moon is involved does not always act as a particularly stabilizing influence and a marriage partner's afflicted Moon here can precipitate periodical changes of residence or unsettling domestic upheavals. The one whose fourth house is involved may experience difficulty in accumulating property as his partner may not wish to undertake commitments in this direction, which leave him with a feeling of being tied down.

The purpose of this contact may be to encourage, in the person whose fourth house is involved, a more sensitive attitude towards his environment and a willingness to change or modify his surroundings so that they coincide more closely with his personality.

Moon in the Fifth House

When the man's Moon falls in the fifth house of his female partner's horoscope, he will be attracted to her by the way in which she deploys her talents, by the way in which she projects herself and by her general attitude to the whole area of creative and pleasurable activities. There may well be some emotional involvement and a display of affection. The man is likely to prove an appreciative audience to his partner, encouraging her to display her talents and enjoying her sense of humour. He may be able to appeal to her sense of the dramatic and assist her in the process of self-dramatization.

Should there be a considerable age gap in the relationship, if the elder's fifth house is involved, he may feel a desire to adopt a parental attitude towards the younger, although if the positions are reversed, the elder may still be inclined to play this role.

This link is usually the signature of a happy association unless the Moon is much afflicted.

The purpose of such a link is to encourage, in the person whose fifth house is involved, an awareness of the fact that he needs to consider the effect of his creative efforts and attempts at self-projection, in relation to the reaction he is likely to evoke in others, and to develop in him an ability to create works that have a more popular appeal. This fifth house accentuation relates particularly to the cultivation of an ability to evoke a sympathetic response in an audience.

Moon in the Sixth House

When the man's Moon falls in the sixth house of his female partner's horoscope, he is likely to have an instinctive awareness of the areas in which she needs support. He will be pleased to supply practical help and will often be able to make suggestions that can improve her general efficiency and often her physical well-being.

He may be able to help her with a number of irksome chores, but if the Moon is afflicted at birth or there are difficult cross-aspects to the Moon, he may be inclined to fuss and worry unduly. He may therefore be more of a hindrance than a help and instead of oiling the wheels and helping things to go more smoothly he may prove to be a source of irritation. In such a situation his partner should be careful not allow his undue concern for her physical welfare to lower her morale.

He will be likely to see his partner as someone to whom he can offer service as a do-gooder, demonstrating to himself that he is capable of sympathetic attention to the needs of others. When the Moon is well-aspected at birth and the cross-aspects are favorable, this can be a very soothing link. When a doctor's Moon is in the sixth house of his patient's horoscope he may take an interest in that patient's welfare over and above the call of duty.

The purpose of this link can be to focus the thoughts of the person whose sixth house is involved on the need to adopt a sympathetic attitude towards those who offer him service, and to give his own services ungrudgingly, without thought of a specific reward or of insisting on the bare minimum agreed upon.

Moon in the Seventh House

When the man's Moon falls in the seventh house of his female partner's horoscope and more especially when it falls in conjunction with the western horizon, he may know instinctively how to complement and balance the most important facets of her personality. This link is sometimes a feature found in the comparison of the horoscopes of married couples. He may be the means of enlarging the circle of her friends, assisting in bringing her into contact with a variety of helpful people and generally making her reputation known more widely. The connection of the Moon with publicity makes the seventh house a good location for the Moon of a publicity agent, if his services should be required. Those who come into contact with a person as the result of the activities of their publicity agent may also have their Moon in his seventh house.

The man with his Moon in this sector of his partner's horoscope will be inclined to regard his partner as an equal and may expect to have his own status as an equal acknowledged, being particularly sensitive about his rights in this respect if the Moon is much afflicted, and having no liking for being patronized. With this link, the couple may share a number of interests and in some cases, if delicate negotiations of a personal nature are required at any time, the one whose Moon is involved may be able to operate as a sensitive go-between.

When the Moon is well-aspected at birth and the majority of cross-aspects are favorable, the association can be a particularly felicitous one and the partner whose seventh house is involved may instinctively recognize in the other a person with whom she would be happy to co-operate.

The purpose of the link is to make the person whose seventh house is involved more aware of the need to adapt and adjust to others, being careful to respect their feelings, and to realize that co-operation entails going at least half-way to meet the other person.

Moon in the Eighth House

When the man's Moon falls in the eighth house of his female partner's horoscope an all-or-nothing type of relationship could develop, with the man's feelings being strongly involved so that the condition of his Moon at birth and the cross-aspects to it from his partner's nativity are likely to be particularly crucial. The relationship is hardly ever likely to be lukewarm and her feelings for the man will either be ardent, with a need to exercise a good deal of emotional self-control, or almost non-existent. Any strong sympathy or antipathy she feels towards him could be due to the quality of a relationship in a previous life, but whatever the reason, it will usually operate as a subconscious impulse whose promptings cannot be denied. She may have the opportunity to benefit from his experiences, as she may be able to make him more aware of the really dramatic happenings in his life that have taught him valuable lessons. If the man allows his imagination to get the better of him he may be inclined to dwell upon the awful possibilities of a situation he has encountered, rather than confining himself to an account of what actually happened.

If the man's Moon is badly aspected, she may have little inclination to enter into any relationship with him. Should a relationship develop, she should exercise great care if she is involved in any financial dealings with him. Quarrels over money and legacies could easily develop and the man may instinctively and sometimes quite unjustly, mistrust her motives and misinterpret her actions where matters involving finance are concerned.

When the Moon is well-aspected, he may be able to help his partner to tap some hidden source of awareness within herself through which she is able to enhance her self-knowledge.

The purpose of the contact is to enable the person whose eighth house is involved to become more aware of the hidden depths of feeling in others and to gain an extra measure of self-control when her own feelings are stirred by them.

Moon in the Ninth House

When the man's Moon falls in the ninth house of his female partner's horoscope, he will want to understand why she believes and acts as she does. He may feel himself attracted to her because he believes he understands her philosophy of life, and he may be able to round out her philosophy as a result of his own personal experiences. The agreement between them, as far as general broad principles go, may only be on a superficial level, but such a mutual understanding has a good chance to grow, because he will be anxious to foster the relationship, which he will value for the way in which it contributes towards his understanding of life.

His travel reminiscences may arouse a spirit of wanderlust in his partner and in some way he may be able to widen her horizons and show her how to go about extending her experience of foreign countries. This link sometimes occurs between the horoscopes of traveling companions, who, by exchanging ideas, are able to add interest to a commonplace journey.

When a parent's Moon is in this position in the horoscope of his offspring, he may encourage the child at an early age to go off on his own, and generally stimulate his interest in travel in the belief that this is the best way for him to complete his education.

If the Moon is much afflicted there may be a complete lack of sympathy with each other's philosophy of life or their spiritual upbringing.

The purpose of this position is to make the person whose ninth house is involved more sensitive to the other person's attitude to life and to appreciate the sentiments and associations that lead him to adopt such a viewpoint.

Moon in the Tenth House

When the man's Moon falls in the tenth house of his female partner's horoscope, and more particularly when it falls in conjunction with the Midheaven of that horoscope, he will instinctively understand what she is aiming at in life, will share her aims and want her to succeed in them. Because of this manifest faith in her abilities, she may be inspired to pull out just the little bit extra that means all the difference between success and failure. He will know how to nurture her ambitions and be able to make suggestions that will help to draw out some of her latent talents. His suggestions may also open up career opportunities for her and he may even feel it incumbent upon himself to adopt a somewhat parental attitude towards his partner, gently pushing her towards a certain goal and being particularly concerned to shield her reputation from attack from any source.

If the Moon is much afflicted, her growing dislike of her male partner may cause him to disparage her reputation, or she may find him something of a responsibility, with the result that she has to put his affairs in order and sometimes answer for him.

There may be a domestic link between the partners and, when the Moon is well-aspected, this is a link frequently found between the horoscopes of husband and wife.

The purpose of this position is to make the person whose tenth house is involved more sensitive to the fact that one's reputation depends, to a large extent, on the goodwill and support of others, and that any blemish in his own reputation may reflect upon the reputations of those around him.

Moon in the Eleventh House

When the man's Moon falls in the eleventh house of his female partner's horoscope he may find himself instinctively drawn towards her. He will be able to appreciate the ideals that she cherishes and will be likely to display a friendly concern for her general welfare. They may first meet through being connected with a group formed for the purpose of pursuing some common ideal.

This is often the index of a real bond of friendship. The purpose of the link is to make the person whose eleventh house is involved more aware of the importance of joining forces with those who share his ideals, and of being ready to accept friendship when it is offered.

Moon in the Twelfth House

When the man's Moon falls in the twelfth house of his female partner's horoscope he may instinctively be able to recognize her problems and may be able to sense her weak points. He will be likely to adopt a particularly charitable attitude towards her and he will be anxious to protect her if he feels she is in a situation where one of her vulnerable points is likely to be exposed to attack. Sometimes his concern can be embarrassing and he may be inclined to worry unduly about her problems or the state of her health. If the Moon is afflicted he may not make allowance for her weaknesses, or he may moodily take offence where none is intended and even tell tales about her behind her back.

If the majority of aspects to the Moon are favorable, he is likely to be well disposed towards her. He may well invite her to confide her troubles to him, but she should make sure exactly where she stands with him, as he may be inclined to concern himself too much with her welfare and go out of his way to initiate action on her behalf when it would have been better to leave well alone.

The purpose of this link is to make the person whose twelfth house is involved more aware as to who can be trusted with his welfare.

MERCURY IN THE HOUSES

One person's Mercury falling in the horoscope of another person acts to stimulate his power to communicate, brings out his ideas or puts him in touch with new thoughts or new sources of information. It places him in a position where he is expected to make a mental response, adjusting his ideas if necessary, and sometimes poses problems that test the degree of understanding he is able to bring to them. Very much will depend upon the sign Mercury is in at birth and upon the aspects it receives, because Mercury is apt to be strongly influenced by these factors.

Mercury in the First House

When a man's Mercury falls in the first house of his female partner's horoscope, or more particularly when it is in conjunction with her Ascendant, the way in which he thinks may appeal to her, and he will be able to derive a mental stimulus by exchanging ideas with her. If Mercury is much afflicted or in adverse aspect to the ascending degree from some other sector of the horoscope, there may be a fundamental lack of understanding between the two at the mental level, even although communication may frequently take place.

He may be the cause of her having to travel more than usual, or he may tend to make her more than usually restless. This can be a very helpful link when the couple have a common interest in intellectual pursuits, otherwise the man may tend to waste too much of his partner's time discussing matters of no real importance.

Mercury in the Second House

When the man's Mercury falls in the second house of his female partner's horoscope he may have a special talent for detecting any shortcomings in the way in which she handles her financial arrangements and he may be able to produce some helpful suggestions as to how she can augment her finances, at the same time showing her how to make a more realistic assessment of her own earning powers. If Mercury is much afflicted at birth or there are a number of adverse cross-aspects to Mercury, any advice he gives her may prove to be ill-founded and any financial transactions with him would probably work out to her detriment.

Mercury in the Third House

When the man's Mercury falls in the third house of his female partner's horoscope, he should be able to communicate freely with his partner and provide her with a source of mental stimulus that can lead her to a better grasp of ideas, unless the cross-aspects from her horoscope to his Mercury are unfavorable. In such cases, his ideas may clash with hers, resulting in arguments and misunderstandings.

This position favors an easy relationship on a "neighbourly" basis. The person whose Mercury is involved may be the means of bringing news or information to the other, or he may act as a go-between, linking him with associates. Any link arising from this redomification of Mercury in another's horoscope may occur through educational activities of various kinds.

Mercury in the Fourth House

When the man's Mercury falls in the fourth house of his female partner's horoscope and more particularly when it is in conjunction with the fourth cusp, he may provide her with an incentive to travel or to become more mobile. In some way he may be able to bring an influence to bear on her domestic scene, implanting ideas in her mind which she will instinctively recognize as relating to her own situation. Although there is sometimes an element of casualness about Mercury's attitude, the fact that Mercury is never very far away from the Sun and Venus may result in these bodies also being in the fourth house of the partner so that the more transitory of Mercury's effects may be less in evidence.

Mercury in the Fifth House

When the man's Mercury is in the fifth house of his female partner's horoscope he may be able to provide her with ideas that act as a spur to her creative imagination. They may have first met through both being interested in the same hobby or through activities connected with children or education. If Mercury is much afflicted at birth or there are a number of difficult cross-aspects to Mercury, he may adopt a too critical attitude towards the creative efforts of his partner or his ideas may hinder rather than help the effective realization of her creative projects.

Mercury in the Sixth House

When the man's Mercury is in the sixth house of his female partner's horoscope he may be able to provide her with valuable know-how about the best way to get jobs done. He may be able to make suggestions about her diet and how she can best maintain her physical fitness so that in periods when she is feeling the effects of stress he may be able to help with effective advice. If the cross-aspects to Mercury are unfavorable, his advice may prove unsettling. Any technical improvements he suggests may only result in new snags arising.

When an employee's Mercury falls in the sixth house of his employer's horoscope, this does not promise a long term relationship unless his Sun also falls in the sixth house.

Mercury in the Seventh House

When the man's Mercury falls in the seventh house of his female partner's horoscope, and more particularly, when it falls in conjunction with her Descendant, he may be able to provide her with ideas that complement and round out her own. In discussions he may be able to put forward a view opposite to hers, giving her the opportunity to compare the two viewpoints and assess their relative merits. He may be instrumental in widening her circle of contacts, so that not only he, but others, can act as a sounding board for her ideas. He will like to consider his partner's ideas in the light of his own different viewpoint. His willingness to co-operate with her on the mental level ensures that discussion and debate with him can bring profitable results, always provided that his Mercury does not receive too many discordant cross-aspects from her nativity. In such cases, emotional or other factors may intervene to arouse prejudices or other distorting factors that may prevent discussions being conducted with a proper degree of objectivity.

The seventh house is a good position for the native to have the Mercury of his lawyer's horoscope re-domiciled, and also for the Mercury of anyone acting as his agent, always provided the majority of aspects are favorable.

Mercury in the Eighth House

When the man's Mercury falls in the eighth house of his female partner's horoscope he may be in a better position to understand her unconscious motivations than most, consequently he may be able to give her valuable hints as to how she might effect some measure of self-transformation. If he appreciates her sense of inner values this can be a most rewarding contact, but it is not always the most comfortable situation for a person to have this subliminal area penetrated by another. This can be rather a crucial position for Mercury and if it is much afflicted at birth and the cross-aspects are unfavorable, he may either wittingly or unwittingly use his knowledge of her inner motivations for his own advantage.

When the balance of aspects to Mercury is adverse it would be unwise for her to enter into any financial transactions with him.

Mercury in the Ninth House

When the man's Mercury falls in the ninth house of his female partner's horoscope, they may have first met while traveling and he may be able to bring to her notice areas that she had hitherto left unexplored. They may both make the same journey at frequent intervals and so get into conversation, thus discovering a mutual interest in the more superficial details of everyday life. Sometimes a deeper level communication will be possible, especially if there are favorable cross-aspects to Mercury, in which case a meeting of minds can take place, resulting in a beneficial exchange of ideas and discussions on the more philosophical aspects of life. If Mercury is much afflicted at birth and there are unfavorable cross-aspects, there may be little agreement between the couple and their discussions may lead to unprofitable arguments or fruitless speculation.

This link sometimes occurs between the horoscopes of distant friends who frequently keep in touch with each other by letter.

Mercury in the Tenth House

When the man's Mercury falls in the tenth house of his female partner's horoscope, and more particularly when it falls in conjunction with her Midheaven, he will be able to appreciate why her ambitions lead her in a certain direction, and to understand what she is trying to achieve. He may be able to make suggestions which help her to further her career, perhaps drawing attention to details she may have overlooked. He will be happy to communicate her achievements to others and perhaps put her in touch with those who can give her assistance. If Mercury is much afflicted at birth and there are adverse cross-aspects, he may be critical of her aims and even spread idle gossip that reflects upon her reputation.

Mercury in the Eleventh House

When the man's Mercury falls in the eleventh house of his female partner's horoscope, she may first be attracted to him because of his conversational abilities and the quality of his intellect. He may be able to understand the ideals she holds dear and be able to put her in touch with those who hold similar ideals. He may also be able to help her make a more realistic assessment of the best way to achieve her hopes and wishes.

If Mercury is much afflicted at birth and receives a number of unfavorable cross-aspects from the partner's horoscope, there may be some basic lack of sympathy between the couple or his suggestions may prove more of a hindrance than a help to her. In some cases he may misrepresent her ideas to others in her circle, placing her relationships in some difficulty as a result.

Mercury in the Twelfth House

When the man's Mercury falls in the twelfth house of his female partner's horoscope he may take a special interest in the way in which she adjusts to life as a whole. He may be particularly aware of her vulnerable points and be in a position to point out any inconsistencies in her behaviour. Any criticism he offers may be helpful in assisting her to avoid pitfalls and if Mercury is well aspected at birth and the cross-aspects are favorable, he may be able to give her much good advice. If the aspects to Mercury are less favorable, he may still give good advice but she may be inclined to resent it or find it particularly difficult to put into practice.

In some cases, when Mercury is involved with a number of adverse aspects, he can be something of an annoyance to his partner, spreading scandal about her behind her back and making direct conversation in such a way as to needle her and play on her weaknesses. Whether or not he is well disposed towards her, his ability to spot her weaknesses may be instrumental in bringing home to her the areas most in need of extra attention and transformation.

VENUS IN THE HOUSES

Venus represents the native's capacity to find areas of harmony between himself and others, where the promotion of a mutually happy relationship can be encouraged and given opportunities to flourish. It assists him to establish pleasant relationships by showing appreciation and projecting charm, while it indicates the qualities in others that will most appeal to his sense of values. When Venus is debilitated or much afflicted, he may be tempted to use any personal charm and physical attractions he possesses to manipulate and offer seductive inducements to others for his own personal advantage, according to the circumstances of the relationship. Venus plays a most important part in all romantic relationships, not only on the physical level but in establishing feelings of harmony at all levels.

Venus in the First House

When the man's Venus falls in the first house of his female partner's horoscope, and more particularly when it falls in conjunction with her Ascendant, this is an excellent omen for their personal relationship and a "classic" contact between the horoscopes of marriage partners. She will be particularly aware of his charm, while her personality may strike an harmonious chord in his psyche. She should feel very much at home with him and enjoy his company as he is likely to encourage her to be her own natural self.

If Venus is much afflicted at birth and the cross-aspects are unfavorable, much of the promise of this position may be diminished and because of his over-possessiveness she may excite his jealousy or envy. Even so, an affectionate link may still exist, though it may be punctuated from time to time by quarrels and emotional upsets.

Venus in the Second House

When the man's Venus falls in the second house of his female partner's horoscope, he may have a particularly beneficial effect upon her, not only in relation to material things but also emotionally and spiritually, for the second house is related to assets at every level of being and to all attributes that help give a feeling of stability. His sense of values will make him particularly aware of her good qualities, giving her a feeling of well-being. He is often likely to go out of his way to assist her.

This link usually signifies a very good understanding between those of opposite sexes, unless Venus is much afflicted at birth and the cross-aspects are mainly inharmonious. In all types of relationship the partner whose afflicted Venus is involved may be a source of distraction to the other, leading him to neglect profitable opportunities and causing him to become careless over financial matters.

Venus in the Third House

When the man's Venus falls in the third house of his female partner's horoscope this will promote a good degree of mental rapport and mutual understanding between them. Entertaining conversational exchanges will usually result, as the man will be likely to encourage his partner to communicate her thoughts and his sympathetic reception of what she has to say will stimulate her to express her ideas in the most pleasing form of which she is capable. He will be able to put forward his own point of view to her most persuasively. The rapport between the two may be diminished if Venus is adversely affected at birth and the cross-aspects from the partner's horoscope are inharmonious.

When Venus is fortified in the nativity and the cross-aspects are beneficial, this is a good link in a teacher-pupil relationship when it is the teacher's Venus that is involved.

Venus in the Fourth House

When the man's Venus falls in the fourth house of his female partner's horoscope, and more particularly when it is in conjunction with the Lower Meridian, she may take an instinctive liking to him and feel very much at home with him. He may assist her to beautify her home or put her in touch with opportunities for improving her environment in other ways or help her to acquire property.

He may be tempted to adopt a parental attitude towards her, with very satisfactory results, unless the cross-aspects to Venus are particularly adverse.

She may, out of admiration, tend to emulate his habits and instinctive reactions, though if Venus is debilitated or much afflicted at birth and the cross-aspects are not helpful, she may be tempted to take the line of least resistance in her dealings with him.

Venus in the Fifth House

When the man's Venus falls in the fifth house of his female partner's horoscope, he may be a source of great pleasure to her and she may always enjoy being in his company. He will tend to be very appreciative of all her creative efforts and will encourage her to present them in the most attractive and dramatic form. This is often an indicator of a romantic association when it occurs between the horoscopes of opposite sexes of a suitable age, though a great deal may depend upon the natal condition of Venus and the cross-aspects to it as to whether such a partnership endures.

This contact is sometimes found in the horoscope of a parent, when a friend's Venus falls in his fifth house and the friend has a special talent for helping him manage his children and making himself popular with them.

Venus in the Sixth House

When the man's Venus falls in the sixth house of his female partner's horoscope he is likely to take much pleasure in rendering her various services and showing her how to perform her chores more easily. There may be an element of reciprocity in this relationship, with the man needing her care and support at some time.

In an employer-employee relationship, the employer's Venus in his employee's sixth house (unless Venus is much afflicted) will usually indicate that he will be concerned to see that working conditions are congenial. Should the position be reversed, the employee's Venus in his employer's sixth house may make his employer too indulgent towards him for his own good.

This is a good house position for a doctor-patient or nurse-patient relationship, when it is the patient's sixth house that is involved.

Venus in the Seventh House

When the man's Venus falls in the seventh house of his female partner's horoscope, and more particularly when it is in conjunction with her Descendant, a high degree of mutual co-operation is possible as Venus is the natural ruler of the seventh house. Such a link is often found between the horoscopes of husband and wife, but if this should duplicate each partner's natal position, each may be inclined to leave the task of establishing harmony to the other and the partnership may suffer as a result.

The male partner may be at particular pains to evaluate his mate's capacity for establishing a happy relationship before he finally commits himself, but once he is satisfied that she can do so, this link promises a particularly harmonious partnership, provided Venus is not much afflicted at birth and the cross-aspects are mainly favorable.

Venus in the Eighth House

When the man's Venus is in the eighth house of his female partner's horoscope this can be a somewhat crucial position and a great deal may depend upon the cross-aspects to Venus. Her feelings towards him will probably be deeply rooted and she may not always be sure of the true reasons for her emotional reactions, whether they be sympathetic or antipathetic.

In a male-female relationship this link can indicate considerable sexual attraction and the partner whose Venus is in the eighth house of the other may seem to be possessed of some mysterious allure. In coming to terms with this source of fascination, the other may gain a great deal of self-enlightenment. When this interchange is present between a couple who are romantically interested in each other, it is wise to check whether there are other indications of affinity of a more durable nature, otherwise much of the interest may be based on physical attraction, which is no great guarantee of a permanent association.

Venus in the Ninth House

When the man's Venus falls in the ninth house of his female partner's horoscope he may, through his example, be able to influence her whole approach to life. His obvious goodwill can produce reactions in her that will increase her interest in gaining a greater understanding of the ideas that motivate his way of life.

He may implant in her mind a greater desire to travel and he may be able to provide transport for her or show her how she can travel more easily or comfortably.

This link encourages a sympathetic rapport and facilitates an atmosphere of goodwill (unless Venus is much afflicted) with the result that she is fascinated by the philosophy of her partner and very amenable to persuasion in this direction. It is a very useful link between the horoscopes of teacher and pupil, when it is the pupil's ninth house that is involved.

Venus in the Tenth House

When the man's Venus falls in the tenth house of his female partner's horoscope, and more particularly when it falls in conjunction with her Midheaven, he may be able to offer her considerable help with her career and provide her with valuable encouragement as she seeks to realize her aims, because he can appreciate the value of what she is attempting to achieve. She will always be able to retain his high opinion of her worth, unless Venus is much afflicted at birth or there are difficult cross-aspects. Even so, this may only signify a temptation on her part to take undue advantage of his generous support. She will find that any demonstration of loyalty towards him on her part will usually be amply repaid.

If the position is reversed, the woman's Venus in the tenth house of her male partner can make her an object of adoration, with a desire on the man's part to place her on a pedestal.

Venus in the Eleventh House

When the man's Venus falls in the eleventh house of his female partner's horoscope this can make for a very happy association and is a link frequently found between the horoscopes of marriage partners. He will be particularly appreciative of her ideals and he may be able to assist her to realize some of her dreams. This link can indicate the possibility of building a friendship based on the highest motives.

If Venus is much afflicted at birth and the cross-aspects are inharmonious, he may be tempted to pursue the friendship for ulterior motives, or she may take undue advantage of his friendly disposition towards her.

Venus in the Twelfth House

When the man's Venus falls in the twelfth house of his female partner's horoscope, in which Venus is naturally at home, he may have a special talent for helping her to adjust to difficult situations and be able to suggest solutions to her when she is faced with complicated problems. He may have a special interest in easing her path as much as possible and may not always say exactly what is in his mind for fear of upsetting her. He can be a sympathetic companion to her and comfort her when she is distressed and may be able to put her in touch with those who can minister to her bodily well-being and spiritual needs. He may be instrumental in introducing her to a study of occult or mystical subjects.

If Venus is much afflicted at birth and the cross-aspects are discordant his influence may have a seductive efffect upon her, causing her consciously or unconsciously to lose sight of her objectives and perhaps exploiting her susceptibilities and playing on her sympathies for his own ends.

In a relationship between a patient and his doctor or nurse, this is a beneficial link when it is the patient's twelfth house that is involved.

MARS IN THE HOUSES

Wherever the native's Mars falls in another person's horoscope it will act to spur that person on and call forth an energetic response from him, requiring him to mobilize his resources for action and generally making life busy for him in that area of life ruled by the house in which Mars is re-domiciled. When the cross-aspects to Mars are favorable he can be a powerful supporter of the other, but if there are a majority of discordant aspects he may be a rival. In some cases he may be a source of destructive opposition, whose antagonism is undisguised.

Mars in the First House

When the man's Mars falls in the first house of his female partner's horoscope and more particularly, when it falls in conjunction with her Ascendant, he will be able to keep her on her toes, challenging her to put forth her best efforts and to summon up her courage in an emergency. He can prove to be a courageous advocate for her cause but he will expect her to display some degree of independence and self-sufficiency. When the cross-aspects are harmonious, this element of challenge will help her to follow his lead and match his performance. His ideas may stimulate her to respond with her own complementary thoughts, thus paving the way to an effective collaboration. This can be very effective in a business partnership, unless Mars is much afflicted at birth and the cross-aspects are discordant, when there may be some likelihood of quarrels through his rashness or over-assertiveness, or through some other aspect of his behaviour that becomes a source of aggravation. His activities may make too many demands on her or his attempts to call forth a more energetic response from her may become annoying through his continual sense of urgency, that leads him to be forever pressing for quick results.

Between opposite sexes of the appropriate age group this link can denote much physical attraction (also when Mars is in close aspect to the rising degree from other sectors of the horoscope) and is frequently observed between the horoscopes of marriage partners.

Mars in the Second House

When the man's Mars falls in the second house of his female partner's horoscope he will be able to encourage her to show more initiative in the handling of her resources, though there is a danger that he may encourage her to overspend or become too adventurous in her financial dealings. He may disagree with her over the way in which she handles her financial problems and will expect her to demonstrate her financial independence, at the same time respecting his own.

If Mars is much afflicted at birth and the cross-aspects are inharmonious, he may envy her financial standing.

Between opposite sexes of the appropriate age group, Mars in this sector can exert a strong sexual stimulus and much may depend upon the cross-aspects as to whether this brings beneficial results.

Mars in the Third House

When the man's Mars falls in the third house of his female partner's horoscope he will be able to provide her with a strong mental stimulus. He will want to know and appreciate the reasons behind her actions and may consult her about problems that require a good deal of clear thinking to unravel. He will be likely to discuss his problems frankly and openly with her, not hesitating to argue and debate her point of view and sometimes challenging her opinions in order to draw her out. He will expect her to have made up her own mind about the issues under discussion and not to have been swayed by the arguments of others or by mere hearsay.

If the cross-aspects to Mars are discordant he may be envious of her mental accomplishments. Discussions between them may need to be kept as objective as possible as any strong disagreement could lead to acrimony.

In some cases, he may be the cause of his partner's having to make frequent travels. This link occurring between the horoscopes of neighbours may denote difficulties between them if the cross-aspects are not particularly harmonious.

Mars in the Fourth House

When the man's Mars falls in the fourth house of his female partner's horoscope and more particularly, when it falls in conjunction with the Lower Meridian, she will probably have an instinctive like or dislike for him according to the cross-aspects to Mars. He will be inclined to appreciate her for what she is. His behaviour may challenge her to take stock of her instinctive reactions to him and to examine some of her habitual attitudes. When the cross-aspects are favorable she will experience a greater sense of security when he is around, but if his Mars is afflicted at birth and the cross-aspects to it are mainly discordant, she will be inclined to regard him as a liability and a source of disruption inimical to the establishment of a calm domestic atmosphere around her.

If this link does exist between two people who have to share the same domestic environment, the one whose Mars is involved will bring a lively influence to bear upon the home environment and things will never be dull while he is around. If the cross-aspects are reasonably harmonious, even if his presence can at times be somewhat exhausting, his absence may bring a lull that is less desirable than his presence. This kind of link can occur in a parent-child relationship, when the parent's Mars in this sector of his child's horoscope may indicate that the parent adopts a rather demanding attitude towards his offspring and expects him to show signs of independence and self-reliance at an early age.

Sometimes the person whose Mars falls here will be a source of extra domestic work to the other, making demands upon him which keep him busy and use up his energy.

Mars in the Fifth House

When the man's Mars falls in the fifth house of his female partner's horoscope he can provide her with an incentive that will stimulate her to be more creative and encourage her to demonstrate her ability to take charge of a situation. Such a link is excellent for companionship unless Mars is much afflicted, when the couple may quarrel over who is to take the initiative or exercise authority. He will be instrumental in providing a challenge to her sense of loyalty and he will greatly appreciate demonstrations on her part that this quality is a basic part of her character.

Between opposite sexes of a suitable age, this can signify an attachment involving the passions but of itself this link is not a guarantee of true affinity.

Mars in the Sixth House

When the man's Mars falls in the sixth house of his female partner's horoscope, he may challenge her to demonstrate her efficiency and technical know-how, at the same time being ready to apply his own skills and knowledge if they are needed. He can give her useful assistance when jobs need doing, though if Mars is afflicted at birth or the cross-aspects are unfavorable, he may not always approve of her way of doing things and he may become impatient if she appears to be taking too much time over the job. Such an attitude on his part can be a source of mutual irritation. If he tends to become overcritical, this may play on her nerves.

She will find that her partner has no trouble in keeping her busy and he may be inclined to dwell on the virtues of work for its own sake and of making efforts for the welfare of others. In an employer-employee relationship, this is a good position for the employee's Mars, though it can signify some lack of initiative on his part.

Mars in the Seventh House

When the man's Mars falls in the seventh house of his female partner's horoscope and more particularly when it falls in conjunction with her Descendant, he will be likely to act in such a way as to test her powers of co-operation and her ability to cope with the give and take of partnership. She will be able to sense that her partner is able to confidently express those qualities that she is inclined to believe she lacks and so she may feel that by collaborating with him she can strengthen her own position. For his part, he may recognize that some of her qualities are complimentary to his own. This mutual recognition can form the basis of a most effective partnership if the cross-aspects to Mars are favorable.

There may be times when the relationship is subject to some friction, when the irritating facets of his personality are more in evidence. He may expect her to involve herself in his own disputes and quarrels. Disagreements may spring up for no apparent reason but the chances of such interruptions to the harmony of the relationship may be diminished if she is always careful to respect his independence and to pay due regard to what he considers to be his rights.

When opposite sexes of a suitable age are concerned, some degree of physical attraction is likely. In some cases, even when Mars is afflicted, marriage can result and if both partners enjoy a good row, no great damage may result, but if there are severe afflictions involving Mars, the partner whose seventh house is involved may suffer mentally and perhaps physically through the cruelty of the other.

Mars in the Eighth House

When the man's Mars falls in the eighth house of his female partner's horoscope, he may make her uncomfortably aware of some of her subconscious motivations that normally operate without her knowledge. In order to satisfy himself about the underlying reasons for her actions, he may try to delve a little more deeply into her subconscious motivations than most people and she may find this type of probing scrutiny a rather uncomfortable process and one she does not wish to encourage. The relationship between them may not really flourish until he feels more sure of the real reasons underlying her actions and in the process of eliciting these she may find that he has been instrumental in causing her to relinquish some of her preconceived ideas. While he is attempting to fathom his partner's psychological depths he may occasionally utter some penetrating comment on her behavior or attitude which strikes a chord in her subconscious mind, ultimately leading her to make deep level changes so that some kind of transformation results.

If Mars is afflicted at birth, his method of getting to know her better may be apt to cause her some displeasure, while if there are strong cross-aspects to Mars from her nativity, their relationship may make no headway at all.

When this link occurs between the nativities of opposite sexes of the appropriate age, it can denote the presence of a strong sex attraction, though not necessarily of a true love relationship.

Mars in the Ninth House

When the man's Mars falls in the ninth house of his female partner's horoscope, he will be able to supply a stimulus to her thinking and challenge her way of looking at life, so that she becomes aware of the necessity to clarify her ideas and give greater force to her arguments.

He will want to know what she thinks about issues that he is interested in and he may use her as a "sounding board" for the purpose of clarifying his own ideas so that even when he asks her advice it may only be to measure it against what he had already decided to do. He may expect her to have clearly defined views on a variety of subjects and attempt to use her as an encyclopaedia. This link encourages a frank interchange of views, but if Mars is much afflicted at birth and the cross-aspects are discordant, the partners' philosophies of life may be so much at variance that true communication becomes impossible.

In some cases, the one whose Mars is involved may be the means of speeding up the other's travel arrangements or place him under the necessity of traveling more than usual.

Mars in the Tenth House

When the man's Mars falls in the tenth house of his female partner's horoscope and more particularly, when it falls in conjunction with her Midheaven (this is where Mars is naturally exalted), he will challenge her to show that she is worthy of her reputation and by so doing help her to produce her best level of performance. He can provide her with a constant stimulus to achievement and may expect her to make strenuous efforts to realize her aims. He will give her his energetic support if he feels she will make a reciprocal effort to achieve success. In some way he may play a fatherly role towards her and he may congratulate himself for his perspicacity in singling her out for encouragement if she subsequently enhances her reputation. This interest in her career may extend to making suggestions as to the most suitable employment for her to follow.

If Mars is afflicted at birth or the cross-aspects are difficult, this may signify a measure of rivalry and even antagonism between the two, but such enmity may spur her on to make greater efforts. He may seek to gain prestige at her expense and, in extreme cases, he may deliberately try to damage her reputation.

An employer whose Mars falls in the tenth house of his employee's horoscope will be apt to be rather demanding towards that employee, but unless the cross-aspects are discordant he will usually be prepared to reward achievement appropriately.

Mars in the Eleventh House

When the man's Mars falls in the eleventh house of his female partner's horoscope he may go out of his way to seek her friendship and may be instrumental in encouraging her to take practical steps towards making her dreams come true. Her aspirations may fire his enthusiasm, which in turn gives her more hope of achieving them.

If Mars is much afflicted at birth she may devote time and energy to the sorting out of his problems as a gesture of friendship, or she may be very concerned about him because of his ill health or difficult circumstances. If the cross-aspects are discordant, little good may come from such a contact and he may be responsible for frustrating one of her most cherished aspirations.

Mars in the Twelfth House

When the man's Mars falls in the twelfth house of his female partner's horoscope a very critical relationship may exist between the two and unless the cross-aspects to Mars are preponderantly favorable, he may not only discover her Achilles' heel but use the knowledge for his own benefit. He may know just how to play on her psychological weaknesses in order to upset her.

Experiences resulting from this type of contact may lead her to make a more effective appraisal of herself and challenge her to be completely honest about herself, while cultivating a straightforward approach to others. Any attempt to cover up her weaknesses may make her seem insincere to her partner. If his Mars is well aspected at birth and the cross-aspects are harmonious, he may be able to help her to work on her weak points and fortify them, shielding her from attack in her more vulnerable areas until she is able to fend more effectively for herself, acting as her champion until he has encouraged her to develop enough self-sufficiency to stand on her own feet.

JUPITER IN THE HOUSES

Jupiter in the native's horoscope shows his capacity for helping and sustaining others in all those matters signified by the house in which it falls in their horoscope. It denotes his ability to expand their resources, bringing them fresh hope and a more buoyant approach to their problems as a result of his own benevolent attitude. It indicates his willingness to give helpful and constructive advice based on a philosophy molded by his own experience. If the contact is discordant, he may be instrumental in making the other person over-optimistic or extravagant. He may make promises that he is not in a position to keep (if Jupiter is much afflicted at birth) or he may act in bad faith and over-dependence on such support may encourage the other to grow careless or to embark upon foolish adventures as a result of the misleading advice he had been given.

Jupiter in the First House

When the man's Jupiter falls in the first house of his female partner's horoscope and more particularly, when it falls in conjunction with her Ascendant, her personality will encourage him to take a benevolent interest in her, resulting in the formation of a rewarding friendship. She will be likely to receive favors from him and his company will always put her in a good humor so that she feels completely relaxed with him. Very often they will find that they share common aspirations and a respect for each other's qualities. She may be doing him a favor by providing an outlet for his altruistic instincts.

He will usually be willing to make allowances for her if she occasionally falls short of the standards that he has come to expect of her, but she may need to be on guard against taking undue advantage of his tolerance and goodwill. He will always be happy to give her advice and assistance if he is in a position to do so. If Jupiter is much afflicted at birth and the cross-aspects are discordant, she may be tempted to presume too much on his generosity or she may grow careless, relying on him to rectify any mistakes she may make. He may encourage her to be more extravagant than her resources permit or to be over-indulgent in other ways, or his advice may either mislead her or be misinterpreted by her.

Jupiter in the Second House

When the man's Jupiter falls in the second house of his female partner's horoscope, he may be in a position to offer her material help or to give her advice which enables her to increase her material resources. He may be instrumental in helping her to cultivate a more realistic sense of values and if she should be in need of financial aid he would be happy to oblige her. Similarly, she could lend him money without risk, unless his Jupiter was much afflicted at birth and the cross-aspects were discordant. In such situations his afflicted Jupiter could denote that he would be likely to encourage her to spend unwisely and his advice might be ill-founded.

In the horoscope of a client this is a good position for his broker's or banker's Jupiter, provided it is reasonably free from affliction.

Jupiter in the Third House

When the man's Jupiter falls in the third house of his female partner's horoscope she may find that he is very easy to talk to and as a result he may monopolize quite a good deal of her time in conversation. If Jupiter is well-aspected at birth and the cross-aspects are favorable he may have a genuine desire to help her expand her everyday knowledge and may be able to pass on quite a good deal of useful information to her.

He will be happy to draw on his own experience though there is a danger that if Jupiter is much afflicted at birth, he may be inclined to boast, exaggerate or even to bluff when he is not sure of his facts and if the cross-aspects are discordant, this could be a source of trouble if she is not able to recognize when he is allowing his sense of proportion to become distorted. Even when Jupiter is well-aspected, she may need to be on the alert to see that he is not telling her what he thinks she would like to hear rather than what she ought to hear.

Unless Jupiter is much afflicted this is a good link between the horoscopes of teacher and pupil, when it is the pupil's third house that is involved.

Jupiter in the Fourth House

When the man's Jupiter falls in the fourth house of his female partner's horoscope and more particularly, when it falls in conjunction with the Lower Meridian, he will often possess a very happy knack of making her feel at home, wherever she may be, and know instinctively how to put her at her ease. It will come naturally to him to adopt a parental attitude towards her and sometimes he may have the power to arouse in her strong memories that relate to her past, with the result that she is able to discover latent talents within herself. Unless there are strong afflictions to Jupiter, he may have the ability to nurture these talents and generally assist in the unfolding of her individuality.

He may be a source of help to her in her home environment, assisting her to make improvements and perhaps generally increasing the value of the property.

When the parent's Jupiter falls in the fourth house of his child's nativity, this can indicate a particularly felicitous relationship. It is also a good link between the horoscopes of a builder and decorator and his client, when it is the client's fourth house that is involved, and between the horoscopes of associates in enterprises connected with farming and mining, always provided the majority of aspects to Jupiter are favorable.

Jupiter in the Fifth House

When the man's Jupiter falls in the fifth house of his female partner's horoscope this can be a very felicitous omen for the partnership. He will wish to make it easier for her to use her creative faculties in the best possible way, and to help her to discover the most effective means of self-expression. He will enjoy giving her pleasure, perhaps providing her with opportunities in this direction she might otherwise have been denied.

At the same time he will value her support and her good opinion of him. She may gain real pleasure through his companionship, especially at social functions and places of entertainment. The relationship may grow through a mutual interest in the theater or the arts, or through the sharing of some congenial hobby.

If she has children he will be benevolently disposed towards them and may like them to regard him as an uncle.

Between opposite sexes of an appropriate age, this link may signify a romantic friendship with much mutual affection.

The relationship may be somewhat less than cordial if Jupiter is badly aspected at birth and the cross-aspects to it are mainly discordant.

Jupiter in the Sixth House

When the man's Jupiter falls in the sixth house of his female partner's horoscope he may be in a position to render her valuable service and may take pleasure in such activities. He may be able to pass on to her some special "know-how" which complements and augments her own and he may be instrumental in introducing her to new techniques that help her to perform her routine chores with greater ease. He will be likely to take a general interest in her welfare and well-being.

This is a useful link in a relationship between a patient and those who have responsibility for his medical care, when it is the patient's sixth house that is involved. An employee's Jupiter falling in the sixth house of his employer's horoscope indicates that he will give his employer loyal and unqualified support, unless Jupiter is much afflicted at birth and the cross-aspects are discordant. When one person's Jupiter falls in this sector of another's horoscope, it usually signifies that he is willing to allow the other to assume a senior status, who may then acknowledge some obligation to see that his interests are looked after.

Jupiter in the Seventh House

When the man's Jupiter falls in the seventh house of his female partner's horoscope and more particularly, when it falls in conjunction with her Descendant, this is very favorable for a most co-operative partnership unless Jupiter is much afflicted. He may take a particular pleasure in working together with her and may be instrumental in putting her in touch with a number of influential contacts, generally widening her social circle. This link often occurs between the horoscopes of husband and wife.

If Jupiter is much afflicted and the cross-aspects are discordant, his exaggerated opinion of his partner could work out to her disadvantage, or throw her off balance so that she will attempt more than she is able to cope with. In some cases he may make her promises he cannot keep, or act in bad faith.

When Jupiter is well-aspected he may have a special interest in making her reputation known over a wider area. In a relationship between a publicity agent and his client this is a helpful link when it is the agent's Jupiter that is involved.

Jupiter in the Eighth House

When the man's Jupiter falls in the eighth house of his female partner's horoscope, he may be the means of making her aware of some hitherto neglected facet of her being, which may have operated either as an asset or a liability to her, with the result that she will either concentrate on enhancing and enriching some special attribute, or on attempting to transform the defect in such a way as to eliminate it as a negative factor, and turn it into a positive source of benefit. He will usually have her best interests at heart. Between opposite sexes of a suitable age this link usually indicates considerable physical attraction, as well as an instinctive appreciation of each other's good qualities, a foundation upon which a solid relationship can be built. If his Jupiter is much afflicted, the man may marry her for her money, though in cases where Jupiter is well supported at birth and the cross-aspects are mainly harmonious, financial transactions between the two will usually present no problems, each acting in good faith towards the other.

The eighth house is a good position for the Jupiter of the native's banker to fall, always provided it is reasonably well-aspected, and the same holds good for all others upon whom he relies his financial transactions.

Jupiter in the Ninth House

When the man's Jupiter falls in the ninth house of his female partner's horoscope, he may be able to introduce her to a wider range of philosophical and religious teachings and in the process give her a greater insight into some of the more abstract problems that she had previously been unable to solve satisfactorily. He will be happy to draw upon his own experience and knowledge in order to help her to expand her understanding and he may have the happy knack of being able to stimulate her ideas on a variety of subjects, helping her to widen her horizons.

She will tend to value his good opinion of her and will trust him with her confidences. This link symbolizes a happy relationship based on mutual trust, unless Jupiter is much afflicted at birth and the cross-aspects to it are discordant.

This is a good link between the horoscopes of teacher and pupil when it is the pupil's ninth house that is involved. The same is true of a guru-pupil relationship, as the one whose Jupiter is involved may be able to foresee the direction in which the other might most profitably develop. The ninth house is also connected with publicity and with publishing and a publisher's Jupiter in this sector of an author's horoscope is a useful talisman for a profitable association.

The one whose Jupiter occupies this house in another's horoscope may sometimes be able to assist him in his travels, arouse an interest in foreign countries and some times provide transport for him.

Jupiter in the Tenth House

When the man's Jupiter falls in the tenth house of his female partner's horoscope and more particularly, when it falls in conjunction with her Midheaven, he may be instrumental in making possible improvements in her status, perhaps as a result of putting her in touch with influential people or through wise advice based on his own professional experience. He may give her a taste for success or by his good opinion of her give her an extra incentive to succeed, so that she does not let him down. He may take pleasure in playing the role of "father" to her, helping her to reach her goals and realize her full potential, because he appreciates the aims she has in mind.

His object will be to strengthen her belief in herself and to encourage her to achieve her ambitions through applying her efforts wisely. If Jupiter is afflicted at birth and the cross-aspects to it are discordant he may cause her to aim higher than she is capable of, weaken her resolve by making her path too easy, or perhaps hamper her progress by giving her bad advice.

When Jupiter in the horoscope of the native's parent or employer falls in his tenth house they will reward his efforts with the appreciation they deserve.

Jupiter in the Eleventh House

When the man's Jupiter falls in the eleventh house of his female partner's horoscope a very rewarding friendship can develop between them. He may be instrumental in introducing her to a wider circle of friends and in helping her to expand her social life in other ways, perhaps introducing her to a group of kindred souls working towards some specific end.

He is likely to appreciate the ideals she holds dear and he may be able to assist her to realize them. He is likely to be her friend in the best sense of the term, making allowances for any temporary lapses on her part. For her part, she may need to guard against taking too much advantage of his generosity of spirit, particularly against taking him too much for granted, as he sets a special store on her friendship.

While this is a good position for another's Jupiter, the position is rather less favorable if Jupiter is debilitated at birth and the cross-aspects are discordant, when too much indulgence, over-optimism or self-esteem may spoil the overall effect.

Jupiter in the Twelfth House

When the man's Jupiter falls in the twelfth house of his female partner's horoscope, he could be the person to whom she is most likely to turn in times of trouble. He may be able to show her how to cope with any deficiencies in her character or temperament that may involve her in disconcerting situations and he will often be able to bolster her self-assurance so that she is able to summon up fresh courage to tackle her problems, which may seem less formidable as a result of his friendly advice. He may be able to work behind the scenes to straighten out her problems and do much to restore her faith in herself.

He will often be very interested in finding out what makes her tick and, while she may feel encouraged to share confidences with him, he may not always be discreet in keeping these confidences to himself, especially if Jupiter is afflicted at birth and the cross-aspects are discordant. If there is a romantic attachment between them, they may have to guard against scandal.

In some cases he will be able to awaken her interest in occultism, mysticism, and all subjects that bring a greater understanding of life's undercurrents, as well as an appreciation of the fact that many of the barriers that appear to divide one area of experience from another are, in the wider sense, purely illusory.

The twelfth house of the native's horoscope is a good position for the Jupiter of his doctor or those who may be called upon to nurse him. Friends with their Jupiter in his twelfth house will be those most likely to rally round when he is ill and be most outgiving when he is in need of sympathy.

SATURN IN THE HOUSES

Wherever the native's Saturn falls in another's horoscope indicates that area where he may be able to teach the other a valuable lesson in life, making him more aware of where his obligations lie, helping him to develop a greater sense of responsibility and self-reliance and generally deepening his understanding. He may be the cause of the other person having to exercise a greater degree of concentration, and having to become more aware of what is of permanent value, so that he is able to discard non-essentials. The native may be tempted to act as the other person's conscience and if Saturn is afflicted, he may project his fears, inhibitions and guilt complexes upon him, tending to act as a damper, attempting to restrict, limit or delay his schemes or to disparage his efforts. He may be the means of indicating to the other exactly what he owes to him.

Saturn in the First House

When the man's Saturn falls in the first house of his female partner's horoscope, and more particularly when it falls in conjunction with her Ascendant, something in her personality may convince him that he can depend upon her. He will value her as a stabilizing influence and as a result she may more effectively develop her sense of responsibility. His conduct may make demands upon her patient understanding and sometimes test her powers of endurance but this is nevertheless an indication of a lasting relationship unless Saturn is much afflicted, when she may never sufficiently overcome her initial distaste for the relationship to develop at all.

When Saturn is well-aspected at birth and the cross-aspects are predominantly favorable, he may be in a position to give her the benefit of his experience in areas that are most helpful to her. She may, at some time, be called upon to undertake responsibility on his behalf or she may feel that it is her duty to perform some special task for his benefit. In some way she may be conscious of the fact that she has to "carry" him and to supply all the buoyancy in the relationship (for this reason he may be all the more inclined to "lean"). Without such an element of buoyancy being supplied by his partner, the association may become over-serious and develop a feeling of heaviness that can diminish the pleasure that otherwise might have been derived from each other's company.

This link sometimes occurs between the horoscopes of marriage partners and when it is the husband's Saturn that is involved the best results are often obtained when the wife is content to acknowledge his greater experience although if Saturn is afflicted at birth and the cross-aspects are discordant, the husband's tendency to project his fears and inhibitions onto her may reduce his wife's enthusiasm for his company and depress the atmosphere between them. He may saddle her with too many responsibilities and may demand overmuch attention from her. She may have to nurse him or cope with some physical affliction he develops or some financial setback he sustains. The circumstances of the relationship often abound with difficulties requiring a great deal of perseverance and self-discipline to overcome. Unless Saturn is well-supported it is usually the husband who will suffer the most.

When this link occurs, both partners must accept the bonds of marriage willingly if the relationship is to prosper. Sometimes this link indicates a childless marriage. The relationship may be a particularly karmic one. The wife may have the opportunity to pay off a karmic debt to her husband.

His attitude may be critical, because he is anxious that any aspects of her personality that detract from her complete integrity may be ironed out, to the mutual benefit of both partners and she may find that she is called upon to overcome some temperamental defect in order to put the relationship on a thoroughly sound basis. The Sun is naturally exalted in the first house and Saturn in the opposite house, so that false pride is particularly obnoxious to Saturn, who seeks to establish the true essence of his partner underlying the mask of her personality, which often does not reflect the real inner nature. This process can be extremely irksome, though the final result may be of lasting benefit.

Such a link often provides the partner, whose first house is involved, with experiences that would not be met with on his own but when Saturn is much afflicted the partners may lose valuable opportunities through the hesitancy of Saturn to commit himself.

Saturn in the Second House

When the man's Saturn falls in the second house of his female partner's horoscope he may be instrumental in showing her how to build up and improve her resources, discarding what is superfluous and retaining only what is essential. She may owe him some debt which can most suitably be repaid on a material basis. When this link exists any debts should always be punctiliously discharged.

If Saturn is well-aspected he may be able to give her a greater sense of security and help to develop in her a more prudent and responsible attitude towards financial affairs, advising her as to the best way to insure against risk and how to avoid doubtful investments. If Saturn is debilitated or afflicted at birth and the cross-aspects are discordant, his cautious and fearful advice may cause her to lose good opportunities for profitable investment or to sustain losses in some more direct way. In some way he may be a source of expense to her. Sometimes he may interfere in her financial affairs thinking to improve her chances of gain, instead causing her reputation to suffer by inadvertently breaking promises she had already made.

On the positive side and when Saturn is well supported, he may be able to save up money for her, teach her frugality and show her how to handle her resources wisely. Sometimes, though, when Saturn is afflicted, his own financial attitudes may demonstrate to her exactly what should not be done! She should not take her partner's financial advice unless his Saturn is well-aspected at birth and the cross-aspects are harmonious and then only if it does not conflict with what her own commonsense and experience tell her. Needless to say, this is not a good position for the Saturn of the native's financial adviser.

Saturn in the Third House

When the man's Saturn falls in the third house of his female partner's horoscope he may be the means of giving her a more stable way of thinking. He may show her how to concentrate more effectively upon her studies and how to sharpen her critical faculties and think in a more disciplined way, so that she is able to distinguish more easily between the essential and the superfluous, becoming less likely to be sidetracked.

In some way he may be the cause of limiting her mobility or act as a source of delay in her travels. In such situations he may be the means of giving her greater time to sit and reflect. In some cases he may be instrumental in making her journeys more arduous. He may ask her to undertake responsible errands on his behalf.

When Saturn is afflicted he may be responsible for causing her relationships with neighbours to deteriorate. She may find his ideas heavy, his conversation boring and his mental approach too thorough and painstaking for her taste. When this link is present between casual associates some care may be necessary on the part of the one whose third house is involved. If the link is present between teacher and pupil, with the pupil's third house involved, the lessons may be heavy going and demand a great deal of mental effort.

Saturn in the Fourth House

When the man's Saturn falls in the fourth house of his female partner's horoscope and more particularly, when it falls in conjunction with her Lower Meridian, he may wish to assume the responsibility of a parent towards her. He may cause her to take more notice of her habitual and instinctive reactions. Unless Saturn is well aspected at birth and the cross-aspects are exceptionally favorable, his influence may be particularly overpowering, especially if the contact was first made when she was very young. His attitude may be overcritical, which can undermine her self-confidence. On the other hand he may expect her to take too much responsibility, especially of a domestic nature, too soon. It may be possible for her to learn a good deal from him but unless the cross-aspects are predominantly harmonious she may not feel particularly comfortable in his presence.

In some way he may encourage her to follow in her father's footsteps.

Saturn in the Fifth House

When the man's Saturn falls in the fifth house of his female partner's horoscope it may be difficult for her to enlist his support for any enterprise she wishes to undertake. He may be inclined to disparage her creative efforts and she may find it difficult to arouse any emotional response from him. There could be a general lack of sympathy between the two which forms a barrier to any real understanding or close association.

At the same time he may be rather demanding in his attitude towards her, as he may find it difficult to believe that she is putting forth her best efforts on his behalf. While his lack of appreciation may be genuine, she should try to examine her own reactions as objectively as possible because she may be expecting to receive his enthusiastic approval without really having done anything to warrant such an expectation. In such circumstances his lack of enthusiasm may represent a well merited criticism of the real quality of her work.

Any feeling of disparagement she feels may result in her making an extra effort just to show how wrong he was. The net result may be that he concludes, that in order to get the best out of his partner he should consistently refrain from being enthusiastic.

Occurring between opposite sexes of a suitable age, this position of Saturn may be seen as a challenge to capture the partner's interest, with Saturn playing hard to get. This is not the happiest augury for a lasting partnership, however, and the husband with Saturn here may be over-stern with the children and lacking in enthusiasm for his wife's social activities. Sometimes such an attitude may be based on envy, with the husband feeling that his wife has some special attribute that he has not.

The lesson for the person whose fifth house is involved is to learn to create for the sake of the result and not in order to gain approbation. On another level his partner may provide him with experiences that lead him to establish greater control over his emotions. If the cross-aspects are discordant, such a partner may be the source of some deep emotional disappointment. If, in addition, Saturn is much afflicted at birth, little joy can result from this link.

Saturn in the Sixth House

When the man's Saturn falls in the sixth house of his female partner's horoscope, he may feel that he has a right to expect some service from her. For his part, he will expect to be fully recompensed for any service that he may render her. He may adopt a critical attitude towards the way she does things and go out of his way to test her efficiency. Although he may appear to be too ready to find fault, he may do so only in order to help her improve her methods and introduce her to more reliable techniques, with the ultimate aim of making her more self-sufficient.

In some way he may be instrumental in keeping her busy or he may occasionally hinder her progress. Unless Saturn is well aspected at birth and the cross-aspects are particularly favorable, this is not a good position for an employee's Saturn, or for the Saturn of anyone who has care of the native's health.

Saturn in the Seventh House

When the man's Saturn falls in the seventh house of his female partner's horoscope, and more particularly, when it is in conjunction with the Descendant, this may be the indication of a very critical relationship. Saturn is naturally exalted in the seventh house and represents the possibility of a permanent relationship, one solid enough to stand the test of time. He will assess her worth as a partner and if she measures up to his standards she will have a friend for life. The snag is that his method of testing her may sometimes prove to be rather irksome. If Saturn is afflicted at birth and the cross-aspects are discordant, she may resent his methods and question his right to test her out in that fashion. She may need to live by the precept "do as you would be done by" but even then this may not guarantee an effusive response from her partner.

He may be demanding, but provided Saturn is well aspected, he will display integrity in the partnership and his reliability will provide her with a challenge to demonstrate a reciprocal dependability.

If he has an afflicted Saturn, she may find it extremely difficult to get on with him and his inflexible approach or lack of enthusiasm may make any true rapport impossible or she may feel that she will never be able to please him.

Provided Saturn is well aspected this can be a good link in a business partnership, though a lawyer's, manager's or agent's Saturn in the native's seventh house is not to be recommended.

Saturn in the Eighth House

When the man's Saturn falls in the eighth house of his female partner's horoscope he will be likely to make her particularly aware of those areas of her psyche over which she normally has little control and if these should be a source of weakness, she may find that he has reservations about accepting her friendship. He may need to know her a long time before he finally makes up his mind to consolidate the relationship. He may act in such a way as to make her uncomfortably aware of certain of her deficiencies and as a result she may feel the need to make some kind of transformation in certain of her attitudes so that the relationship can operate more smoothly.

If Saturn is afflicted at birth and the cross-aspects are discordant, this relationship may give rise to an enmity on either side which is difficult to account for on any rational grounds. Even when there are few afflictions to Saturn he may be prevented by some vague sense of foreboding from entering wholeheartedly into a relationship with her. It is almost as if he were debating within himself whether he could trust her with his life. He may demand most convincing proofs of her integrity before he really feels at home with her. Naturally, this is hardly the best basis on which to form a really satisfactory relationship and his reservations and sometimes ultra-cautious attitude may well turn her against him. The relationship may call for a great deal of tolerance and a willingness to make sacrifices on her part if it is to prosper.

Sometimes this link is present between the horoscopes of those who are called upon to face some great danger together and who, in the course of the experience, are able to recognize each other's essential nature as it stands revealed in the face of extreme adversity. Sometimes this link indicates that the relationship will come about through a death and, in extreme cases, the one whose Saturn is involved may be the cause of the other's death.

This is not a happy position for the Saturn of anyone who has responsibility for handling the native's finances, as it often indicates that the native will suffer loss through his agency.

Saturn in the Ninth House

The man's Saturn falling in the ninth house of his female partner's horoscope indicates that he may be instrumental in focusing her thoughts upon religious or philosophical issues, leading her to adopt a more serious attitude to the important issues in life. The claims of orthodox values and the wisdom of ancient teachings may be brought more into her consciousness through his agency. He will be likely to encourage her to cultivate a greater feeling of responsibility in relation to the propagation and conservation of knowledge and to follow her own line of self-development in such matters. If Saturn is much afflicted at birth and there are discordant cross-aspects, the two may never see eye to eye over matters relating to religion or to the general understanding of life as a whole.

In less exalted matters, he may be a person who relies upon her for transport, or who brings her responsibilities connected with foreign countries. He may in some way be responsible for hampering her mobility or be the cause of a certain amount of unavoidable travel or correspondence.

When a parent's Saturn falls in the ninth house of his child's horoscope he may send the child to boarding school or be particularly demanding of him in relation to the educational standards he expects him to attain.

Saturn in the Tenth House

When the man's Saturn falls in the tenth house of his female partner's horoscope and, more particularly, when it falls in conjunction with her Midheaven, he may play some definitive role in relation to her career. If he should be her employer, he may make considerable demands on her, but if Saturn is well aspected at birth and the cross-aspects are favorable, he will reward her strictly according to her deserts.

He may act in such a way as to test the strength of her ambition and if he occasionally goes out of his way to thwart her best endeavors and retards her progress, she may find that in the long run such action has strengthened her will to succeed. He may delay recognition until such time as she is really fitted for advancement and by so doing save her from failing in a new undertaking through insufficient experience. He will encourage her to develop a realistic approach to her responsibilities.

He may be inclined to adopt a rather parental attitude towards her, taking a paternal interest in her progress and even attempting to play the "heavy father" if Saturn is much afflicted. He will be likely to tell her the truth about herself and his critical appraisal of her performance is usually calculated to assist her to attain a higher level of achievement and self-development, unless Saturn is much afflicted, when he may be inclined to envy her position.

He is likely to assess her prestige on her actual performance and not on hearsay. His concern is that she will be able to do complete justice to herself and her potentialities when she is called upon to display her talents.

If Saturn in the horoscope of an older rival falls in the native's tenth house, this rival may stand in the way of the native's progress.

Saturn in the Eleventh House

When the man's Saturn falls in the eleventh house of his female partner's horoscope he will take a practical interest in helping her to achieve her ideals if she is prepared to work hard to bring them about, and if he believes that they are truly worthwhile and within the bounds of possibility to achieve.

A strong friendship can grow as a result of this link but she will need to convince him that she is a solid and dependable person who will not take the friendship for granted. He will expect her to contribute her full share to the friendship and sometimes he may make claims on her friendship at an inconvenient time, with the result that she has to make sacrifices in order to respond as he would wish. He may try to put her friendship to the test by making some demand upon her that would limit her freedom in other directions. He will always be willing to place his experience at her disposal.

If Saturn is much afflicted at birth and the cross-aspects are discordant, she may feel antipathy towards him, with the result that she prefers to avoid rather than to cultivate his company.

Saturn in the Twelfth House

When the man's Saturn falls in the twelfth house of his female partner's horoscope there may be some difficulties in the relationship. He may expect her to be reliable and self-sufficient in those very areas where she is likely to be most vulnerable. In consequence, she may not feel particularly at ease in his presence and he may occasionally bring one of her weaknesses to light in a disconcerting way, arousing her resentment and his doubts about her ability to act consistently or wisely. As a result, he may be instrumental in making her more aware of those areas of her psyche where she is most vulnerable, thus giving her an incentive to eradicate such shortcomings.

When other cross-aspects are favorable, he may work behind the scenes to strengthen her position but if Saturn is afflicted at birth and the cross-aspects to it are discordant, he may work against her in secret to undermine her position and frustrate her plans.

In some cases she may be placed in a position where she has to shelter him or generally render him aid or assistance; he may make testing demands upon her sympathetic and charitable instincts.

URANUS IN THE HOUSES

Wherever the native's Uranus falls in another's horoscope indicates that area where he is able to show the other a radically new way of looking at things and tackling problems, encouraging him to break away from outdated attitudes of thinking and to develop a more forward-looking policy. It shows where he can arouse the other's latent sense of originality. The revolutionary new outlook of Uranus may cause problems to the other, especially if Uranus is afflicted in the nativity and the cross-aspects are discordant, when the native may expect him to change course too rapidly or to alter his conduct too radically. The native's intransigent attitude may be the cause of friction in the relationship and sometimes his unpredictability may stretch his companion's powers to the utmost. The function of Uranus in this context may be to challenge the other person to see things in a new perspective, recognizing the principle behind the phenomenon and transcending any limitations imposed by his own fears, by the need to observe popular conventions, and by the dead-weight of the past.

The native may be the means of sowing, in the other's mind, seeds of discontent with his present circumstances increasing his feelings of tension and perhaps nervousness until he manages to adapt more readily to the alterations that seem desirable.

Uranus in the First House

When the man's Uranus falls in the first house of his female partner's horoscope, and more particularly when it falls in conjunction with her Ascendant, some unusual facets of his personality may capture her attention. Between opposite sexes of the same age there can be a dynamic attraction. He will usually take the initiative in the association although afflictions to Uranus may denote some tension as to which partner is to exercise the initiative. Even so, the fascination between them may remain and the relationship will never descend to the commonplace. He may encourage her to try out new ideas and to develop hitherto neglected aspects of her personality. In some cases, he will be the means of introducing an element of novelty into her life, putting her in touch with a new circle of friends and bringing her into contact with a completely new environment.

He may challenge her, perhaps not wittingly, by his own being and life style, to make changes in herself and as the process of making such drastic changes in one's way of living and thinking is rarely a congenial one, she may find such a challenge places her in a very uncomfortable position.

When Uranus is afflicted at birth and the cross-aspects are discordant, he may want to dictate to her what she should do in certain circumstances and his manner may be such as to make her tense and nervous. He may be the cause of her breaking with old associates and may finally disappear from her life as suddenly as he entered it.

Uranus in the Second House

When the man's Uranus falls in the second house of his female partner's horoscope he may inspire her to re-examine the way in which she handles all the resources at her disposal as well as her whole attitude to the establishment of her security. He may encourage her to cultivate a more happy-go-lucky attitude towards financial matters and, unless the cross-aspects are very good, his advice on how she should improve her financial position may need to be very carefully examined before she decides to act on it. He may suddenly place her in a position where she is called upon to foot the bill unexpectedly and if the cross-aspects are discordant he may find ingenious ways of parting her from her money.

Needless to say, this is not the best place for the Uranus of anyone who has the task of dealing with the native's finances.

Uranus in the Third House

When the man's Uranus falls in the third house of his female partner's horoscope he may be the means of giving her an entirely new slant on life, putting her in touch with new sources of information that give her the opportunity to develop quite different mental perspectives.

The physical attraction, which is quite often a feature present in first house contacts, is transferred to the mental realm so that a high degree of mental rapport becomes possible, provided the cross-aspects to Uranus are not too discordant, in which case his way of thinking may seem to be too abnormal to merit serious attention. Even so, she may at some later date suddenly become aware of the principle behind the ideas he was trying to convey to her.

He may have the capacity to keep her mentally alert and on her toes at all times, and his way of thinking may challenge her to get back to first principles and remind her that, in certain circumstances, issues are not always clear-cut and that theories based on incomplete evidence may have to be modified considerably in the light of new information.

He may be instrumental in helping her to bring about changes in her environment and may suggest valuable, time-saving cuts in her methods of travel.

Uranus in the Fourth House

When the man's Uranus falls in the fourth house of his female partner's horoscope and more particularly, when it falls in conjunction with her Lower Meridian, he may have a very unsettling effect, not only upon her domestic atmosphere but also upon her instinctive and habitual way of life.

In some ways he may cause her to re-examine her ideas resulting from her parental upbringing, her domestic arrangements and the whole basis she operates from. His influence may be felt by her as a challenge to cultivate the habit of acting more spontaneously. If Uranus is much afflicted at birth and the cross-aspects to it are discordant, he may thoroughly disrupt her life and make her position untenable. He may follow an unusual occupation which upsets her normal routine.

In a parent-child relationship, the parent whose Uranus falls in the fourth house of his child's horoscope may be the cause of constant changes in the child's domestic environment, sometimes as a result of moving house, and he may be instrumental in determining the child's career.

Uranus in the Fifth House

When the man's Uranus falls in the fifth house of his female partner's horoscope he may be able to give considerable assistance to her creative and artistic efforts, stimulating her originality. Unless Uranus is much afflicted she will find that his ideas often give her a vision of new possibilities, so that she becomes more open to inspiration. He may be instrumental in bringing new opportunities for the development of her social life and in giving her a new attitude to the use of leisure. His hobbies may provide her with a new interest.

Between opposite sexes of a suitable age this link can stimulate a mutual romantic interest but of itself it does not guarantee any permanency in the relationship.

If Uranus is afflicted at birth and the cross-aspects are unfavorable, the two may be at cross-purposes and he will either have a poor opinion of her creative efforts or he may cause her to waste time in leisure pursuits that are unworthy of her talents.

Uranus in the Sixth House

When the man's Uranus falls in the sixth house of his female partner's horoscope he may be able to suggest effective new ways of doing things and introduce her to labor-saving devices that help to make her work easier. By comparison with his methods, she may feel that hers are cumbersome and less efficient, and without necessarily consciously suggesting it, he may cause her to overhaul her own methods to see what improvements can be made.

He may introduce her to new diets or arouse her interest in new keep-fit methods and other ways to improve her health. She may revise her attitude to service and to those who occupy a subordinate role, as a result of his own ideas on the subject. He may call upon her to perform some unusual service on his behalf.

Unless Uranus is well aspected at birth and the cross-aspects are preponderantly benefic, something about his presence may prove unsettling to her and she may sense that his attitude towards her is rather critical, even if he does not express it in words. There may be a tendency for him to set her nerves on edge. At some time she may have cause for concern over his health.

This is not a good position for the Uranus of anyone who ministers to the native's health or who is responsible for providing him with manufactured foods or goods. Neither is it a good position for an employee's Uranus, especially if afflicted, as this person may question his methods and try to improve upon them, sometimes with disastrous results. He may also grow restless after a short period and seek other employment.

Uranus in the Seventh House

When the man's Uranus falls in the seventh house of his female partner's horoscope, and more particularly, when it is in conjunction with her Descendant, he may place her in a position, perhaps unconsciously, where she has to make some radical change in order to maintain the relationship on an even keel. He may be responsible for introducing her to a whole new circle of people. If Uranus is afflicted at birth and the cross-aspects to it are discordant, he may want to interfere with her relationships and may be the cause of breaking up her relationship with somebody else. In some cases he may try to come between her and her husband or attempt to dictate to him what he should do.

This link indicates a type of relationship that is likely to remain delicately poised, being subject to abrupt changes of course, either through erratic tendencies on the part of the man or through circumstances that arise with disconcerting suddenness. He may enter her life suddenly and depart with equal suddenness. In the case of a romantic association, although he may exercise some fascination over her, she would not be well advised to marry him unless the cross-aspects between the two nativities were particularly harmonious. Even so, this link may indicate periods of enforced separation due to the occupation of one of the partners involving much travel or as a result of unforeseen circumstances.

As a result of such an association, she may decide to change her line of approach to other people.

The link is not to be recommended in cases of a business partnership unless novelty and originality are the keynotes of the enterprise.

Uranus in the Eighth House

When the man's Uranus falls in the eighth house of his female partner's horoscope, the relationship may be a particularly significant one. Her experiences with him may lead her to undertake some radical self-appraisal with the result that she is able to effect a transformation in some important aspect of her being. He may be the means of bringing her into touch with some teaching or discipline that is particularly connected with obtaining greater self-knowledge, thus facilitating work on the self. He may stimulate her interest in the general area of occultism and he may enable her to view the phenomenon of death in a new light, as the beginning of a new life rather than the end of an old one.

At a less exalted level, he may be the means of interesting her in a study of economics, though in practical financial matters he might not be the best one for her to entrust with any financial matters, as he might be inclined to act in an erratic manner. If the two are marriage partners, there could be a contest between them over who should exercise control over the family budget.

Between opposite sexes of a suitable age, this link may denote considerable physical attraction, but if Uranus is afflicted at birth and the cross-aspects to it are discordant, any unduly experimental attitude on the part of either may lead to undesirable complications.

Uranus in the Ninth House

When the man's Uranus falls in the ninth house of his female partner's horoscope, he may be instrumental in causing her to review her whole philosophy of life. His views on philosophy and religion may differ greatly from her own and he may be able to put her in touch with ideas and teachings that shed new light on some of the problems that puzzled her and challenge her to revise her attitudes to some aspects of human experience. He may bring to her notice new books that stimulate her to branch out in new directions and to think along more original lines.

He may be the means of stimulating in her a greater interest in foreign countries and travel abroad or he may be able to suggest easier and more speedy methods of getting from place to place.

If Uranus is much afflicted at birth the challenge he poses to her thinking and outlook may be so drastic that she rejects his ideas totally, or they may be so extraordinary or disturbing that she finds herself completely unsettled or filled with apprehension.

Uranus in the Tenth House

When the man's Uranus falls in the tenth house of his female partner's horoscope and more particularly when it falls in conjunction with her Midheaven, he may dramatically affect the course of her career, perhaps suddenly providing her with an opportunity for advancement or, through his own example, causing her to ask herself whether she is doing the right job and going the right way about bringing her aims to fruition.

In some way he may strike her as a rather erratic type of person and, as people are known by the company they keep, she may sometimes feel that her reputation is not entirely enhanced by the association. If his behaviour does strike her as being rather extraordinary, he may provide her with a useful example of how not to conduct herself!

When Uranus is afflicted at birth and the cross-aspects are discordant, his impact upon her affairs may be highly disruptive. She may well regard him as a person she could never work for or allow to direct her life.

If the Uranus of the native's employer falls here, he may expect the native to show a considerable degree of initiative and adaptability, being alert to changing situations and on his toes to take advantage of every new opportunity that comes along.

If a parent's Uranus falls here he may attempt to dictate to the native which occupation he should follow, or he may encourage the native to strike out on some original line of his own.

Uranus in the Eleventh House

When the man's Uranus falls in the eleventh house of his female partner's horoscope he may be instrumental in introducing her to societies and organizations dedicated to the furtherance of some ideal that she cherishes, or he may put her into touch with a wide variety of friends. He may be able to give her a new understanding of the concept of brotherhood. Uranus is the natural ruler of the eleventh house and his independence may sometimes make him appear rather casual and if she is to engage in a close association with him she may have to be prepared to meet him more than halfway. In times of emergency he may react surprisingly and offer help when she least expects it.

If Uranus is afflicted at birth and the cross-aspects are discordant, she may never choose to seek his company in the natural course of events. If they are brought together by chance she may feel distinctly uncomfortable in his presence.

Uranus in the Twelfth House

When the man's Uranus falls in the twelfth house of his female partner's horoscope the relationship may be a particularly challenging one as he may cause her to call forth all latent powers of sympathy and understanding in an effort to find the best way of dealing with him. She may feel some tension in his presence but if the cross-aspects are harmonious and Uranus is well aspected at birth he may be instrumental in shedding new light on her problems and in helping her to adjust more satisfactorily to life as a whole, though before this end is achieved she may have to make some fundamental alterations in her emotional and intellectual attitudes. He may propose drastic remedies to her and if she has faith in him and is prepared to adopt them, she may achieve surprising results. He may be able to work behind the scenes on her behalf with great effect.

If Uranus is afflicted at birth he may have the knack of making her feel ill at ease and inadequate in some way and she may have the feeling that he is hatching some secret plot to take advantage of her weakest points. She may imagine that he is strongest where she is weakest, though if she attempts to copy his methods she may only make matters worse.

This is not a good location for the Uranus of the native's doctor or those who have charge of his nursing.

NEPTUNE IN THE HOUSES

Wherever the native's Neptune falls in another's horoscope indicates that area of life where the other may be able to establish a sympathetic rapport with him. In some way he will be able to get through to the native's more idealistic and charitable side so that he may be prepared to make sacrifices to help him. The native's idealism may stir up a similar emotion in the other or, in some cases, an unfulfilled yearning or some subtle dissatisfaction with his present condition. In some way the native will leave him with a feeling of vague uneasiness that he cannot satisfactorily account for. The native may allow the other person to invoke in him a mood of euphoria that leads him to turn his back on the hard facts of life and in turn the native's false optimism may lull the other into a false sense of security.

When the native's Neptune is afflicted, the other person may experience some subtle feeling of being out of his depth with him and he may be tempted to relax his own moral code if the native displays a lack of scruple in certain matters. The native may not be able to get a clear picture of what the other is driving at. He may thus act to confuse him or waste his time, sometimes involving him in material loss or damaging his reputation. The native may take undue advantage of the other's sympathetic nature.

The native's actions may challenge the other to make absolutely certain that he is registering the correct impression of the native's intentions, to find a rewarding outlet for his charitable instincts and to make a practice of looking at life from a more poetic standpoint.

Contemporaries will have Neptune more or less in the same area of the zodiac, so that the aspects at birth become a particularly crucial factor.

Neptune in the First House

When the man's Neptune falls in the first house of his female partner's horoscope and, more particularly, when it falls in conjunction with her Ascendant, he may find that his most effective channel of communication with her is through her emotions and charitable impulses. He may be the means of causing her to feel more deeply about the underprivileged. He may be able to interpret her dreams and explain her fantasies, though she may have to watch that he does not foster her illusions. His effect upon her may be very relaxing and soothing. He may either consciously or unconsciously show her how to dramatize herself more effectively. Especially if the two are contemporaries, there may be a need for her to guard against identifying herself with his emotions and allowing him to sway her sympathies unduly.

If the cross-aspects to Neptune are favorable he may be able to show her how to attain her heart's desire although, unless her desires are free from the wish for personal advantage at the expense of others, she may find that what appeared to promise so well ends by being a source of much disappointment.

When Neptune is badly placed at birth and the cross-aspects to it are unfavorable, the two may get a totally wrong picture of each other or he may prove to be completely unreliable. In some way he may be a source of disappointment to her, not necessarily because of any deliberate action on his part and perhaps because of some misapprehension on her part. In extreme cases, he may intentionally set out to mislead her and involve her in scandal that is damaging to her reputation.

Neptune in the Second House

When the man's Neptune falls in the second house of his female partner's horoscope she would be wise not to allow him to influence her financial arrangements. Ideally he may inspire her with ideas about how to distribute wealth for the greater welfare of the poor and needy, but in the hard light of day such schemes may turn out to be impracticable and of no real service. Nevertheless he may in some way test her ability to loose hold of her purse strings and adopt a more open handed attitude towards her finances.

She may feel tempted to buy his goodwill through demonstrations of generosity and, if his Neptune is much afflicted at birth and the cross-aspects to it are discordant, he may try to impose on her charitable impulses or exploit her gullibility. Her lesson may be to become a shrewder judge of other people's motives. Envy may lie at the root of their financial relationship.

He may paint rosy pictures of how she can improve her financial standing, though she may find if she takes his advice that she is soon out of her depth or circumstances outside her control may intervene to upset her most carefully laid plans. She may need to scrutinize all his suggestions with as much commonsense as she can muster before she adopts them, but she would often find it safer to ignore his ideas entirely. Sometimes he may have lucky "hunches" which work well for him, but as soon as he gives her the benefit of his foresight, something goes wrong and she fails to capitalize on his advice.

Neptune in the Third House

When the man's Neptune falls in the third house of his female partner's horoscope his impact upon her mental processes may be to help her to develop her powers of imagination and poetic appreciation. He may challenge her to transcend the process of commonsense reasoning by adding an extra dimension of intuitive awareness and he will perhaps have the gift of picturing ideas so that they are more vividly communicated to her, or he may have the ability to glamorize education and learning processes so that she becomes more interested in them. Sometimes she will need to think very clearly in order to avoid a certain amount of mental confusion, and the mental images he conjures up may be capable of more than one interpretation. He may be able to persuade her to take a less cut and dried view of education and knowledge, giving her the inclination to widen her basis of study, learning to abjure the doctrine of exclusivism: i.e., that because "A" is right, "B" must be wrong.

He may be able to pick up her thoughts telepathically and teach her how to increase her powers of intuition.

If Neptune was afflicted at his birth and the cross-aspects to it are discordant, he may appear to her to be consistently wrong-headed and she may find that his opinions, or what she imagines to be his opinions, lead her astray or cause her to become muddle-headed.

He may give her false information about travel schedules, amenities or even be the cause of her making a fruitless journey, though if the aspects to Neptune are predominantly favorable he may implant a desire to travel in her mind through his fascinating accounts of foreign journeys, and perhaps encourage her to travel by sea or air.

In a teacher-pupil relationship this is not a good position for the teacher's Neptune unless the cross-aspects to it are particularly favorable.

Neptune in the Fourth House

When the man's Neptune falls in the fourth house of his female partner's horoscope and more particularly when it falls in conjunction with her Lower Meridian, he may exercise some subtle influence over her domestic atmosphere. Her instinctive reactions and habit patterns will either meet with his sympathetic approval or with an unreasoning distrust. Her experiences with him may tend to loosen the effect of her parental upbringing and, if Neptune is much afflicted, may tempt her to throw overboard some of the principles carefully instilled into her in her childhood. Sometimes he may exercise some subtle claim on her hospitality or know exactly how to play on her charitable instincts so that she feels under an obligation to offer him shelter and support.

If he should be acting on her behalf in relation to the acquisition or disposal of property or real estate, she may find that the negotiations have been mis-managed or even that some element of deception is present. If Neptune is much afflicted at birth and the cross-aspects to it are discordant, he may squander her estate or encourage her to do so. He may try to trick her out of her birthright or in some way involve her in scandal, causing her to neglect some vital precaution, or be the cause of some subtle deterioration in her domestic atmosphere.

If the Neptune of one of the native's parents falls in his fourth house, he may find that he is tied to that parent as a result of his infirmity or chronic illness.

Neptune in the Fifth House

When the man's Neptune falls in the fifth house of his female partner's horoscope he may be able to increase her artistic vision and add a subtle new dimension to her creative powers. He may inspire her to display her personality more dramatically and bring a new sense of idealism into those activities nearest to her heart. He may be instrumental in widening the scope of her leisure time activities. If they are of a suitable age, this link may encourage dreams of romance or shared romantic fantasies. If Neptune is much afflicted the net result may at best be somewhat disappointing and at worst may lead to some subtle and unpleasant travesty of the love relationship.

This contact can challenge her to live up to the highest romantic ideals she may cherish and remind her that true love may demand complete surrender and a readiness to sacrifice all for the beloved. It may cause her to develop a greater intuitive recognition of the fact that she is the object of someone's affection and teach her to elevate and refine the nature of her own affection.

He may subtly drain away her vitality or encourage her to dissipate it in fruitless enterprises. At best he may provide her with the inspiration to reach the heights of creative endeavour.

Neptune in the Sixth House

When the man's Neptune falls in the sixth house of his female partner's horoscope, she may find that he is the cause of impairing her efficiency in some way. He may have the effect of blurring the sharp focus that she is usually able to bring to bear upon her technical operations. He may be very sympathetic towards her problems and he may also inspire a more idealistic attitude on her part towards rendering service.

If Neptune is well aspected at birth and the cross-aspects to it are favorable, he may have a soothing effect upon her but, if the planet is afflicted at birth and by the cross-aspects, he may have little appreciation of her methods or he may offer impractical suggestions that throw her off course with the result that she feels she would have been better off without his help or advice.

In an employer-employee relationship this is not a good place for the employee's Neptune as he may fail to interpret directions correctly or have an unfortunate knack of creating or attracting muddle and chaos. He may lose a good deal of working time through illness. If the employer's Neptune is in this position he may be vague or careless in passing on his instructions and even though he may be concerned about his employee's welfare, practical measures in this direction may be slow to appear.

Neptune in the Seventh House

When the man's Neptune falls in the seventh house of his female partner's horoscope and more particularly when it falls in conjunction with her Descendant, she may feel that he is the ideal partner for her. However, unless Neptune is well aspected at birth and the cross-aspects to it are favorable, she may find that she has allowed herself to be deluded by a mirage of unattainable bliss, and the wonderful union she had envisaged may never be realized. In some way he may remain elusive and out of reach, even if they should marry, although some fascinating glamour often remains to suggest the eternal promise of some mystic communion.

It might perhaps be better if she did not have cut and dried ideas about partnership with him because the whole object of her experience with him may be to accustom herself to the idea of allowing complete freedom of thought and action to others, not attempting to bind them to her and relying only on those links brought into being by compassionate understanding and a feeling of spiritual identity.

In some way he may be instrumental in widening her circle of associates.

When Neptune is much afflicted at birth and the cross-aspects to it are discordant, it may be impossible for her to establish a satisfactory rapport with him, as he may seem to be unreliable and completely lacking in practical virtues. Sometimes he may deliberately misrepresent her and try to damage her reputation. The purpose of such a link may be to make her more intuitively aware of the elements of compatibility in another person and to bring home to her the need to make sacrifices if a truly harmonious partnership is to be found. This contact may also help her to realize that a compassionate understanding of the temperamental differences between people helps to dissolve the barriers between them.

This is not a good position for the Neptune of the native's lawyer or of anyone he may nominate to act on his behalf.

Neptune in the Eighth House

When the man's Neptune falls in the eighth house of his female partner's horoscope she may become aware of some subtle discontent engendered by the relationship, perhaps born of an unconscious recognition of the need for some vital element of transformation in her being. Such a feeling may be so vague that she finds it difficult for the desire to work changes in herself to gather impetus. As time passes the general feeling of un-ease may gradually assume such proportions that the last remnants of her resistance are finally dissolved.

This can be an excellent link if they share a latent or developing interest in the occult and in after-death states of consciousness, but there may be a great need to guard against developing a woolly-minded attitude to these affairs. In no realm is it more important to be strictly practical and great care should be exercised on her part if his Neptune is afflicted at birth and the cross-aspects to it are discordant. In some cases he may play on her fear of death and the unknown.

If there is a sexual relationship between them this link can pose problems of unfulfilled desire.

This link is rarely an entirely comfortable one since he may be instrumental in causing her to realize that self-transformation can only be achieved through some degree of sacrifice—of some part of the lower nature, leading to a purification of the desires.

This is not a good position for the Neptune of the native's business partner or anyone who handles his business affairs. Any relatives whose Neptune falls here may challenge his right to an inheritance.

Neptune in the Ninth House

When the man's Neptune falls in the ninth house of his female partner's horoscope he may have a very uplifting and spiritualizing effect upon her whole outlook on life. Through his vision she may be encouraged to widen her frontiers and cultivate a more receptive attitude towards ideas. The experiences they undergo together may undermine any tendency she may have had to pay undue reverence to dogma, and bring her a more compassionate understanding of formal religious teaching. If his Neptune is prominently placed and much afflicted he may attempt to give her ideas a communistic slant. If the cross-aspects to his Neptune are unfavorable he may arouse false hopes or blur her clear understanding of religious and philosophical issues.

As her tutor he may have the power to rouse her imagination and invest subjects she had hitherto regarded as commonplace with a new appeal. His glowing accounts of experiences encountered abroad may stimulate in her a restless desire for travel. In many ways he may be instrumental in helping to widen her horizons spiritually, mentally and physically. The two may first have met while travelling by sea or air.

If Neptune is much afflicted she may find him a false prophet.

This is not a good position for the Neptune of the native's publicity agent.

Neptune in the Tenth House

When the man's Neptune falls in the tenth house of his female partner's horoscope and more particularly, when it falls in conjunction with her Midheaven, the ideal outcome of their association could be for him to inspire her to spiritualize her conscious aim in life so that she sets her sights high and lifts her thoughts towards ever higher endeavour.

There is often a risk, however, that the more progress she makes, the more unattainable the goal may seem to be and so she may tend to lose heart. If the association occurs in early life, he may be held up to her as a shining example of what can be done and, far from being spurred on to emulate such an example, she may feel disheartened, or that the comparison is unfair because his talents may lie in a very different direction from hers, or that she has been denied the golden opportunities that he enjoyed.

He may set much store by the value she places on his reputation.

When his Neptune is afflicted and the cross-aspects to it are discordant, he may subtly distort her aims or cause them to become blurred. If there is a close link between them she may have to sacrifice her career in some way on account of his illness and infirmity. In a situation involving rivalry, he may maneuver her out of a promotion, subtly undermine her position or bring her good name into disrepute, either by scheming to involve her in scandal, or perhaps unwittingly as a result of some carelessness or misunderstanding on his part.

Neptune in the Eleventh House

When the man's Neptune falls in the eleventh house of his female partner's horoscope he may appear to her to be a particularly desirable friend, but if her motives for seeking his friendship are to some extent ulterior she may find that the association turns out to be very different from what she had expected. To outward appearances, he may seem to be in a position to satisfy her most extravagant hopes and fondest wishes.

She may find that the friendship flourishes best when it is kept on a "loose rein." Contact on a regular basis is not favored by this position of Neptune, which often indicates an "easy come," "easy go" type of relationship. Sometimes this link is present between the horoscopes of those who are separated geographically by an expanse of land or sea, when the differences in their experience may prove highly diverting to each other.

Sometimes his ill health or unfortunate circumstances may call for sacrifices on her part and bring out the compassionate side of her nature. He may be instrumental in introducing her to a group formed with the object of furthering some ideal, or in enlarging her circle of friends, some of whom may have artistic interests or talents. The couple may gain much pleasure in leisure time activities together.

Her experiences with him may be designed to teach her how to cultivate friendship on the basis of "no strings attached" and to accept the fact that it is not possible to live all the time in a state of heavenly bliss.

Neptune in the Twelfth House

When the man's Neptune falls in the twelfth house of his female partner's horoscope the effect of this association may depend very much on the state of her twelfth house, as well as on the aspects to his Neptune at birth and the cross-aspects to the two nativities. Her association with him may in some subtle way enable her to adjust more easily to life's problems and encourage her to develop a more relaxed attitude towards them.

On the other hand, if the aspects to Neptune were preponderantly discordant, the relationship could easily lead her to seek some form of escapism, which could result in her becoming more deeply involved with her difficulties and leave her further than ever from a final solution.

In some way he may be able to arouse her most charitable and kindly instincts, opening the way for her to help some of those who are underprivileged, or he may be in need of her sympathies himself.

A mutual interest in psychic matters or mysticism may first bring the couple together, but unless Neptune is well aspected and the two charts blend well together, the resultant experiences may not live up to their expectations and may, in extreme cases, be quite unpleasant.

If his Neptune is afflicted at birth and the cross-aspects to it are discordant, he may either play her false or lure her into a situation where she becomes the cause of her own undoing either through some inherent weakness or through failing to be true to herself.

The main purpose underlying the association may be to sharpen her intuitive recognition of those really in need of her sympathy and support, and to be on her guard against foolishly confiding her secrets, exposing her weak points to others. It may challenge her to sacrifice all those aspects of her personality that work against her best interests and hamper her spiritual progress.

PLUTO IN THE HOUSES

Wherever the native's Pluto falls in another's chart shows where he will be likely to cause that person to discover some hidden part of himself so that he eventually finds that he has developed an entirely new outlook in relation to the matters signified by that sector of his horoscope. As a result the other will either be compelled to transform, or will recognize the necessity of transforming, his attitude to such matters. The native's approach to life, his achievements, or what he requires from the other person may cause that person to draw on resources that he did not realize he possessed, and challenge him to produce a level of performance that he did not previously consider possible. The other may feel pressurized by his attitude or suffer some vague form of discomfort. In some cases it may seem as if the native is able to exercise an almost hypnotic influence over the other, willing him on towards some particular line of action. In some way the native may be instrumental in presenting him with an opportunity to make a total overhaul of his motivations and habit patterns, bringing him to the realization that the true reasons leading him to act in a certain way are not the same as those which he outwardly recognizes as being their source. A great deal may depend on the planet or group of planets in the other's nativity that are aspected by the native's Pluto.

Because Pluto travels more slowly than any other known planet, except for the brief periods when it comes within the orbit of Neptune, the tendency will be for the native's Pluto to fall in the same house in a contemporary horoscope as the other's Pluto. In the case of an older generation, the native's Pluto may fall in the following house to the older person's Pluto and in the case of the younger generation, the native's Pluto may fall in the preceding house to the younger person's Pluto. When this type of interchange occurs, the native may bring some influence to bear on those of the younger generation he contacts by bringing about some kind of re-orientation in their attitude to the things signified by the house preceding their own Pluto and this will, in turn, cause them to make changes in the area of their being ruled by the house containing their own Pluto. The situation can be reversed in the native's relationships with the older generation, when the re-orientation can occur in the matters signified by the house succedent to that in which the older person's's Pluto is placed.

Pluto in the First House

When the man's Pluto falls in the first house of his female partner's horoscope and more particularly, when it is in conjunction with her Ascendant, he may find himself attracted to her by some potentiality she appears to possess, or by some facet of her being which is not immediately apparent to others. The real reason for their relationship may be to develop within her an urge to be more and more her essential self. He will be more concerned with the qualities which she does not immediately display to the world and he may challenge her, perhaps not wittingly, to become conscious of some hidden motive for action that she was not aware of, having perhaps suppressed it for some psychological reason. As a result she may find that he has been the means of her effecting some kind of transformation in herself that makes her a more complete and integrated person.

In some cases there can be a kind of Svengali element in such a relationship, with the man hypnotizing his partner with the result that she feels under a compulsion to act in a certain way or to adopt certain beliefs. If Pluto is much afflicted at birth and the cross-aspects are discordant, the relationship may be particularly harmful to her. She may make him aware of some deep-seated maladjustment in his own psyche, which he then projects on to her or holds her responsible for, with the result that enmity arises between them.

This link often signifies a particularly karmic relationship in which a great deal of emotive force has been built up between the two in a previous incarnation together. There may be a good deal of unfinished business to be resolved and the relationship is almost certain to have some deep significance, with considerable potentialities for mutual benefit or harm, according to the nature of the cross-aspects involved.

An involvement in dangerous circumstances together may give her cause to ponder upon the nature of death, and lead her to re-examine her attitude about the possibility of an after-life.

Pluto in the Second House

When the man's Pluto falls in the second house of his female partner's horoscope, her experiences with him may cause her to become aware of the most deep-seated motives that regulate her attitude to money and possessions. The way he acts may cause her to ask herself on what her standard of values is really based, and to re-examine her whole attitude towards the question of security. If the cross-aspects to Pluto are particularly harmonious he may be the means of bringing her much financial gain.

If his Pluto is afflicted at birth and the cross-aspects to it are discordant, he may be instrumental in involving her in losses which cause her to reflect that true wealth cannot be measured satisfactorily on any material basis.

When this link is present, she would be well advised not to allow him too much say in how she conducts her financial affairs, even though he may appear to take a special interest in them, and even if she feels that he can help her to achieve some spectacular breakthrough on the financial front.

Pluto in the Third House

When the man's Pluto falls in the third house of his female partner's horoscope he may exercise a powerful effect on her way of thinking, though there can sometimes be an element of reciprocity and some of her ideas may eventually assume a significance for him that he did not at first realize they contained. His ideas may challenge her to think in a new way and put her in touch with areas of knowledge that eventually lead her to adopt an entirely new way of looking at things. At the same time she should not allow him to try and coerce her into merely copying his own thought patterns.

When a parent-child relationship is involved, the parent's Pluto falling in the child's third house is likely to denote that he has a special interest in the child's education and he may want to dictate exactly how the education should develop.

Pluto in the Fourth House

When the man's Pluto falls in the fourth house of his female partner's horoscope or more particularly, when it falls in conjunction with her Lower Meridian, the relationship may make her conscious of some of her instinctive and habitual responses that were previously almost automatic. She will be likely to have strong feelings for him based on an instinctive feeling of attraction and repulsion and in some way he may invoke vivid memories of some past experience, possibly related to a previous life, that takes hold of her to such an extent that she may find that it has a striking psychological effect upon her.

He may exercise some strong influence over her domestic environment and perhaps over her career. If the cross-aspects to his Pluto are discordant, he may affect her career adversely, bringing to light some long forgotten misdemeanour on her part that reflects on her good name.

In a parent-child relationship, where it is the parent's Pluto that is involved, he may have had a great influence upon the child's early upbringing or the child may have unconsciously tried to copy him or if the cross-aspects were discordant, he may have avoided following that parent's example at all costs. The parent may want to dictate what career the child should follow and he may be keen for his child to follow in his own footsteps. He may try to urge the child to leave home as soon as possible or alternatively to hold on to him as long as possible, according to the nature of the cross-aspects to Pluto.

Pluto in the Fifth House

When the man's Pluto falls in the fifth house of his female partner's horoscope, he may in some way be responsible for making her aware of some latent creative talents which he may enable her to develop with dramatic effect, either by example or suggestion.

When the couple are of a suitable age a very strong emotional link can exist between them, though a great deal may depend upon the cross-aspects to Pluto as to the nature of any involvement and the way it develops. There will be a tendency for many of her contemporaries to have their Pluto re-located in this same house, so that this stimulus may indicate a susceptibility to become emotionally involved with them. The net result may be to encourage her to investigate the underlying motives that give rise to this susceptibility. If she finds that her passions are becoming unduly involved she may find that she is eventually compelled to transform her whole attitude and approach to affairs of the heart.

In some way he may have a far-reaching influence upon her attitude to leisure, the pursuit of pleasure and her spare time activities. If she has children and Pluto is afflicted at birth and the cross-aspects to it are discordant, his influence over her children may be undesirable.

In a parent-child relationship, when it is the parent's Pluto that is involved, he may either encourage the child to express himself with perfect freedom or try to dictate the pattern of her leisure time activities and interfere in her love affairs. If it is the child's Pluto that falls in the parent's fifth house, there may be a strong karmic link. The parent may become completely absorbed in the child's life.

Pluto in the Sixth House

When the man's Pluto falls in the sixth house of his female partner's horoscope, he may in some way make demands upon her services. He may take a special interest in the way she does things and if her technical know-how is not adequate, she may find the association with him a continual challenge to her to overhaul and improve her methods.

This may not be a particularly comfortable relationship from the woman's point of view as it may make her feel like a "probationer" continually under the scrutiny of her partner, and the purpose of such a relationship may be to test how efficiently she is able to become more aware of her inner attitude towards giving service to others and towards the acceptance of service from them. As a result of her experiences in this relationship she may have to totally revise her attitude towards working in a subordinate capacity, also her attitude towards those who may serve her in a similar capacity.

She may find that this person has some subtle but far-reaching effect upon her health, perhaps because she feels (there may be no real justification for this) that he is too demanding and too critical of her efforts. He may be able to suggest ways in which she can improve her diet or show her new exercises that promote fitness, and his own way of life may provide her with a challenge to adopt a routine similar to his.

If Pluto is well aspected at birth and the cross-aspects to it are favorable, this could be a good position for the Pluto of the native's doctor, especially if the native suffered from some deep-seated condition, but anything less than a well-supported Pluto in the native's sixth house could signify that he was subjected to treatment that ultimately did him more harm than good.

Pluto in the Seventh House

When the man's Pluto falls in the seventh house of his female partner's horoscope and more particularly, when it is in conjunction with her Descendant, the relationship with him may test to the utmost her capacity for total co-operation. Her experiences with him may cause her to explore the real nature of her inner motivations relating to partnership and to ask herself what she really requires of her partner. He may expect her to display total dedication to the partnership between them, and may be instrumental in making her aware of a hidden side of herself that needs to be entirely transformed and integrated into her conscious awareness before she can enter into a completely satisfying relationship with him.

If they are married, the relationship may be a particularly karmic one. As the seventh house is related to her attitude to the world at large he may have a definitive effect upon her political outlook.

Should Pluto be afflicted at birth and the cross-aspects to it be discordant, she may never really come to terms with him and a stage may be reached where he adopts an attitude of permanent hostility towards her. There may be something in her own attitude that makes him aware of some deep-seated disturbance in his own psyche which forms a continuing obstacle to an harmonious relationship between them.

Pluto in the Eighth House

When the man's Pluto falls in the eighth house of his female partner's horoscope, he may be the cause of her becoming aware of some of the most deep-seated and subconscious motivations that govern her behaviour. Unless Pluto is particularly well aspected this contact may be rather an uncomfortable one as it can arouse in her an uneasy awareness that the solution of many deep-seated problems may lie only in a willingness to submit herself to a rigorous self-discipline, especially when the desire nature is involved.

This association may encourage a growing inner conviction that attempts to gain greater self-control may eventually lead her to ac- acquire more power over circumstances and even over other people. Consequently she may gradually build up within her a growing conviction that it would be well worth the effort to attempt to bring about some measure of self-transformation.

Any temptation to surrender power to her partner would be unwise, nor would it be advisable for her to let him have too much influence over her financial affairs, unless his Pluto was well aspected at birth and the cross-aspects to it were particularly favorable. If she is interested in occult matters her association with him may lead her into deep waters and if the cross-aspects to Pluto were discordant, she could become involved in some unpleasant experiences. In some cases, when the cross-aspects are particularly favorable, he could be instrumental in helping her to clear away deep seated repressions, and in bringing into her conscious awareness some of the hitherto hidden urges that had dominated her actions without her having realized it. He may bring her a greater insight into the nature of death, making her aware of the possibility of an after-life.

When the two are of a suitable age this link may indicate a high degree of physical attraction unless the cross-aspects to Pluto suggest otherwise.

Pluto in the Ninth House

When the man's Pluto falls in the ninth house of his female partner's horoscope he may have a great effect upon her religious views and upon her general philosophy of life. His ideas may challenge her to examine her own ideas in depth, perhaps to a degree she had not before contemplated. In the process she may uncover some unconscious motivation that appeared to compel her to adopt a certain kind of outlook.

The result of the association may be to awaken a keen desire on her part to widen her horizons drastically, both figuratively and literally, giving her a taste for foreign travel or a greater interest in other countries. She may obtain publicity through him which can result in changes according to the cross-aspects involved. If these are discordant, his beliefs may be greatly at variance with hers and he may try to sweep away some of her cherished beliefs or to sow the seeds that lead to her developing a philosophy of life that is against her own best interests.

Pluto in the Tenth House

When the man's Pluto falls in the tenth house of his female partner's horoscope and, more particularly, when it falls in conjunction with her Midheaven, he may exercise some degree of control or influence over her career, or be the means of her entertaining certain ambitions. If the cross-aspects are discordant, he may in some way damage her reputation.

As a result of this association she may adopt a more definitive attitude to positions of power and authority. She may find that in the process she becomes aware for the first time of some hidden motivations that had hitherto governed the direction of her ambitions, and her whole attitude toward making her way in the world. If he should happen to be her rival for a position and succeeds at her expense, the experience may speed up the process referred to above. In some cases, should the cross-aspects be favorable, she may gain promotion as a result of his death.

The purpose of such a link can be to help her to transform her aims and to test her integrity when she is called upon to occupy positions of influence.

In a parent-child relationship, when it is the child's tenth house that is involved, the parent may try to dictate the course of his career and may want him to follow in his footsteps. An employer's Pluto in the tenth house of his employee's horoscope may indicate that the employer is likely to be rather demanding.

Pluto in the Eleventh House

When the man's Pluto falls in the eleventh house of his female partner's horoscope he may be instrumental in putting her into touch with groups or societies dedicated to the furtherance of some particular ideal. As a result of their experiences together she may feel a need to examine in some depth the real reasons underlying her most cherished hopes and wishes, and to re-define her attitude towards communal activities of all kinds.

He may have a very strong impulse to seek her out as a friend and if the cross-aspects to Pluto are favorable she may share this impulse. The relationship may generate a good deal of intensity and her experiences with him may determine to some extent her attitude to all her friends. Should the cross-aspects be discordant the two may have little in common or the friendship may be abruptly terminated, perhaps by his death.

Pluto in the Twelfth House

When the man's Pluto falls in the twelfth house of his female partner's horoscope the association can be a very critical one unless Pluto is well aspected, because the experiences she shares with him may make her uncomfortably aware of those elements in her character that are apt to play her false when she is under pressure. An even more disturbing factor may be her realization of subconscious compulsions towards certain types of action or of weaknesses that she had not known about before this relationship started. As a result she may feel that he is in a position to exploit her Achilles' heel and perhaps insidiously undermine her position. For his part he may not consciously wish to act in this way at all, but any feeling of insecurity on her part may transmit itself to him in such a way that he believes her to be unreliable or a bad risk.

In some way her experiences with him may be the cause of her making a deep-level examination of those areas of her being that are most likely to play her false in an emergency and to overhaul her general adjustment to life as a whole. She may find herself placed in situations that bring sudden moments of illumination which lead her to transform her whole outlook on life.

Her experiences with him may involve some claim on his part upon her sympathies and charitable impulses and he may be instrumental in changing her views about the sick, the suffering and the underprivileged. He may involve her in some kind of underground activity and, if Pluto is much afflicted, enterprises of an illegal and immoral nature. Her connection with him may arise through the treatment of some illness or psychological trouble she is suffering from. In some cases his behaviour may accentuate her health problems.

CHAPTER 9

The Relationship Horoscope Method of Calculation

The essential quality and the potentials of a relationship between any two people can be symbolized within the framework of a single horoscope, calculated according to a technique discovered by the author and tested by him over a number of years. The idea first occurred to him when compiling examples of progressed and converse directions for inclusion in *The Technique of Prediction,* in which the system of Secondary Directions was amplified to include not only the traditional "day for a year" measure but also a "day for a month," a "day for a week," and a "day for a day."

The last named measure was so described in order to draw attention to the fact that transits (a "day for a day") were an integral part of the complete system and, since the three other measures were calculated both in terms of time elapsed after birth (progressed) and time elapsed before (converse, or perhaps more logically, "regressed"), to draw attention to the fact that "converse transits" were also valid.

Now it follows that, with any two individuals, there must be a moment in time when the date of the progressed "day for a day" measure in the case of the elder coincides with the date of the converse "day for a day" measure in the case of the younger. This represents a meeting point in time equidistant between the birth dates of these two individuals, a halfway point which should theoretically provide an astrological summary of the inherent possibilities of a relationship between them. This common point in time will be found to represent accurately the potentiality of the relationship (and this potentiality always exists, whether or not it materializes through an actual meeting between the two.)

When the place of birth of two individuals differed, it also seemed logical to calculate a halfway point in space by finding the mean of the two latitudes and the two longitudes and basing the house cusps on the tables for the mean latitude.

The writer's experience over the years has satisfied him that the relationship horoscope based on this formula (i.e., the determination of space-time medians) is valid in its own right and, since no relationship is static, this chart can be directed by any preferred system with excellent results. Unless the relationship was formed at birth (as it would have been, for instance, between parent and child) it will usually be found that the first meeting has occurred under strong positive directions which also activate key areas in the nativities of the two concerned. It follows that, except in the most unusual cases, such indications of the time of the first meeting can only be calculated in retrospect, after a relationship has been formed. Even so, they can provide a valuable check on the accuracy of the relationship chart. The impact of the relationship on both of the parties concerned will be shown by the cross-aspects between the relationship horoscope and each individual nativity.

When the times of birth of the partners are unknown it is obviously not possible to define an exact meeting point in time but, as in the case of natal horoscopes, a good deal of useful information may be elicited from a consideration of the sign positions of the planets on the day and their mutual aspects. If the exact time of only one of the partners is known, this too will preclude an exact placing of planets in houses. In such cases a sunrise chart or solar house chart is a useful substitute, though less comprehensive than an exact horoscope. There is also the possibility that a wrongly stated time of birth can distort the house positions but these hazards are not, of course, confined to the comparison horoscope.

Twins born close together in time will have a relationship chart that almost mirrors their nativities, symbolizing the sometimes astonishing rapport that may exist between them. This emphasizes the point that, in order to expand the information given by the comparison chart, it is necessary to observe how each partner's nativity relates to it.

The method of calculating the relationship horoscope is as follows:

1. Note down the birth date of both partners and calculate the exact number of days between the two birth dates. If the period spans several years, the calculation may be expressed in years and days, provided due attention is paid to the incidence of Leap Years.

2. Divide the time difference by two.

The following example will show how the calculation should be made:

Duke of Windsor	Date of Birth	23rd June, 1894
Duchess of Windsor	Date of Birth	19th June, 1896
		(leap year)
Difference between the two birth dates		1 year 362 days
Divide by two		363½ days
Halfway date		21st-22nd June, 1895*

In order to simplify the calculation of the mid-point in time between the two birth times, each should first be expressed in terms of Local Mean Time. The final result will give the Local Mean Time for the Meridian of the relationship horoscope.

Duke of Windsor	10.12 p.m. L.M.T.
(L.M.T. at London is the same as G.M.T.)	
Duchess of Windsor	5.15 a.m. L.M.T.
Difference between 10.12 p.m. on 21st June and	
— 5.15 a.m. on 22nd June	7h 03m
Divide by two	3h 31½m
Add 3h 31½m to earlier time to give meeting	
point in time	1h 43½m a.m. L.M.T.
	22nd June

In order to make the above calculation as clear as possible it should perhaps be added that 21st June, 1895, is 363 days after the Duke's day of birth, while 22nd June, 1895 is 363 days before the Duchess's day of birth. The 363 days after the Duke's birthday are

---

*When the time distance between two dates of birth does not divide by two, it is necessary to take a period of 48 hours in order to define the exact half-way point between two birth times.

not completed until 10.12 p.m. L.M.T. on 21st June and the 363 days prior to the Duchess's birthday are not completed until 5.15 a.m. on the 22nd June.

It will usually be found that this mid-point in time does not produce a Midheaven which exactly concides with the mid-point between the two natal Midheavens. This is because our measurement of time is an approximation made necessary by the irregularity of the earth's orbit and does not exactly tally with Sun Time. The calculated time is used to determine which of the opposing mid-points between the two Midheavens to choose, in this case 26 Capricorn 27. The resultant Local Mean Time can then be adjusted by the small amount necessary to produce the required Midheaven.

The meeting point in space is determined as follows:

Latitude of births
 Duke of Windsor   51 N 32
 Duchess of Windsor   39 N 18
  Total   90(N)50
  Divide by two   45 N 25

Had the place of the Duke's birth been 51 S. 32 it would have been necessary to have subtracted the half difference (45°25') from the larger number:

 Latitude of birth   51 S 32
 Subtract half difference   45   25
 Latitude of relationship horoscope   6 S 07

The meeting place Longitude is calculated similarly:

 Duke of Windsor   0 W 05
 Duchess of Windsor   76 W 38
  Total   76(W)43
  Divide by two   38 W 21 ½
      =Longitude of relationship horoscope

If one Longitude is East of Greenwich and the other West, the same procedure as in the case of North and South Latitude applies, as in the example given above.

It does not matter whether the point in space determined by the mid-point Latitude and Longitude falls in the middle of an ocean —it is purely symbolic and a spacial median.

The data for the relationship horoscope has now been established and the chart can now be calculated for 1.44 a.m. L.M.T. 22nd June, 1895, (Lat. 45N25; Long. 38W21) in the usual way.

This type of relationship horoscope need not be limited to contacts between living people. Comparisons may be made with outstanding figures of the past or with ancestors of the native, who, by virtue of their works or the general quality of their life have made some special impact on the native. The horoscopes of towns or cities that have played a significant part in the native's life may similarly be combined with the native's horoscope, provided the necessary data relating to the town or city is available. Organizations with which the native is connected may also prove to be a fruitful subject for examination by this method. Should he so desire, there is no reason why the native should not use the system to see how he might relate to any public figure or person whose data are known to him, always bearing in mind that though the number of potential contacts he might make is vast, in actual fact he can only establish meaningful contact with a relatively limited number of his fellow beings.

In the next chapter we shall examine in some detail the application of some of the methods of comparison outlined in previous chapters, together with examples of relationship horoscopes derived from partnerships involving the interplay of a variety of human passions and predicaments.

CHAPTER 10

Examples of Horoscope Comparison

The Windsors

The romance between Edward VIII of England and Mrs. Wallis Warfield Simpson aroused enormous interest from the moment it first became known that the King was considering the possibility of making her his wife. From the start it was made clear to King Edward by the British Establishment that such a marriage would give rise to intricate constitutional problems. The King England is the titular head of the Church of England, and that Church was not prepared to give its blessing to the remarriage of those whose previous marriages had ended in divorce. King Edward was unable to persuade Parliament to modify this situation in any way, and so he found himself faced with the choice of marrying Mrs. Simpson (who had been married twice before) and renouncing the throne, or staying single and retaining his kingly status. Thus it was that he chose to abdicate and marry the bride of his choice. As a result, he and his wife were virtually ostracized by the royal family and they never came back to live in England, preferring to establish their main residence in the more gracious atmosphere of Paris.

An English astrologer had predicted many years before the event that the Duke of York would ascend the throne. As he was only the second in line of succession, such an elevation could only have occurred through the removal of his elder brother, the Prince of Wales. Writing in the August, 1894, issue of *The Astrologers' Magazine,* Sepharial commented on the Prince of Wales' horoscope:

> "In marriage, the native will seek abroad for a partner and an attachment outside his own country will be contracted, but owing to the planet Uranus being retrograde, the affair will be liable to fall through.... The figure lacks entirely the essentials of a royal horoscope and the position of Jupiter, ruler of the tenth house in its fall in Gemini, confirms this prognostic."

Raphael, commenting on the same horoscope in the 1924 Ephemeris, wrote:

> "It is not altogether a very fortunate map. It cannot really be said that the figure is one which would be expected for a successful monarch. In regard to marriage the influences are conflicting."

The position of Jupiter in Leo, close to the Midheaven of the Duke of York's horoscope and in wide trine to Mars (also in closer sextile to Pluto, though Raphael would not have known this at the time he made his prediction), was the reason for Raphael's forecast that the King's second son would eventually succeed to the throne. A well-supported Jupiter in Leo in the tenth almost inevitably means a rise in life, and for a Prince, the only rise commensurate with his position is to be crowned King!

The question thus arises as to whether the abdication of Edward VIII was, in fact, part of the cosmic plan. His brother's nativity indicated a rise in life, and as long as Edward remained on the throne, this rise would be denied to his brother. There are also deeper implications. It is a proven precept of mundane astrology that the horoscope of a ruler reflects the destiny of the country he rules. Within three years of King Edward's abdication, Britain was at war. Had Edward VIII still been on the throne, Raphael's prognostication: "Should he come to the throne we should be involved in a disastrous war" would have been implemented and Britain would have had a monarch whose horoscope was far less favorable to the conduct of a successful long term war than his brother's.

Jupiter in the Duke of York's horoscope was retrograde in 8°36' Leo. In Mrs. Simpson's nativity it was in 8°48' Leo. Mrs. Simpson was some six months younger than the Duke of York and in that period Jupiter had turned direct and returned to almost the same position that it occupied in the Duke's natal chart. The retrograde Jupiter in the Duke of York's horoscope may represent the round about way in which he came to the throne. Edward VIII's horoscope has 8°14' Aquarius rising. This is cast for a slightly later time than the officially stated time of birth, which gives 3° Aquarius rising. My own rectification was completed many years ago and the Ascendant was not arranged to fit the particular requirements of the present exercise!

When the Horizon or Meridian of one person's horoscope conjoins one of the planets in another's nativity, he will be the means of activating that planet in the other's horoscope. Thus it was that the man who later became the Duke of Windsor was the means of elevating his brother to the throne, and of making it possible for his bride to become a Duchess.

The Pre-Natal Epoch, which confirms the birth horizon, is cast for 19th October, 1893, when Venus is in 8 Sagittarius, a degree from the natal Midheaven of the Duke of Windsor. Venus in Sagittarius is a classic indication of marriage to a foreigner and its placement on the natal Midheaven shows how the romance involved matters relating to status and authority, as well as indicating the great public interest it aroused. Nowhere was this interest more lively and acute than in the United States, where the bride was born. It is no surprise, therefore, to find that the position of Uranus in the U.S.A. horoscope falls in 8°50' Gemini, in opposition to the Duke's natal Midheaven and pre-natal Venus and that, in one of the several versions of the United States' horoscope, the same degree of Gemini rises.

These positions combine to give a Venus-Uranus opposition involved with the royal Meridian. This piquantly focuses attention on the fact that a foreign bride (Venus in Sagittarius) and an American divorce (U.S.A. Uranus) combined to bring into question the possibility of Edward VIII marrying a divorcee and still remaining on the throne.

It is worth noting that the Part of Marriage in Mrs. Simpson's horoscope is in 21°03' Capricorn, with an antiscion degree in 8°57' Sagittarius. The U.S.A. Venus in 2°20' Cancer is almost exactly conjunct the Duke's natal Sun.

It is also not without significance that the horoscope for the United Kingdom (7th December, 1922, London, 3.21 p.m. G.M.T.) has 9°43' Gemini rising and Uranus in 9°49' Pisces. Additionally, the Sun is in 14°45' Sagittarius in the seventh house (royal marriage to a foreigner) and opposes the Duke's Neptune (renunciation, abdication) in 14°00' Gemini.

There is an exact balance between the horoscopes of the Windsors in terms of the distribution of the planets by hemisphere. The

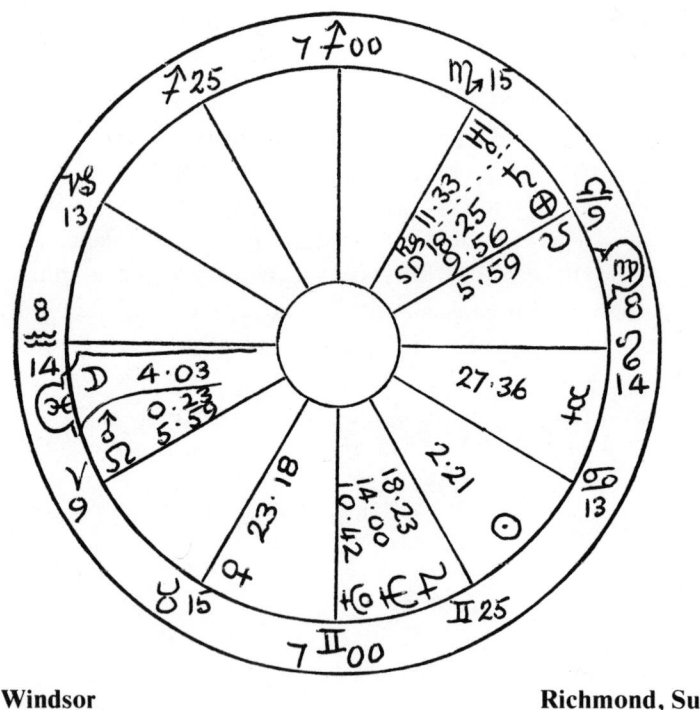

Duke of Windsor
23 June 1894

Richmond, Surrey
10.12 p.m. G.M.T.

Duchess has seven planets in the Eastern Hemisphere; the Duke has seven planets in the Western Hemisphere. A majority of planets in the eastern half of the horoscope signifies that the native will have the opportunity to take the initiative in life and that his fate rests largely in his own hands. A majority of planets in the western half suggests that the native's freedom of action is restricted to some extent by his duties and obligations to others. Matters of protocol and the demanding standards expected of the monarch have always operated as an inhibiting factor in the life of the ruler of the country, and the Duke of Windsor, with the independent Aquarius rising, the Ascendant squared by an elevated Uranus and the assertive Mars squar-

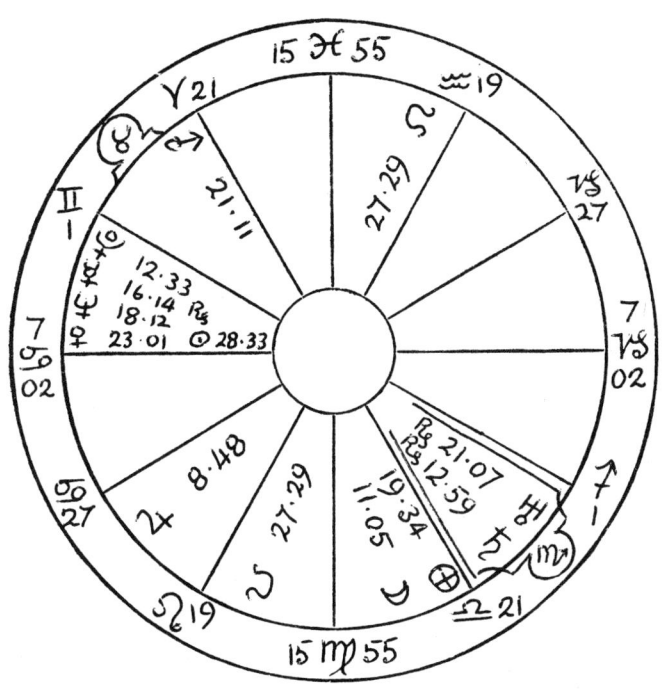

Duchess of Windsor
19 June, 1896

Blue Ridge Summit,
Baltimore
5.22 a.m. E.S.T.

assertive Mars squaring the Sun, was no doubt often more exasperated than many of his predecessors by the necessity of conforming to the demanding requirements of the monarchy. The Moon in Pisces, disposing of the kingly fifth house Sun, introduced the element of renunciation, which led up to the abdication, as a primary factor in his psychological make-up.

A further confirmation of this situation occurs in the 1922 horoscope of the United Kingdom, which practically coincided with the Duke's first Saturn return. Saturn in his nativity is in Libra in the eighth house, relating to his capacity to act responsibly and wisely in matters connected with marriage and challenging him to effect a transformation in his whole attitude to the acceptance of responsibility and to cultivate a keener awareness of the direction in which his duty might lie.

The majority of the planets in the Duchess's horoscope by quadruplicity and triplicity, fall in mutable and air signs, producing a Gemini synthesis and accentuating the twelfth house, which contains five bodies in Gemini. Four of the Duke's planets fall in her twelfth house, including Jupiter, which frustrated his attempt to secure royal status for her, especially as Jupiter is debilitated in Gemini, though she did, of course, attain the rank of Duchess.

The Duke had four planets in cardinal and four in mutable signs, and four planets in air and four in water signs so that there is no clear cut majority on which to base a synthesis. Both luminaries in water signs and an angular Neptune indicate a somewhat stronger emphasis on the water element, matching his partner's Ascendant, while her Gemini majority blended with his air Ascendant. His three Gemini planets, operating at the instinctive fourth house level, enabled him to achieve an effective understanding with his Gemini partner.

In matters relating to romance and marriage, the Venus zodiac plays a principal role. If we equate the position of Venus in Wallis Simpson's nativity with 0 Aries by moving it backwards 2 signs 23 degrees 1 minute, we can find the location of the other planets relative to Venus in 0 Aries by deducting the same amount of arc from their longitudes. The following important contacts then appear:

UNDERSTANDING HUMAN RELATIONS

Duchess of Windsor
(Venus Zodiac)

Duke of Windsor
(Tropical Zodiac)

Venus 0 Aries .... Mars 0⅓ Aries
Sun 5½ Aries .... N.Node 6 Aries
Mercury 23 Pisces,
    Mars/Pluto 23½ Aquarius .... Venus 23½ Taurus
Moon 18¼ Cancer .... Saturn 18½ Libra
Mars 28 Capricorn. .... Mercury 27⅔ Cancer
Pluto 19 Pisces .... Jupiter 18⅓ Gemini
Asc. 14 Aries,
    Venus/Uranus 14 Gemini .... Neptune 14 Gemini
Sun/Venus 2¾ Aries .... Sun 2⅓ Cancer

Equating the Duke's Venus with 0 Aries we get the following positions in the Duke's horoscope, in terms of the Venus Zodiac, which form close aspects with the Tropical positions of the planets in his partner's horoscope:

Duke of Windsor
(Venus Zodiac)

Duchess of Windsor
(Tropical Zodiac)

Asc. 14¾ Sag. (own trop.
  Neptune 14 Gemini;
  Jupiter/Pluto 14⅔ Gemini). .... Mercury/Pluto 13¾ Gemini
Moon 10½ Capricorn .... Moon 11¼ Libra
Mars 7 Aquarius; Sun 9 Taurus
  (own Asc. 8¼ Aquarius). .... Jupiter 8¾ Leo
Uranus 18 Virgo; Pluto 17½ Aries
  (own Jupiter 18⅓ Gemini). .... Neptune 18¼ Gemini
Neptune 20½ Aries .... Uranus 21 Scorpio

Activities involving the Venus principle will bring into play, in the nativity, the special relationship of each planet to Venus as indicated by its planetary distance from Venus. This distance can be expressed in terms of a 360 degree zodiac (which is nothing more than a cycle of relationship) in which Venus plays the role of 0 Aries. When the Duke planned to marry Mrs. Simpson, he activated the positions of the planets adjusted to the Venus Zodiac.

Thus it was that he met the situation with an obstinate refusal to compromise (Mars Aries □ Sun Cancer) which was related immediately to his natal horizon through the conjunction of the adjusted Mars and the square of the adjusted Sun involving his Tropical Ascendant. These two planets in terms of their position in the Venus Zodiac then formed a T-square with his partner's Jupiter in Leo so that the question of her being refused any kind of royal status acted to increase his determination to go ahead with the marriage at all costs. His adjusted Ascendant also fell in opposition to his natal Neptune, which was therefore placed in a seventh house position as soon as matters relating to marriage arose in the Duke's life.

The combination of the radical fourth house Neptune with Jupiter, the debilitated ruler of the tenth house, had already led Sepharial to suggest that "the figure entirely lacks the essentials of a royal horoscope." The addition of Pluto (undiscovered at the time of Sepharial's pronouncement) to this conjunction acted to intensify the restless desire for freedom indicated by the original conjunction, while at the same time adding the element of compulsion in that the constitutional requirements of his royal position demanded that he should observe certain moral and legal niceties that others in less exalted positions could happily ignore. Faced with the choice of either renouncing the throne of England or the woman he loved, he chose the former, as indicated by the radical fourth house stellium.

Increasing attention is now being paid to the special connection of the lunar nodes with relationships of all kinds, based on the fact that they mark the points where the Moon crosses the ecliptic, putting itself in alignment with the Sun and Earth. Significant relationships in the life are usually those which have previously been established in a past incarnation. It may well be that when positions of the natal planets have been translated into their equivalent in the Nodal or Draconic Zodiac they may show, through their cross-aspects to other nativities, those contacts which have been carried over from a previous incarnation. When the Duchess of Windsor's natal planets are translated into terms of the Draconic Zodiac the following important contacts then appear:

UNDERSTANDING HUMAN RELATIONS

Duchess of Windsor
(Draconic Zodiac)

Duke of Windsor
(Tropical Zodiac)

Mars 23½ Taurus . . . . Venus 23½ Taurus
Sun 1 Leo . . . . Mars 0½ Aries
Asc. 9½ Leo (own Jupiter 8¾ Leo) . . . . Asc. 8¼ Aquarius
Jupiter 11 Virgo. . . . . Pluto 10¾ Gemini
M.C. 19 Aries. . . . . Saturn 18½ Libra
Moon 13 Scorpio (own Saturn 13 Scorpio) . . . . . Uranus 11½ Scorpio
Saturn 15½ Sagittarius
  (own Mercury 16¼ Gemini) . . . . Jupiter/Neptune 16 Gemini

The first two contacts listed are particularly related to attraction between the sexes while the Duchess's adjusted Ascendant is almost on the Duke's natal seventh cusp (marriage in a previous life?). Additionally, this adjusted Ascendant falls within a degree of her natal Jupiter, bringing into play the question of royal status. Status is also connected with the Midheaven, and her adjusted Midheaven falls in opposition to his natal Saturn in Libra (marriage difficulties).

Since the proposed marriage entailed a great deal of heart-searching on the part of the Duke and his intended bride, it is not surprising that a certain number of the contacts listed do not indicate an easy path.

The Duke's planets, translated into his Draconic Zodiac, produce the following contacts:

Duke of Windsor
(Draconic Zodiac)

Duchess of Windsor
(Tropical Zodiac)

Moon 28 Aquarius   N.Node 27½ Aquarius
Sun 26 Gemini . . . . Sun 28½ Gemini
Mars 24 Pisces . . . . Sun/Venus 25¾ Gemini
                                                            Venus 23 Gemini
Venus 17½ Taurus . . . . Saturn/Uranus 17 Scorpio
Neptune 8 Gemini (opposition own M.C.) . . . . Jupiter 8¾ Leo
Jupiter 12 Gemini   Pluto 12½ Gemini
Saturn 12½ Libra . . . . Moon 11¼ Libra

The conjunction of the Draconic Moon with his partner's Lunar North Node is highly significant and equivalent to a Moon-Ascendant conjunction. With the Draconic Sun also involved, the relationship is shown to be a particularly close one, while the Mars-Venus square also denotes a strong physical attraction. Neptune is translated to a position exactly opposing the Duke's own radical Midheaven, suggesting that the tendency to abdicate from positions of responsibility was a pre-disposition brought over from the past. His re-allocated Jupiter-Saturn trine now coincides almost exactly with his partner's Moon-Pluto trine.

Because questions of title and position were involved one would expect to find the Solar Zodiac positions activated. The re-adjusted planets of both partners make no fewer than seven close cross-aspects in each case. The following appear to be the most significant:

Duke of Windsor   **Duchess of Windsor**
(Solar Zodiac)   (Tropical Zodiac)

Venus 21 Aquarius. . . . . Mars 21 Aries, Venus 23 Gemini,
                                                                  Uranus 21 Scorpio
Mars 28 Sagittarius. . . . . Sun 28½ Gemini
Uranus 9 Leo (opposition own Asc.)
   Pluto 9 Pisces (quincunx own Fortuna) . . . . Jupiter 8¾ Leo
Neptune 12 Pisces . . . . Pluto 12½ Gemini

Duchess of Windsor   **Duke of Windsor**
(Solar Zodiac)   (Tropical Zodiac)

M.C. 18 Sagittarius (opposition own Neptune) . . Jupiter 18½ Gemini
Mars 22¾ Capricorn (sextile own Uranus)
Uranus 22¼ Leo (sextile own Venus) . . . . Venus 23 Taurus
Pluto 14 Pisces . . . . Neptune 14 Gemini
Asc. 8½ Aries (trine own Jupiter)

In both cases there is a Neptune-Pluto square and a Venus/Mars/Uranus configuration involving a Venus-Uranus square. In addition, the Duchess's Pluto/Mercury/Neptune conjunction in the Solar Zodiac now brackets the position of her Tropical Midheaven.

UNDERSTANDING HUMAN RELATIONS

The question of where the Duke's duty lay focuses attention upon the Saturn Zodiac. Most of the cross-aspects formed by planets transposed into this zodiac are strenuous ones. The following appear to be the most important:

Duke of Windsor **Duchess of Windsor**
(Saturn Zodiac) (Tropical Zodiac)

Sun 14 Sagittarius
   (opposition own Neptune)......... Mercury/Pluto 14⅔ Gemini
Moon 15½ Leo .... Saturn/Uranus 17 Scorpio
Mars 12 Virgo (□ own Neptune/Pluto) .... Pluto 12½ Gemini
Uranus 23 Aries;   Mars 21¼ Aries
   Pluto 22¼ Scorpio...................... Venus 23 Gemini,
M.C. 18½ Taurus................... Venus/Mars 18⅔ Taurus

Duchess of Windsor **Duke of Windsor**
(Saturn Zodiac) (Tropical Zodiac)

Asc. 24 Scorpio........................... Venus 23½ Taurus
Venus 10 Scorpio........ Uranus 11½ Scorpio; Pluto 10¾ Gemini
Mars 8¼ Virgo .... M.C. 7 Sagittarius
Uranus 8½ Aries (□ own Asc.;
   trine own Jupiter)...................... Asc. 8¼ Aquarius

In view of the prominent role played by Jupiter in the Duchess's nativity and its conjunction with the Duke's seventh cusp, it is interesting to note that a number of significant cross-aspects emerge when the planets of each partner are transposed into the Jupiter Zodiac. The following appear to be the most important:

Duke of Windsor **Duchess of Windsor**
(Jupiter Zodiac) (Tropical Zodiac)

Moon 15½ Sagittarius   M.C. 16½ Pisces,
   (opposition own Neptune)............. Mercury 16¼ Gemini
Uranus 23 Leo (□ own Venus)................ Venus 23 Gemini
Neptune 25½ Pisces .... Sun/Venus 25¾ Gemini
Pluto 22½ Pisces; Asc. 20 Scorpio............ Uranus 21 Scorpio
M.C. 18⅔ Virgo (□ own Jupiter).......... Neptune 18½ Gemini

259

Duchess of Windsor
(Jupiter Zodiac)

Duke of Windsor
(Tropical Zodiac)

Sun 19¾ Aquarius
N.Node 18¾ Libra. . . . . Saturn 18½ Libra
Mercury 7½ Aquarius (opposition own Jupiter);
    Neptune 9½ Aquarius. Asc. 8¼ Aquarius
Venus 14½ Aquarius. . . . . Neptune 14 Gemini,
    Jupiter/Pluto 14⅔ Gemini
Mars 12¼ Sagittarius. . . . . Neptune/Pluto 12¼ Gemini
Asc. 28¼ Aquarius (trine own Sun)

Jupiter 18½ Gemini

Some of the antiscion degrees throw additional light on the relationship:

Duchess of Windsor
(Antiscions)

Duke of Windsor
(Natal)

Uranus 9 Aquarius. . . . . Asc. 8¼ Aquarius
Sun 1½ Cancer. . . . . Sun 2⅓ Cancer
Mars 9 Virgo;
    Venus 7 Cancer (conjunct own Asc.). . . . . M.C./Pluto 8⅔ Pisces
Moon 19 Pisces . . . . Jupiter 18⅓ Gemini

The antiscion of the Duchess's Uranus falling on the Duke's Ascendant indicates that she was a person who had the potential ability to change the course of his life dramatically, while he was able to actualize the promise of her fifth house Uranus. This could be interpreted as signifying unusual love affairs which challenged her, through the sign position of the planet and its quincunx to Venus in the twelfth house—renunciation—to effect some measure of self-transformation in this area of life. The conjunction between the two Suns is a close link, while the emergence of Venus as an angular factor through its involvement by antiscion with her own Ascendant not only registers the fact that her romance with the Duke brought her world-wide prominence but also matches the angular position of the Duke's pre-natal Venus, which fell on his natal Midheaven.

Her antiscion Mars squared the Duke's Midheaven and more exactly conjoined his Midheaven/Pluto mid-point. It also fell on the United Kingdom (1922) Uranus and in square to the Ascendant of that horoscope.

The Duke's antiscion degrees forming contacts additional to those noted above are as follows (the relationship of the antiscion degrees based on the natal positions in the right hand column above are identical):

Duke of Windsor　　　　　　　　　　　　　**Duchess of Windsor**
　(Antiscions)　　　　　　　　　　　　　　　　　(Natal)

Moon 26 Libra . . . . Sun 28½ Gemini, N.Node 27½ Aquarius
Venus 6½ Leo (opposition own Asc.). . . . . Jupiter 8¾ Leo
M.C. 23 Capricorn . . . . Part of Marriage 21 Capricorn

In terms of the comparison between sign and house position there is an interesting soli-lunar interchange. The Duke had the Moon in Pisces matching his partner's Sun in the twelfth house and he had the Sun in Cancer, matching her Moon in the fourth house. Additionally, he had Venus in the third house, she had Venus in Gemini. He had Saturn in the eighth house, matching her Saturn in Scorpio. The soli-lunar interchanges focus attention upon the fourth and twelfth houses and their connection with situations involving virtual exile and renunciation, while the Venus-Saturn interchanges stress the depth of the relationship and some of the disappointments it entailed.

There is a revealing conjunction, in terms of house position, between the Duke's Sun and his partner's Saturn. Both bodies are respectively about 12/30 of the way through the Placidian fifth house and therefore, according to the system of domal analogues (see page 59), both are in a position equivalent to 12 Leo. The Sun in the fifth house is a classic indicator of kingly power, while Saturn in the fifth acts to limit, frustrate or deny such power, or to make the native uncomfortably aware of the responsibilities of his position. Through his partner, the Duke had cause to weigh these responsibilities with great earnestness and to decide where his true path of duty lay.

The Sun and three of the Duke's planets fall in his partner's twelfth house, emphasizing the importance of her own stellium there. His Mars in Aries falls in her tenth house, but his energetic efforts to persuade the government to introduce a law permitting a morganatic marriage, which would have allowed him to marry a commoner and remain King, were unavailing as his Sun and Jupiter were imprisoned in her twelfth house. The challenge of the twelfth house stimulates the native to arrive at a comprehensive understanding of life, so that all his problems can be seen in their true perspective and then dealt with in such a way as to resolve all tensions.

The apparently trivial fact that both were addicted keenly to solving jig-saw puzzles is probably not without significance, for this pastime involves the development of a sense of overall perspective and an awareness of how all the parts can be related to each other and fit together to make an ordered and significant whole.

Her Gemini stellium fell in his fourth house, activating in particular the Neptune-Pluto conjunction, which often cuts a person off from his birth place, and gives a tendency to seek to establish new roots on a more universal basis.

A comparison of the interplay between the pre-natal epoch planets of one partner and the birth planets of the other is often highly revealing. The Duke's pre-natal epoch, cast for 19th October, 1893, 1:41 a.m. G.M.T. at London, makes the following contacts with his partner's nativity:

Duke of Windsor　　　　　　　　　　　　**Duchess of Windsor**
(Pre-natal Epoch)　　　　　　　　　　　　　　(Nativity)

Sun 26 Libra............Sun 28½ Gemini, N.Node 27½ Aquarius
Moon 8 Aquarius; Venus 8¼ Sagittarius
　　(conjunct natal M.C.)......................Jupiter 8¾ Leo
Mercury 14¼ Scorpio......................Saturn 13 Scorpio
Mars 11 Libra ....Moon 11¼ Libra

Each of the faster moving bodies forms close and significant aspects to the Duchess's nativity, while the Moon-Mars conjunction is a contact frequently found in relationships where sexual attraction is involved.

The Duchess's pre-natal epoch, cast for 13th September, 1895, 1:09 p.m., E.S.T., Baltimore, makes the following contacts with her partner's horoscope:

Duchess of Windsor (Pre-natal Epoch)	**Duke of Windsor** (Nativity)
Venus-Mars 29 Virgo;	
Jupiter 1½ Leo	Mars 0⅓ Aries
Saturn 4 Scorpio	Moon 4 Pisces
N.Node 12 Pisces	Neptune/Pluto 12 Gemini

The Duchess was born at Blue Ridge Summit, Baltimore, at a latitude of 39N.18. It is a curiosity that the Duke's birthplace, Richmond, near London, has a latitude of 51N.32, so that each birthplace has almost the co-latitude of the other. The Duchess's Vertex falls at 24½ Scorpio in opposition to the Duke's Venus, while the Duke's Vertex at 10 Virgo stands at the mid-point of his partner's Moon-Jupiter sextile and in square to his own Pluto.

THE RELATIONSHIP HOROSCOPE

The relationship chart, the calculation of which was explained in the previous chapter, is particularly revealing. The Moon is applying to the conjunction of the Sun, and Venus and Mars are in conjunction, two of the classic indications of sexual compatibility, and a clear pointer to the possibility of marriage between the two. In addition, the mid-point of the luminaries coincides with the mid-point of the Duke's Sun/Jupiter and the Duchess's Sun/Venus. Venus and Mars are both in the royal sign Leo, emphasizing the question of royal status that was to arise, and the square of Uranus to Venus indicates the Duchess's previous divorces that were eventually to deny the possibility of her husband being allowed to remain on the throne after he had married her. The very close trine between the Sun and Saturn shows the strength of the partnership and the fact that it endured until their relationship was terminated by the Duke's death. The very close conjunction of Mercury and Jupiter in Cancer denotes a great deal of mental sympathy.

The Lunar Nodes fall across the Duchess's Meridian, with its special connection with public and private life and also with position status and the establishment of roots. The square of Saturn, ruling

264   SYNASTRY

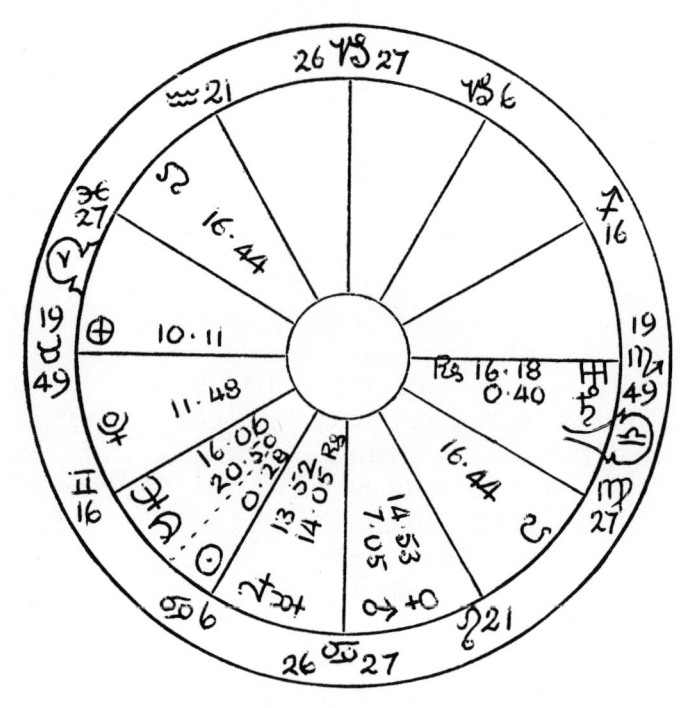

Windsors/Relationship
22 June 1895

45N25, 38W19
4.27 a.m. G.M.T.

the tenth, to Mars in Leo can be taken as an indication of the inflexible attitude of the British Establishment towards the marriage of the monarch to a divorcee, and their refusal to bring in legislation to make it possible for the King to marry and still remain on the throne.

The Moon is close to the Duke's Jupiter and the mid-point of the Duchess's Venus/Neptune, while Fortuna opposes the Duke's Uranus in Scorpio (which is quincunx Pluto) and opposes the Duchess's Saturn (also quincunx Pluto). The early years of the partnership were no doubt a highly testing time for them both, suggesting possibilities of self-transformation through abnegation and self-control, together with a new dedication towards some chosen path of duty.

In 1931, when they first met, the converse Sun in the relationship horoscope was in trine to the radical Midheaven and the progressed Venus was applying to a trine of the Ascendant, of which it was the ruler. The progressed Ascendant had reached the conjunction of the radical Sun and the trine of the radical Saturn. The converse relationship Midheaven was a degree away from the opposition of the Duchess's radical Venus.

At this time the Duke's progressed Mars was in 21½ Aries, conjunct his partner's Mars. His converse Descendant at 27 Gemini had moved back to the conjunction of her radical Sun. The Duchess's progressed Midheaven was in 20 Aries, bringing her progressed Ascendant to 2 Leo, conjunct her progressed Sun and converse Jupiter. Her progressed Mars squared the relationship Venus and opposed the relationship Uranus, while her progressed Jupiter had just passed the conjunction of the relationship Venus.

When they married, in 1937, the Duke's converse Sun was in conjunction with the relationship Ascendant and the Duchess's converse Sun, traveling a degree away from her partner's, had just passed the relationship ascendant. In addition, her progressed Mars was in the same degree as her converse Sun, applying to the opposition of her progressed Uranus which had, characteristically, been on the seventh cusp of the relationship horoscope during the whole period of their relationship. It was many years before it finally moved away from this close opposition of the relationship Ascendant. This interplay of disruptive aspects mirrors accurately the crisis precipitated by their proposed marriage.

In the relationship horoscope itself the progressed Sun had reached the mid-point of Venus/Mars and the progressed Mercury opposed the Midheaven. At the same time the converse relationship Venus had moved back to 27 Gemini, separating from the conjunction of the Duchess's natal Sun and in trine to her North Node, while the converse relationship Mars in 11 Cancer was in square to her Moon and in trine to the Duke's Uranus.

When the Duke died, the converse relationship Venus had reached 16 Taurus forming a T-square with its own radical position and Uranus, thus bringing out the full force of the square between the two planets in the radix. The converse Mars in the relationship figure was in 20 Gemini, at the mid-point of the Duchess's Venus-Neptune conjunction and in quincunx to her radical Uranus. The converse relationship Midheaven in 12 Scorpio was aligned with the Duchess's natal Saturn in that degree and her husband's Uranus in 11½ Scorpio, while the progressed Ascendant was applying to the square of the radical Saturn in Scorpio.

Associate Angles

Finally, a survey of the Associate Angles (see page 61) shows that a number of important contacts appear when these are calculated. The couple first met in London, the Duke's birthplace, so that the angles in both cases are based on the Tables of Houses for the latitude of London.

Duke of Windsor (Associate Angles)		**Duchess of Windsor (Natal Positions)**
When Sun rises	M.C. is 27 Aquarius	N.Node 27 Aquarius
When Moon is on M.C.	Asc. is 8 Cancer	Asc. 7 Cancer
When Moon is on I.C.	Asc. is 16 Scorpio	Saturn/Uranus 17 Scorpio
When Moon rises	M.C. is 20 Sagittarius	Venus/Nept. 20½ Gemini
When Venus is on I.C.	Asc. is 18 Capricorn	Sun/Jupiter 18 Cancer
When Venus sets	M.C. is 15 Virgo	M.C. 16⅓ Pisces
When Mars sets	M.C. is 0 Cancer	Sun 28½ Gemini
When Uranus is on M.C.	Asc. is 5½ Cancer	Asc. 7 Cancer
When Uranus rises	M.C. is 27 Leo	S.Node 27 Leo
When Uranus sets	M.C. is 17½ Capricorn	Sun/Jupiter 18 Cancer
When Pluto is on M.C.	Asc. is 15½ Virgo	M.C. 16⅓ Pisces
When Pluto sets	M.C. is 12 Libra	Moon 11 Libra

The associate angles of six planets only have been tabulated. Out of a possible 24 contacts, 12 are present (only conjunctions and oppositions should normally be considered, and these confined to close orbs). It is significant that three of the Moon's associate angles make contact with the Duchess's planets (the Moon being a general significator of the wife) and that the divorce planet Uranus is also involved in three such contacts.

The Duchess's associate angles calculated for her birthplace produce very few striking contacts and confirm the dictum that the angles should be calculated for the place where the native happens to be at the time of the forming of a significant relationship. Here are the results based on the angles calculated for London. They are less numerous than those listed above. In view of the prominent part played by the Duchess's Jupiter in the relationship it is not surprising to find that it forms the basis of three significant contacts.

Duchess of Windsor **(Associate Angles)**		**Duke of Windsor** **(Natal Positions)**
When Moon is on M.C.	Asc. is 11 Sagittarius	Pluto 11 Gemini
When Mars is on I.C.	Asc. is 18 Sagittarius	Jupiter 18⅓ Gemini
When Jupiter is on I.C.	Asc. is 13 Gemini	Neptune/Pluto 13 Gemini
When Jupiter rises	M.C. is 18 Aries	Saturn 18 Libra
When Jupiter sets	M.C. is 7 Sagittarius	M.C. 7 Sagittarius
When Pluto is on I.C.	Asc. is 18 Aquarius	Jupiter/Saturn 18⅓ Leo
When Pluto rises	M.C. is 7½ Aquarius	Asc. 8¼ Aquarius
When Pluto sets	M.C. is 13 Libra	Saturn/Fortuna 14 Libra

FREUD, ADLER AND JUNG

Here we have a relationship based mostly on the intellectual level. For some years these prominent psychoanalysts worked together, inspired by a common interest in the fundamental causes of human behaviour. Freud was some 16 years older than Adler and 19 years older than Jung. He invited Adler to join him in his work in 1902 and the two men continued in partnership until 1911, when they found that they were no longer able to reconcile the theoretical differences that existed between them. Jung first met Freud in 1907 and thereafter became his foremost disciple but their association ended in 1912 when, as in the case of Adler, Jung found that his own theories were leading him away from Freud's doctrines.

Thus, while the three men were originally drawn together by a consuming interest in psychology and a mutual admiration for each other's talents in this field, they gradually reached a stage where their individual theories became so divergent that they had to separate in order to carry on their professional activities.

Sigmund Freud was the founder of psycho-analysis, with its methods of free association of ideas and an emphasis on the sex drive as the underlying motive of human action and reaction. Adler seemed to place more emphasis on the creativity angle and while the sex force has an obvious connection with creativity, Adler was not happy with what he considered to be Freud's over-accentuation of the sex factor. He stressed the importance of striving towards perfection to compensate for feelings of inferiority. He also considered that the root of all important problems are social, and that the society in which man operates has a great bearing on his psychological reactions. He stressed the uniqueness of each individual and this, combined with his emphasis upon the importance of the social unit, is very typical of his Sun in Aquarius. His solar position clashed directly with Freud's horoscope.

For Adler, the determining factors were subjective psychological factors, such as opinions and values, unified under the life goal. For Freud the determining factors were, in the last anlaysis, objective biological factors such as instincts, especially sex, and past events.

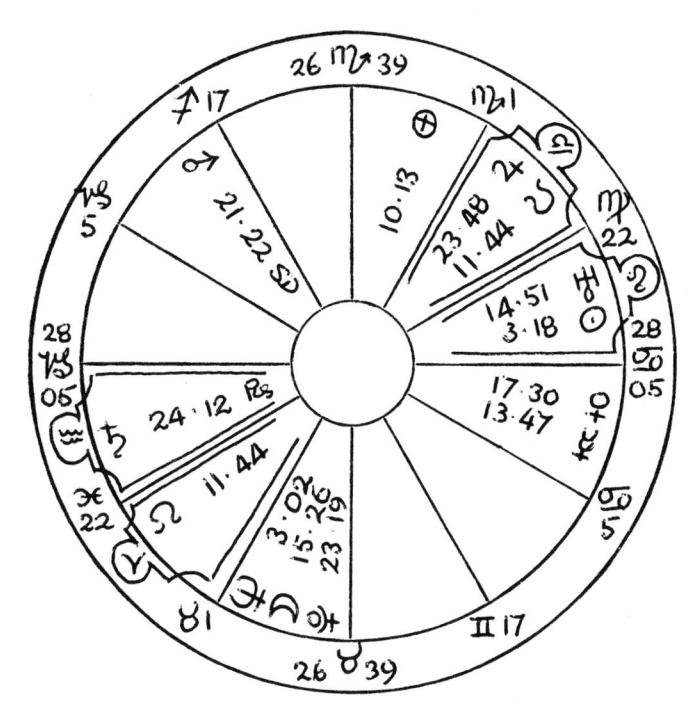

Carl Jung
26 July 1875

Thurgau, Switzerland
7.44 p.m. C.E.T.

Carl Gustav Jung was the founder of analytical psychology. He rejected Freud's emphasis on sex as a root of psychological disharmongy and placed less emphasis on childhood factors in favor of more recent conflicts. He stressed the will to live as a prime factor in determining an individual's psychology. His division of types into introvert and extrovert has posed its own problems to astrologers, who hoped to fit this neatly into a pattern of positive and negative signs. His classification of the four primary divisions of the mind as thinking, feeling, sensation and intuition has been a great help to many astrologers in broadening their understanding of the natal horoscope.

There are strong cross-aspects between all three horoscopes involving the luminaries and planets in close aspect to them:

Freud	Adler	Jung
Sun 16⅓ Taurus	Sun 18½ Aquarius	Moon 15½ Taurus
Mercury/Pluto 16 Taurus	Pluto 16 Taurus	Uranus 14¾ Leo
Uranus 20½ Taurus		
M.C. 14 Leo		

Freud's Sun-Uranus conjunction in the seventh house suggests tensions generated when working in partnership. Pluto on the seventh cusp in quincunx to Mars indicates a tendency to become involved in disputes with partners. (These aspects also indicated that the nature of his work was apt to attract to him people with deep-seated problems.) Between them the three men built up a powerful grand cross in the very center of the fixed signs. Jung's Moon, involved with the Suns of his two colleagues, no doubt indicated an initial attraction, but the triple involvement of Uranus, Pluto and their respective contacts with the luminaries in each case heralded the eventual break-up of their association.

Adler's Pluto on Freud's Sun could initially have operated to impress Freud with Adler's ability to delve into the subconscious but he probably went on delving too long for Freud's comfort, and began to cast doubts on some of the master's theories.

Pluto has a great deal to do with psychoanalysis. The function of Pluto is to transform and liberate. That which is not susceptible to this process is then either eliminated or destroyed. Its function in relation to consciousness is to make us aware of what may have remained dormant or hidden (though nevertheless acting as a strong motivating factor) so that we can come to terms with it and make it an integral part of our conscious awareness or transform it into a source of new power, at the same time making an effort to discard those elements which we can recognize as being of no further use. Hypnosis, sometimes used to probe the secrets of the mind, is also related to Pluto. All three men have Pluto prominent. Freud has it on the western horizon, Jung has it on the lower meridian and Adler has it mid-way between the eastern horizon and upper meridian

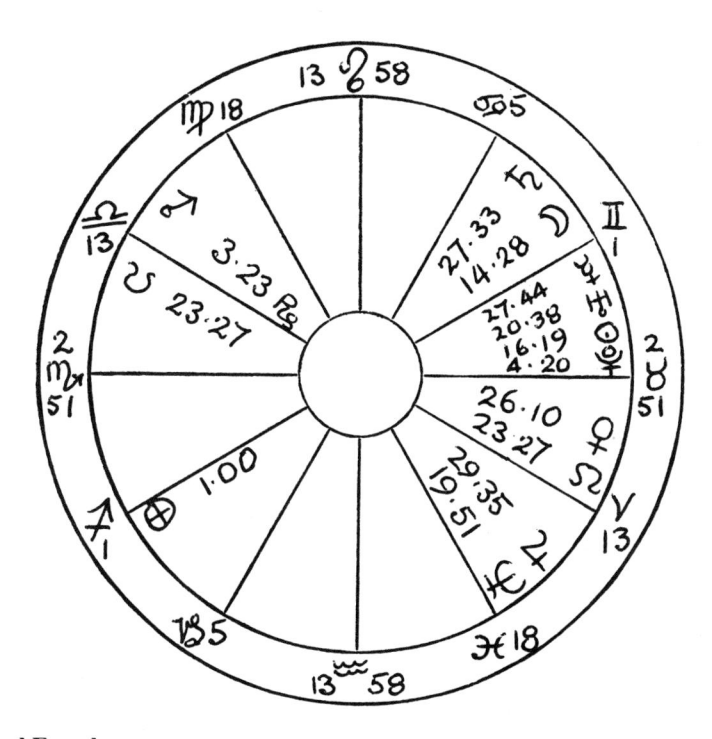

Sigmund Freud
6 May 1856

Freiburg, Moravia
6.15 p.m. C.E.T.

(which represents a mundane position of 15 Aquarius, emphasizing its zodiacal position in 16 Taurus).

The following additional Pluto connections between the three horoscopes are significant:

Freud	Adler	Jung
Pluto 4 Taurus	Moon 5 Taurus	Neptune 3 Taurus
Asc. 3 Scorpio	Antiscion Mars 4 Scorpio	Sun 3 Leo
(Sun pre-natal 25 Leo: Antiscion 5 Taurus)		Antiscion Pluto 6 ⅔ Leo

The close Sun-Neptune square in Jung's horoscope is a reminder of his careful analysis and interpretation of his patients' dreams as a means of solving their problems.

The strong Pluto emphasis in the contacts between the three nativities no doubt relates to the fact that it was the practice for newcomers to the Freudian school to be psychoanalysed. Doubtless the three colleagues took a keen interest in each other's psychological reactions!

Both Freud and Jung had Mars in quincunx to Pluto, so that the special relationship of the quincunx to the sign Scorpio places an extra emphasis upon Pluto. This aspect also has an affinity with the analytical sign Virgo. Adler has the two planets in wide square.

The capacity for mental rapport between the three colleagues is shown by the following contacts:

Freud	**Adler**	**Jung**
1. Antiscion Mercury 2¼ Leo Asc. 2¾ Scorpio	Moon 5 Taurus	Sun 3¼ Leo Neptune 3 Taurus
2. Moon 14½ Gemini	Jupiter/Uranus 15¾ Gemini	Antiscion Mercury 16¼ Gemini
3. Uranus 20½ Taurus	Antiscion Mercury 21 Scorpio Sun/Mars 22 Aquarius	Mars/Jupiter 22½ Scorpio Pluto 23½ Taurus

1. Freud's Mercury antiscion is at the zenith of his horoscope and links closely with Jung's Sun-Neptune square, perhaps providing the stimulus that led to Jung's deep level exploration of the world of dreams.

2. Jung's antiscion Mercury conjunct Freud's Moon provides the possibility of a sympathetic mental rapport between the two.

3. Adler's antiscion Mercury evokes a strenuous response from his two colleagues, providing the possibility of stimulating Freud's originality and Jung's enthusiasm.

Jung's third house planets have already figured in the above tabulations. Both of his colleagues have three planets which fall within the area of his third house, showing a continual sparking off of ideas in this area, underlining the fact that all three men were

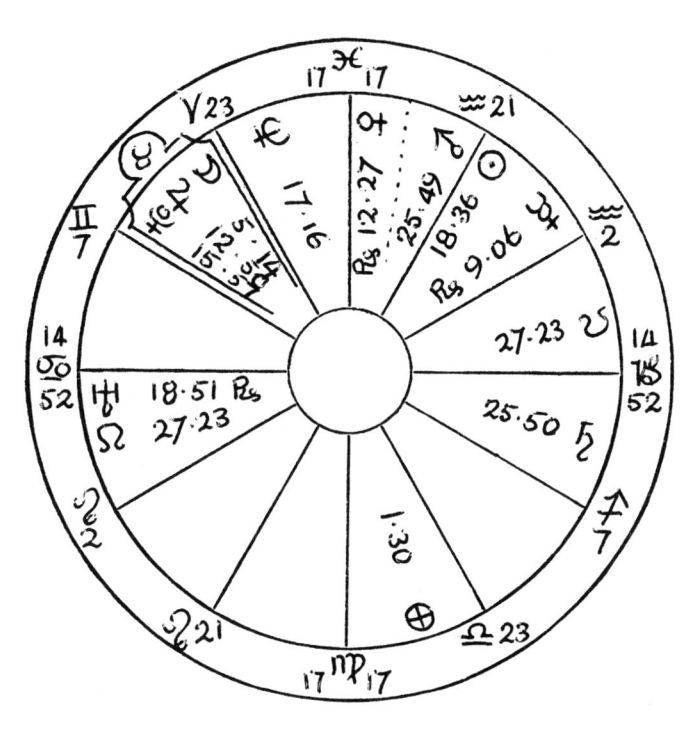

Alfred Adler
7 February 1870

Vienna, Austria
1.58 p.m. C.E.T.

deeply concerned with investigating the human mind. The ninth house is also important in this context. Adler's Sun is on his own ninth cusp, Mars and Venus are bodily in the ninth house. We have already tabulated some of the main contacts involving Adler's Sun. His ninth house Mars functions through the original and independent sign Aquarius and the various cross-aspects (tabulated below) from the nativities of his two colleagues give some indication of the debates and disagreements that must ultimately have resulted in the three parting company:

Freud	Adler	Jung
Sun Pre-natal 25 Leo	Mars 25¾ Aquarius	Saturn 24½ Aquarius
Antiscion Pluto 26 Leo	Antiscion Moon 24¾ Leo	Pluto 23½ Taurus
Jupiter Pre-natal 28 Aquarius		Antiscion Neptune 27 Leo
Mercury 27¾ Taurus	Domal Sun 26 Scorpio	M.C. 26⅔ Scorpio
Domal Saturn 23 Scorpio		Antiscion Sun 26⅔ Taurus
Antiscion Asc. 27¼ Aquarius	Saturn 25¾ Sagittarius	Mars 21⅓ Sagittarius
		Jupiter 23¾ Libra

26°-27° Leo/Aquarius is related by Maurice Wemyss to "an understanding of human nature" and the Sabian Symbols related to this axis and the degrees in square to it, suggest the powers resulting from the cultivation of a healthy, well co-ordinated and well-integrated mind. These cross-aspects indicate the main areas of disagreement between the three men. Jung's rising Saturn, strongly placed in Aquarius and squaring his Midheaven, fell on Adler's ninth house Mars. A fundamental difference of viewpoint is suggested by this conjunction. It was Freud who brought the two men together, so in a way he was responsible for precipitating the clash. His Mercury squared Adler's Mars and Jung's Saturn, while the antiscion of his Pluto opposed this conjunction of the two men's malefics, adding a compulsive element to the combination. Freud had Saturn in square to Mars. Both Adler and Jung had Saturn in sextile to Mars (a contact indicative of an ability for laborious probing and checking). Jung's Mars was close to Adler's Saturn, while Adler's Mars, conjoined Jung's Saturn and squared his Pluto. Jung's Jupiter trine to Adler's Mars and the conjunction of Freud's pre-natal Jupiter with the same point may have helped to postpone the final break-up until all three had profited as much as they were able to from the collaboration.

An examination of the planetary positions in the three horoscopes expressed in terms of the subsidiary planetary zodiacs places a strong emphasis upon several areas, some of which are tenanted in the individual nativities, while others are not. Of those tenanted, the largest accumulation centers around 16-18 degrees of the fixed signs, one of the principal areas of stress between the three horoscopes. For the purpose of this investigation only those subsidiary zodiacs that seemed most appropriate were used: those based on the natal position of the Sun (relating to inner motivation and outer prominence), Mercury (mental orientation), Saturn (sense of duty and the operation of karma), Pluto (inner compulsion and psycho-analytical potential) and the Dragon's Head (relationships in general).

Below are the Tropical positions of the natal planets in the middle of the fixed signs and the transposed positions falling in the same area:

Tropical Zodiac	Solar Zodiac	Pluto Zodiac
Adler Sun 18½ Aquarius	Freud Mars 17 Leo	Freud Neptune 15½ Aquarius
Pluto 16 Taurus	Jung Mars 18 Leo	Jung Mercury 20½ Taurus
Jung Moon 15½ Taurus		N.Node 18½ Aquarius
Uranus 14¾ Leo	**Mercury Zodiac**	
Freud M.C. 14 Leo	Adler Saturn 16¾ Aquarius	**Draconic Zodiac**
Sun 16 Taurus	Jung Neptune 16¾ Aquarius	Adler M.C./Venus 17½ Scorpio
Uranus 20½ Taurus		Jung M.C. 15 Scorpio
(Sun/Uranus = 18¼)	**Saturn Zodiac**	
	Adler Jupiter/Pluto 18½ Leo	
	Freud Sun 18½ Aquarius	
	M.C. 16½ Taurus	
	Jung N.Node 17½ Taurus	
	Mercury 19½ Leo	

Such an accumulation of subsidiary positions all concentrated in the same area serves to accentuate and activate the stresses already indicated by the clash between the tropical positions.

Jung's natal Mars in 21 ⅔ Sagittarius and his Jupiter/Saturn mid-point in 24 Sagittarius are also the focus of a number of subsidiary zodiac placements:

Solar Zodiac	Saturn Zodiac
Adler Mercury 20½ Pisces	Adler M.C. 21½ Gemini
Jupiter 24½ Gemini	Freud Neptune 22⅓ Sagittarius
Jung Jupiter 20½ Gemini	Jung Moon 21½ Gemini
Asc. 24¾ Virgo	Uranus 20⅔ Virgo
Pluto Zodiac	**Draconic Zodiac**
Adler Mercury 23 Sagittarius	Adler Uranus 21½ Pisces
Jung Moon 22 Pisces	Neptune 20 Sagittarius
Uranus 21½ Gemini	Jung Neptune 21 1/8 Aries

Other natal areas stimulated by the subsidiary zodiac positions, though to a lesser degree, are 3° of the fixed, 18°-19° of the mutable and 26°-28° of the cardinal signs.

Of the two areas not involved in major contacts between the charts of the three psychoanalysts, the most tenanted area was about 22° of the cardinals. 21°-22° Cancer, Capricorn has been designated by Maurice Wemyss (*The Wheel of Life,* Vol. III) as an area related to the study of astrology, while Dennis Elwell (*Astrology,* Vol. 42, No. 2) has observed that the same area is frequently tenanted in the horoscopes of sadists. This distinctly unflattering association appears in better perspective when it is realized that astrology offers its practitioners an opportunity to take a dispassionate and objective view of the people whose horoscopes they study. A similar dispassionate and objective view is present in the attitude of the sadist towards his victim. In the latter case the capacity is developed to an extreme, which leads to anti-social behaviour; in the former the capacity is used to make an objective analysis of individual psychology—it is this ability which enabled Freud, Adler and Jung to attain pre-eminence in their respective studies.

These are the subsidiary planetary positions involving this special area:

	Solar Zodiac		**Draconic Zodiac**
Adler	Venus 23¾ Aries	Adler	Sun 21¼ Libra
Jung	M.C. 23½ Cancer	Freud	M.C. 21½ Cancer
	Saturn 21 Libra		Sun 23½ Aries
	Pluto 20 Capricorn	Jung	Sun 21½ Cancer
			Neptune 21⅓ Aries

Mercury Zodiac	**Saturn Zodiac**	**Pluto Zodiac**
Freud Nept. 22½ Capricorn	Adler Uranus 23 Libra	Freud Mercury 23⅓ Aries
	Neptune 21½ Cancer	Venus/Saturn 22⅓ Ar

Only the Draconic Zodiac, with its special connection with relationships shows participation by all three. The involvement of all three Suns in a T-square with Freud's Midheaven at the fulcrum (showing him to be the leading figure in the partnership) is highly significant.

A secondary area (also relevant to psychoanalysis) involved about 12° of the cardinals connected, according to Maurice Wemyss, with logic and memory:

Solar Zodiac	Pluto Zodiac	Draconic Zodiac
Freud Mercury 11½ Aries	Freud Sun 11¾ Aries	Freud Neptune 11¾ Aries
Jung Moon 12¼ Capricorn		Jung Jupiter 12 Libra
		(Saturn 12½ Aquarius)
		Adler Mercury 11¾ Libra

THE RELATIONSHIP HOROSCOPES

The relationship horoscopes of the three men promised little chance of a permanent association. The partnership chart of Freud and Adler, cast for 23rd March, 1863, at 3.50 p.m. L.T. 49N35, 14E50 has Sun conjunct Neptune opposition Saturn. The Moon in 21 Taurus conjoins Freud's Uranus and squares Adler's Sun. Mercury in Pisces is in square to Mars in Gemini, a rather disputatious combination, with Mars in the fourth house, suggesting that disagreements would finally bedevil the partnership. At the time they parted company, the converse relationship Sun was in 15 Aquarius, squaring Adler's Pluto, and the progressed Sun was in 20 Taurus, conjunct Freud's radical Uranus. Both men had Sun/Uranus contacts in their nativities.

The relationship horoscope of Freud and Jung, cast for 15th December, 1865, 6.41 p.m. L.T. 49N13, 11E20, had the Moon in 25½ Scorpio, in opposition to Freud's Mercury/Uranus mid-point and Jung's Pluto in 23 Taurus. When their association ended, the progressed relationship Midheaven had reached to 23 Taurus. At the same time, progressed Sun squared progressed Saturn, and progressed Mars squared converse Sun, while the converse Midheaven was in 17½ Aquarius, in square to Freud's Sun/Uranus mid-point.

The partnership between Adler and Jung was summarized by a relationship horoscope cast for 1st November 1872, 4.42 a.m. L.T. 47N52, 12E50. The luminaries in Scorpio were squared by Uranus. The Ascendant in 15 ⅔ Taurus was conjunct Adler's Pluto and Jung's Moon and in square to Jung's Uranus. It was also conjunct the Sun of Freud, the man who brought them together. Mercury in 21 Scorpio opposed Pluto in 20 Taurus.

All three relationship horoscopes contained a major aspect between Mercury and Pluto, a combination indicating the possibility of achieving a penetrating mental analysis of their patients.

The three colleagues worked together at Freud's Institute in Vienna. Freud's Associate Angles, calculated for the Latitude of Vienna make some particularly significant contacts with the planets of his associates:

Freud (Associate Angles)	**Adler** (Natal Planets)	**Jung** (Natal Planets)
When Sun is on M.C. 26 Leo rises	Mars 25¾ Aquarius	Saturn 24½ Aquarius
When Sun is on I.C. 14½ Capricorn rises	Asc. 14¾ Cancer	Mercury 13¾ Cancer
When Sun rises 22¼ Capricorn is on M.C.	Asc./N.Node 21 Cancer	Venus/Desc. 22¾ Cancer
When Moon is on I.C. 25¼ Aquarius rises	Mars 25¾ Aquarius	Saturn 24¼ Aquarius
When Moon sets 11 Libra is on M.C.		N.Node 11¾ Aries
When Moon is on M.C. 17¼ Virgo rises	M.C. 17¼ Pisces	
When Mercury is on M.C. 4⅓ Virgo rises		Merc./Jupiter 3¾ Virgo
When Mercury is on I.C. 28 Cap. rises	S.Node 27⅓ Capricorn	Asc. 28 Capricorn
When Mercury rises 29½ Cap. is on M.C.		
When Mercury sets 18 Virgo is on M.C.	M.C. 17¼ Pisces	
When Mars is on I.C. 26½ Cancer rises	S.Node 27⅓ Cancer	
When Saturn rises 26 Aq. is on M.C.	Mars 25¾ Aquarius	Saturn 24½ Aquarius
When Uranus is on I.C. 20¾ Cap. rises	Asc/N.Node 21 Cancer	
When Neptune is on M.C. 16⅔ Cancer rises	Asc/Uranus 16¾ Cancer	Venus 17 Cancer
When Neptune rises 25½ Sag. is on M.C.	Saturn 25¾ Sagittarius	
When Neptune sets 17 Gemini is on M.C.		Moon/Venus 16½ Gemini
When Pluto is on M.C. 17¾ Leo rises	Sun 18½ Aquarius	
When Pluto sets 14¾ Leo is on M.C.		Uranus 14¾ Leo
When N.Node is on M.C. 10¼ Leo rises	Mercury 9 Aquarius	

UNDERSTANDING HUMAN RELATIONS   279

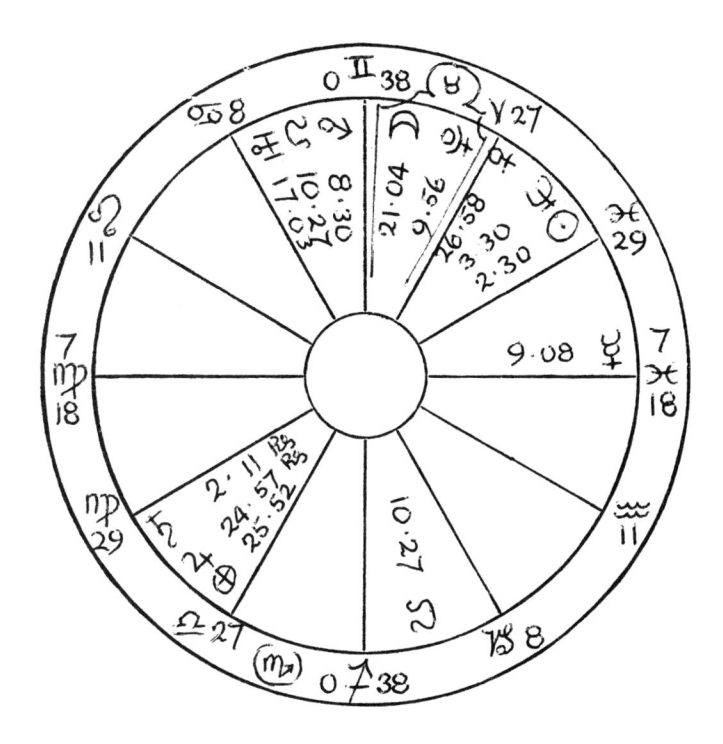

Freud/Adler Relationship
23 March 1863

49N35, 14E50
2.52 p.m. G.M.T.

Both Jung and Freud had the Sun and Uranus in the seventh house, in Freud's case only 4 degrees apart, so it is hardly surprising that they did not continue in double harness together for long. Jung's Uranus was near Freud's Midheaven and Freud's Uranus squared his own Midheaven. What was important in the meeting of these three most acute minds was that each sparked off new ideas in the other, although at the end of the day, Freud remained more or less true to his original doctrines. (It was he who had Mercury in Taurus.) Jung and Freud both had Mars in the eleventh house and Venus in the sixth. Helpfully, Freud's singleton Mars was in sextile to Jung's Sun, Adler's Cancer Ascendant was the complement of

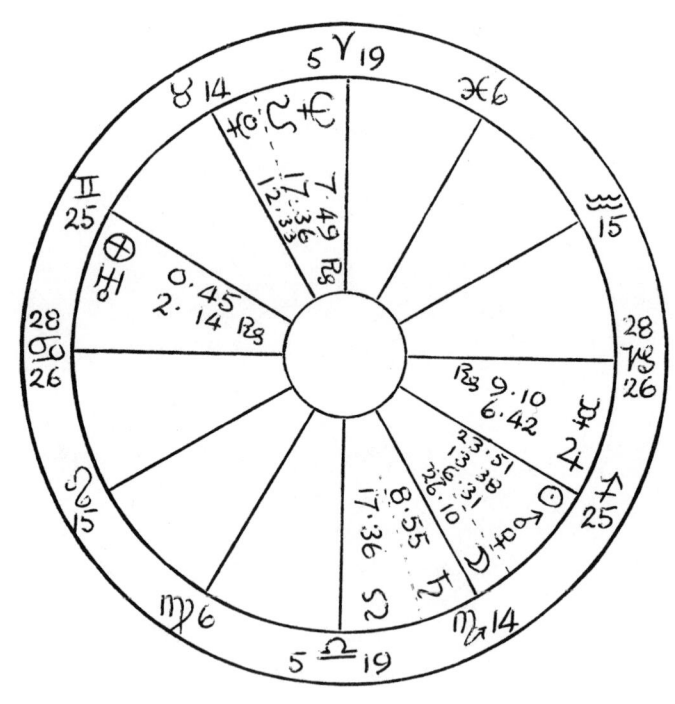

Freud/Jung Relationship
15 December 1865

49N13, 11E20
5.57 p.m. G.M.T.

Jung's Capricorn Ascendant and his South Node was conjunct Jung's Ascendant. Jung's Jupiter in 23 Libra fell on Adler's fifth cusp and on Freud's South Node, a link helpful to co-operation.

Freud's nativity indicated difficulties in working in partnership with others, perhaps on account of a certain amount of intransigence and so he attracted to himself colleagues who eventually broke away from him because they could no longer accept some of his working hypotheses. Nevertheless, had these three not come together and worked together, the world of psychoanalysis might have been the poorer. There is a lesson in chart comparison here in that strenuous conflicts between horoscopes of individuals are not necessarily a warning that they might not work together to each other's mutual benefit, but that it might be a good idea to accept beforehand that

UNDERSTANDING HUMAN RELATIONS 281

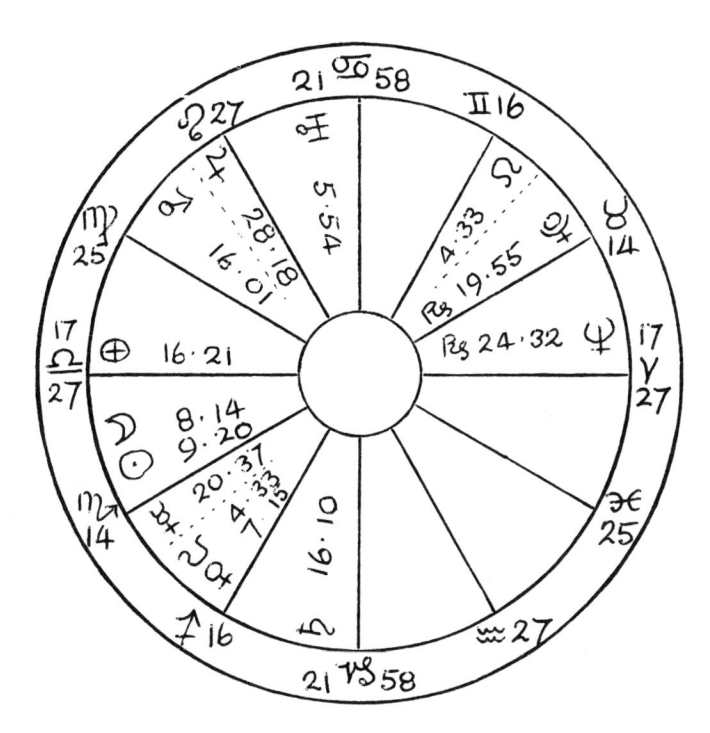

Adler/Jung Relationship 47N52, 12E50
1 November 1872 3.51 a.m. G.M.T.

there would come a time in such relationships when each would grow away from the other as their ideas matured and so while a short term relationship could confer great advantages on each member of the partnership, a long term relationship might not only be inadvisable but virtually impossible.

Adler, with the Sun conjunct Mars in Aquarius, and Uranus rising, Jung with the Sun in Leo, and Saturn rising in Aquarius squared by Pluto, and Freud with his Sun conjunct Uranus in a fixed sign, all had the astrological signatures of rugged individualists, as no doubt their work demanded they should be. Thus it was that after a period of co-operation which was virtually an incubating period for the ideas of Adler and Jung, the three men went their separate ways.

THE MANSON FAMILY

On August 9th, 1969, four members of a gang of drop-outs were sent by their leader on an expedition which was to result in the brutal butchery of five people. The leader of the gang, Charles Manson, was described as a kind of evil guru, regarded by his 26 young followers (20 of whom were female) as some kind of superman. (They usually called him "God" or "Satan.")

The London Observer (22nd July, 1973) carried an article by Peter Wilby in which he reported that Professor Robert Zaehner, Spalding Professor of Eastern Religions at Oxford University and a Fellow of All Souls, an acknowledged authority on drugs and mystical experience, had stated that Manson's philosophy and actions could be traced directly to Indian religious teachings, although Manson's contact with such teachings could mainly have been through various semi-oriental sects in the Los Angeles area, whose understanding of the original texts may have been somewhat less than perfect and in some degree distorted.

According to one Hindu text, "The man who knows me (Brahman) as I am loses nothing that is his, whatever he does, even though he should slay his mother and father, even though he should steal or procure an abortion. Whatever evil he does, he does not blanch." Manson, pointed out the Professor, did not blanch. On the absolute plane, killing and being killed were equally unreal. "Once you have truly got rid of all sense of ego, you will find that you can murder to your heart's content and feel no remorse at all."

This was the kind of doctrine that Manson preached to his followers, many of whom appeared to be motivated by a burning desire to reform the American pattern of society, which they regarded as responsible for the growing problems of atmospheric pollution, the perpetuation of racial prejudice and the existence of corruption in high places.

Television interviews with some of the "family" at the time of the murder trial revealed them as gentle, unassuming creatures, talking of "love" and "peace" and full of admiration for their leader. One of those interviewed was Lynette Fromme, who later attempted to assassinate President Ford. It was almost impossible to imagine the gentle, apparently harmless young girl seen in the interview playing the role of a ruthless killer. Such behaviour only becomes credible in the light of the suggestion that Manson exercised some hypnotic power over his acolytes and so blinded them to the absolute incongruity of indulging in bloody murders in order to establish their ideals of "love and peace." He is known to have used drugs and sexual magic in order to render his family more susceptible to indoctrination. Their respect for him was no doubt increased by the fact that he had undergone a ritual crucifixion and experienced what the Zen Buddhists call "The Great Death" and achieved "enlightenment" (a supreme lightning flash that shatters the time barrier) during a 45 mile walk in the desert.

Elsewhere, (See *American Astrology*, May and June 1974. Reprinted in *The Astrologer's Quarterly*, Autumn and Winter 1974, Vol. 48, Nos. 3 & 4.) the writer has demonstrated how the span of a Great Age can be subdivided into 360 parts to give a "time degree" for each 6 year (approximately) subdivision. Jesus of Nazareth was born when the time degree was 7 Taurus. Charles Manson (note the resemblance to "Son of Man") was born with this degree rising and Jupiter in the opposite degree in Scorpio. He also had the Mars-Neptune conjunction, present in the horoscope of Jesus. His Mercury in 2 Scorpio 59 opposed the time degree operative when Christ was crucified.

Manson's history hardly appears to be that of a Messiah in the making. He was born out of wedlock and spent 17 of his first 33 years behind bars for crimes involving the stealing of cars and forgery. Over the years he developed a burning hatred of society which festered in his brain. The gospel he preached to his followers was that the rich were "pigs" who needed purging. The diagnosis of one psychologist was that he carried locked up inside himself a tremendous amount of repressed anger and hostility towards all mankind, and getting the young women of his gang to commit these killings was his way of working off this pent up animosity. Manson's behaviour was dictated by a perverse desire to punish the affluent.

The fact that he personally did not take part in the killings is made understandable by the comments of a fellow ex-convict who described him as a strangely passive person who, if he was attacked, would sulk rather than strike back.

In his search for suitable victims on whom to wreak vengeance, Manson recalled a half-forgotten grudge against Tony Melcher, Doris Day's son, who was responsible for refusing to have one of Manson's songs (he liked to imagine himself as a wandering minstrel) recorded. Tony Melcher had rented his house to film director Roman Polanski and his wife Sharon Tate, who had appeared in "Valley of the Dolls." Curiously, two other leading actresses in this film suffered misfortunes at the same time.

Thus it was that on the fateful August 9th, Manson dispatched his four disciples on their grisly expedition, not particularly caring who might have rented Tony Melcher's mansion and certainly unaware that four guests were visiting the house that evening, though Roman Polanski was in Europe, directing a film. The raiders, clad all in black, were Charles Watson, Susan Atkins, Linda Kasabian and Pat Krenwinkel. Watson was armed with a revolver, while the girls carried sheath knives.

On their way to the house they saw a young man, Steven Earl Parent, leaving the caretaker's cottage, where he had been paying a visit. In spite of Susan Atkins' pleas and protests that he was not part of their "assignment," Watson shot him, firing three bullets. They then severed the telephone wires to the house, after which Watson climbed in through a window and then admitted the others to the house.

First, the gang tied up their victims. What followed has been described as an orgy of hacking, stabbing and shooting. That Sharon Tate was pregnant caused the intruders no concern at all and, while Susan Atkins held her, Watson stabbed her sixteen times.

When the four returned to the gang's hideaway they were criticized by Manson for "sloppy work" and three of them were sent the next day to do a "proper" job on a rich grocer and his wife, selected at random by the remorseless "guru."

Of the principal actors in the tragedy, only the horoscopes of Charles Manson, Susan Atkins and Steven Earl Parent are known.

UNDERSTANDING HUMAN RELATIONS 285

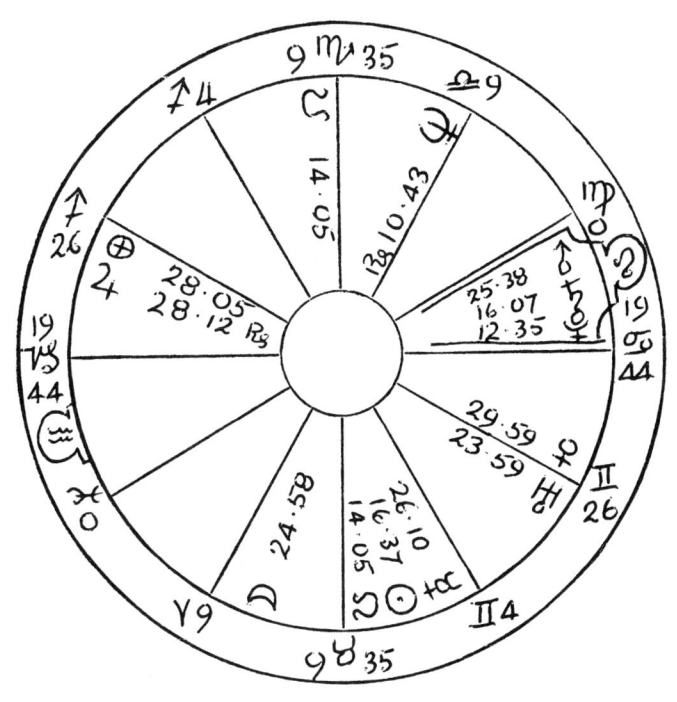

Susan Atkins
6 May 1948

San Gabriel, California
11.21 p.m. P.S.T.

Atkins was the daughter of two alcoholics. Her ambition was to be a dancer. She had fallen foul of the law at 18, when driving round Oregon with two friends, and was put on probation for two years. Her nativity is notable for the way in which the fire signs are accentuated. Three malefics in Leo occupy the seventh house and of these, Mars is involved in a grand trine with the Moon and Jupiter, also in fire signs. The Moon-Jupiter trine is isolated by hemisphere, both mundanely and nodally. The Ascendant ruler, Saturn, is beseiged by Mars and Pluto in the seventh.

Thus she is shown to be heavily dependent on other people, wishing to saddle them with the responsibility (Saturn in the seventh) for her actions and to blame them for arousing her aggressive impulses (compare Adolf Hitler, Mars in seventh). She is likely to attract to herself those who have the ability to stir up her deep-seated impulses to use power in a dramatic way (Pluto in Leo in the seventh). Leo is the sign ruling the affirmation in the Lord's Prayer, "Thy Will be done on Earth as it is in Heaven." The tendency to be swayed by older people (Sun square seventh house Saturn) and the violent nature of the Leo stellium led her to be attracted to Charles Manson, who imbued her and his other followers with the doctrine that it was their divine mission to purge the world of degenerate and sinful characters. A sense of identification with this mission would give her a feeling of exhilaration (Jupiter in Sagittarius trine Moon/Aries trine Mars/Leo) and righteousness, having its foundation in an imagined religious justification (Jupiter/Sagittarius). That her philosophy of life was apt to be distorted by the subtle persuasiveness of others is shown by Neptune in Libra in conjunction with her ninth cusp.

Some kind of sexual involvement is also suggested by the Venus-Uranus sextile to Mars and the close Venus-Jupiter opposition. Like Charles Manson, she has a Sun-Saturn square. In passing it is worth noting that an eclipse of the Sun took place in 18½ Taurus three days after she was born. Manson's Sun was in 19 Scorpio. Her Mars in 25 Leo opposes the position of the Sun on St. Valentine's Day, the day on which the Chicago massacre organized by Al Capone took place. Both St. Valentines were said to have been martyred.

Susan Atkins was Manson's principal lieutenant. The mid-point of Atkins' Venus-Neptune falls at 20 Leo and the mid-point of her Mars-Saturn at 20½ Leo and his natal Saturn in 21¾ Aquarius. The mid-point of his Sun-Venus conjunction is 19 Scorpio.

The mid-point of her Venus-Mars is 27 Cancer and the mid-point of her Mars-Jupiter is 26¾ Libra. His Pluto is in 26 Cancer and his Uranus is in 28½ Aries. The prominence of Venus and Mars in these contacts in the case of Atkins and of Mars, Saturn, Uranus and Pluto in the case of Manson, suggest some of the sexual overtones of the relationship and the compelling influence he was able to wield over her.

UNDERSTANDING HUMAN RELATIONS 287

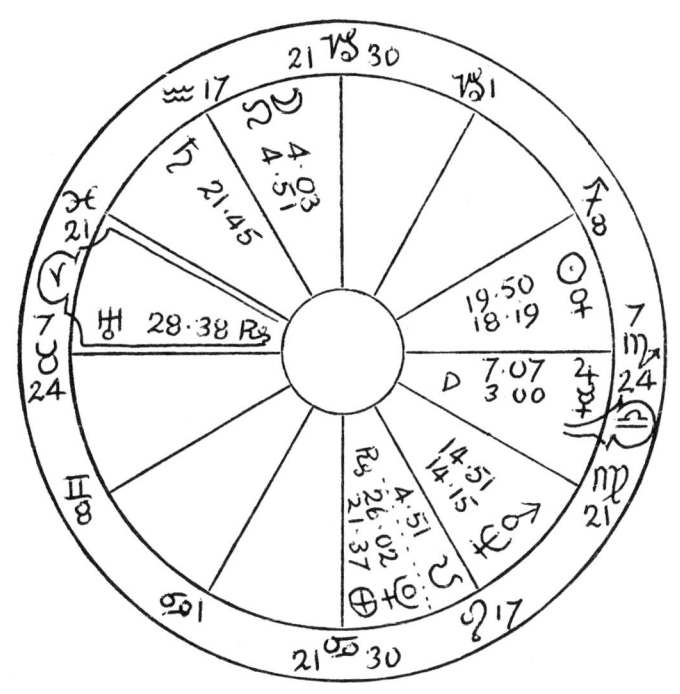

Charles Manson
12 November 1934

Cincinnati, Ohio
4.46 p.m. E.S.T.

His Jupiter falling close to her Midheaven, and his Sun and Venus in her tenth house would have led her to accept his claim to an exalted status. Her Sun falling in his Ascendant would have impressed him with her capacity to act as his second in command. His Saturn in her first house would also give him confidence in her reliability, while she would tend to value his greater experience of life. His Uranus falling in her third house, close to her Moon, would stimulate in a very original way her compelling need to strike out for herself in some revolutionary new line of thought, while his Pluto in her seventh, squaring her Moon, would challenge her to attempt some drastic transformation of her mental attitudes (perhaps through hypnotic influence). His fifth house Mars-Neptune conjunction falling in her eighth house could well relate to the practice of some kind of sexual magic together, besides giving him some uncomfortably accurate insights into her subsconscious motivations.

Atkins' Mars-Saturn-Pluto stellium falls mainly in Manson's fifth, her Saturn being practically on the cusp. This could have introduced a particularly jarring note into their relationship and, in view of the grand cross formed by the stellium and her Sun with Manson's Sun and Venus in square to Saturn, an element of mutual frustration and fatal involvement involving the pursuit of power. Her Neptune falls in his sixth house, so that she may have gained a feeling of "spiritual" uplift through regarding herself as his disciple, though sometimes failing to carry out his instructions efficiently, as evidenced by the raid on the Polanski mansion. Her Jupiter in Manson's eighth is another factor that would increase his trust in her, and her Venus-Uranus opposition to Jupiter denotes the possibility of a considerable amount of physical attraction between the two. Her crusading Moon in Aries in his twelfth house suggests a protective and solicitous attitude towards him and a desire to involve herself actively in any form of service that would contribute to his welfare.

The close proximity of her Midheaven to his Descendant and of his Midheaven to her Ascendant is a very powerful link between them. Her North Node falls on his Ascendant, combining with the grand cross formed by their two Suns and the planets in square to them, a suggestion of a very powerful yet possibly disastrous connection in a previous incarnation.

The interplay between the nativities of Manson and Parent is highly significant. Here are some of the salient features: Manson has the Sun in Scorpio square Saturn. This Saturn was a degree away from Parent's Sun. Manson's pre-natal Saturn was also in the same degree. Manson's natal Mars-Neptune conjunction, a key factor in his horoscope, was in exact opposition to his own pre-natal Sun in 14½ Pisces and in exact opposition to Parent's Venus, close to Jupiter and Mars. Manson's pre-natal Mars in 23 Pisces fell on Parent's Lower Meridian. Manson's pre-natal Mars, Saturn and Sun were therefore involved with key points in Parent's activity. Additionally, his natal Mars-Neptune conjunction was also involved. Except

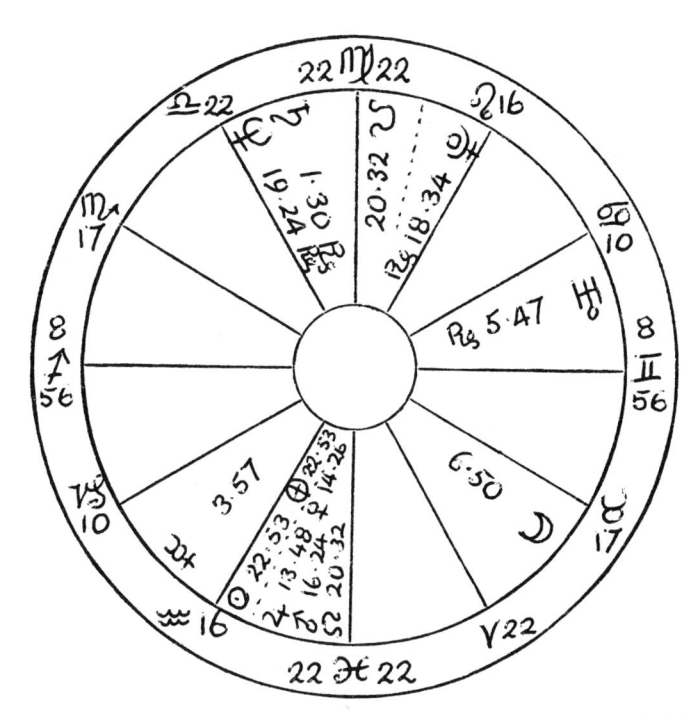

Steven Earl Parent
12 February 1951

Pasadena, California
1.59 a.m. P.S.T.

for the Sun, the luminary representing the will, all the other factors were malefic, and it was Manson who was held principally responsible for Parent's murder, even though he was apparently unaware of his existence.

Manson's natal Pluto fell at the mid-point of Parent's Uranus-Pluto. Parent's Pluto was in opposition to his own Sun and so the Sun-Saturn square in Manson's chart dovetails with the Sun-Pluto opposition in the victim's. Parent's Moon was within a degree of Manson's Ascendant and the antiscion of this Moon was 23 Leo in opposition to Manson's Saturn.

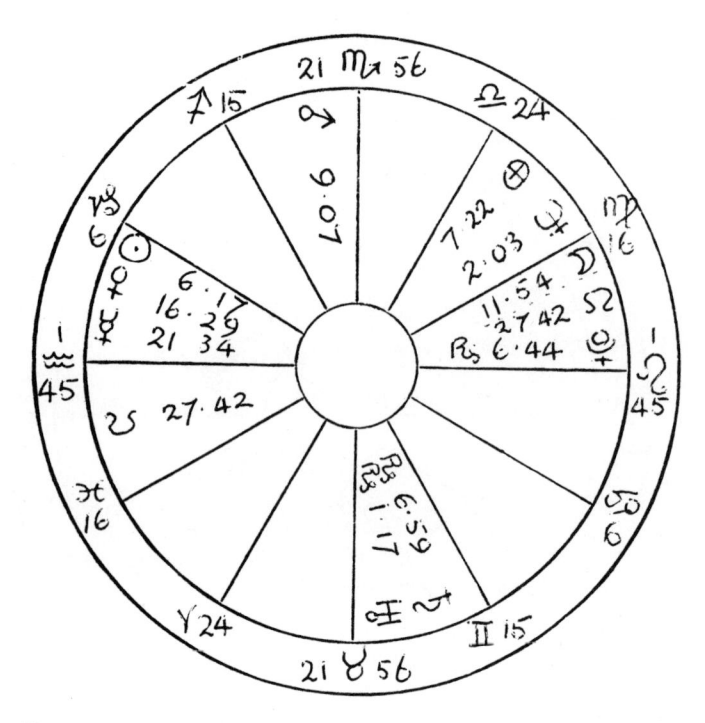

Manson/Parent Relationship
28 December 1942

101W20, 36N38
3.38 p.m. G.M.T.

The antiscion of Parent's Ascendant was the degree of Manson's Midheaven. The antiscion of Parent's Sun in 7 Scorpio fell right on Manson's Descendant and Jupiter. One is tempted to suggest that there must have been some fatal link between the two men, rooted in the past, even though the killing appeared to be a completely unrelated and unpremeditated crime.

THE RELATIONSHIP HOROSCOPES

The Manson-Parent relationship horoscope, cast for 28th December, 1942, 8.54 a.m. L.T., 26N38, 101W20 with a Midheaven of 22 Scorpio, at once directs attention to Manson's Sun square Saturn and Parent's Sun opposition Pluto. The Ascendant in 1 Aquarius is in a close grand trine with Uranus and Neptune. More ominously, Mars is in 9 Sagittarius on Parent's Ascendant, and Saturn is in 7 Gemini. The relationship horoscope was nearly 17 years old when the murder took place. The converse secondary directions measuring to 17 years bring the Sun back to 8½ Sagittarius and Saturn, being retrograde, has moved to 9 Sagittarius. These positions signed Parent's death warrant. Converse Mars had moved back to 20 Scorpio, to Manson's natal Sun and the mid-point of Parent's Sun-Pluto opposition.

According to the law, although Manson was not present at the killing of Parent and the others who were murdered on that night, he was held to have instigated the crime and therefore found guilty. It is significant that the planets seem to deliver a similar verdict, thus appearing to link human law with cosmic justice.

Although Susan Atkins was not the one who shot Parent, the relationship chart between the two still shows a number of afflictions. Her radical Sun exactly squared Saturn (an aspect in the charts of nearly all those involved in the night's ghastly happenings) and as her Saturn was bracketed by Mars and Pluto, these two also squared her Sun. The mid-point of her Mars and Pluto was in conjunction with Parent's Pluto, while the mid-point of her Mars-Neptune closely opposed Parent's Mars.

The Atkins-Parent relationship horoscope, cast for 24th September, 1949, 12.49 p.m. L.T., 34N05, 118W07 has Neptune close to the 16 Libra Midheaven but the most striking feature is the Ascendant in 27 Sagittarius which picks up her natal Jupiter in 28 Sagittarius and her Uranus-Venus mid-point. Her Jupiter and Venus were thus involved in their relationship and it was she who pleaded with Charles Watson not to shoot Parent. Her plea was in vain, however, as the elevated Neptune in the relationship horoscope probably dictated.

The progressions of the relationship horoscope are interesting. Because of the fairly unique circumstances in which their encounter took place, their first meeting was also their last meeting and the bringing of their relationship to life actually heralded the finish of the relationship. Nevertheless, the relationship chart indicated the cir-

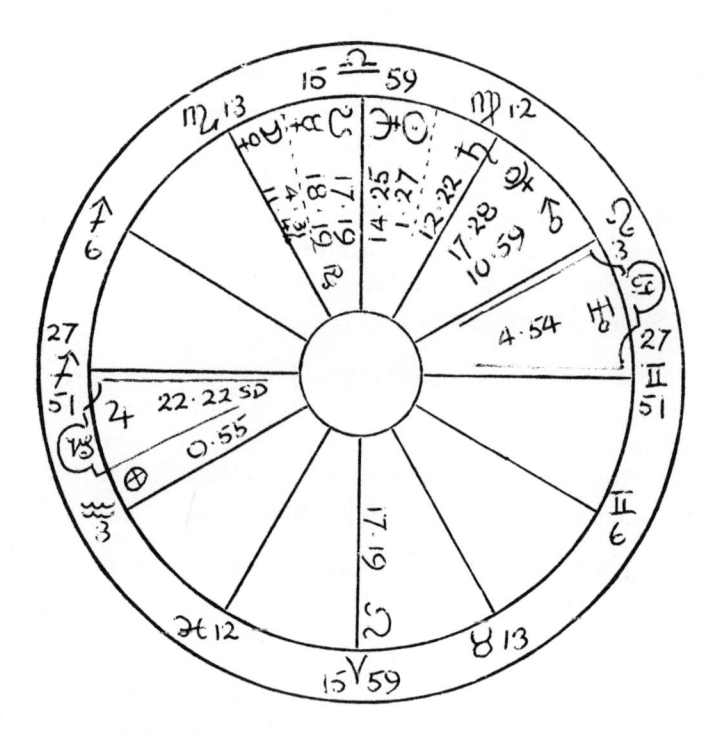

Atkins/Parent Relationship
24 September 1949

118W07, 34N05
8.38 p.m. G.M.T.

cumstances of their meeting, for the progressed secondary Mars had reached 23 Leo, in opposition to Parent's Sun (and in conjunction with the Antiscion of Manson's Ascendant), and Saturn had progressed to 14¾ Virgo, conjunct Manson's crucial Mars-Neptune conjunction and in opposition to Parent's Venus. The converse relationship Venus in 16 Libra also indicates Atkins' bid to save Parent's life and, as far as this passing episode is concerned, the planets appear to have absolved her from blame. But the later events of the night carried no such absolution.

UNDERSTANDING HUMAN RELATIONS 293

Of a large number of cross-aspects derived from the planetary zodiac positions, the following are the most striking:

Manson (Draconic Zodiac)*	Atkins (Tropical Zodiac)	Parent (Tropical Zodiac)
Uranus 24 Gemini	Uranus 24 Gemini	
Mars/Neptune 9 Scorpio	M.C. 10 Scorpio	
Pluto 21 Virgo		M.C. 22½ Virgo
M.C. 16¾ Pisces		Mars 16⅓ Pisces

(Pluto Zodiac)

Mars/Neptune 18 Taurus (opp. own Sun/Venus)	Sun 16½ Taurus Saturn 16 Leo	Pluto 18½ Leo
Moon 9 Libra		
Jupiter 11 Cancer	Neptune 10¾ Libra	
Uranus 2½ Capricorn		Saturn 1½ Libra
Saturn 26 Libra (square own Pluto)		

(Solar Zodiac)**

Moon 15 Gemini		Mars 16⅓ Pisces
N.Node 15 Gemini		Jupiter 13¾ Pisces
Jupiter 17¼ Pisces		Venus 14½ Pisces
Asc. 17½ Virgo		
Mars 25 Capricorn	Moon 25 Aries	
Neptune 24½ Capricorn	Mercury 26 Taurus	
Saturn 2 Cancer		Saturn 1½ Libra
Uranus 8¾ Virgo		Asc. 9 Sagittarius
Pluto 6¼ Sagittarius		Moon/Uranus 6¼ Gemini

(Mars Zodiac)***

Moon 20 Leo		
N.Node 20 Leo	Mars/Saturn 20¾ Leo	Sun/Pluto 20¾ Scorpio
Mercury 18¼ Aries	Asc. 19¾ Capricorn	Neptune 19½ Libra
Asc. 22⅔ Scorpio		
Jupiter 22⅓ Taurus		Sun 23 Aquarius
Uranus 13¾ Scorpio		
Pluto 11¼ Aquarius	N.Node 14 Taurus	
	Pluto 12½ Leo	
	Neptune 10¾ Libra	

*The positions are almost the same in the Lunar Zodiac.
**The positions are almost the same in the Venus Zodiac.
***The positions are almost the same in the Neptune Zodiac.

294 SYNASTRY

Parent (Mars Zodiac)*	Atkins (Tropical Zodiac)	Manson (Tropical Zodiac)
Moon 20½ Taurus	Mars/Saturn 20¾ Leo	Sun 19¾ Scorpio
Mercury 17½ Aquarius		Saturn 21¾ Aquarius
Venus 28 Pisces	Jupiter 28¼ Sagittarius	
Jupiter 27⅓ Pisces	Venus 30 Gemini	
Uranus 19⅓ Cancer	Asc. 19¾ Capricorn	
Asc. 22½ Sagittarius	Uranus 24 Gemini	
(Pluto Zodiac)		
Venus 25¾ Libra	Uranus 24 Gemini	Pluto 26 Cancer
Mars 27¾ Libra	Moon 25 Aries	
Jupiter 25 Libra	Jupiter 28 Sagittarius	
Saturn 13 Taurus	Neptune 12⅔ Leo	
Uranus 17½ Aquarius		Sun 19¾ Scorpio
		Venus 18¼ Scorpio
Asc. 20⅓ Cancer	Asc. 19¾ Capricorn	M.C. 21¾ Capricorn
(Solar Zodiac)		
		Neptune 14¼ Virgo
Moon 14 Gemini		Mars 14¾ Virgo
Venus 21 Aries		
Jupiter 21½ Aries		M.C. 21¾ Capricorn
Mars 23½ Aries		
Saturn 8⅔ Scorpio	M.C. 10 Scorpio	Jupiter 7 Scorpio
		Asc. 7½ Taurus
Uranus 13 Leo	Neptune 12⅔ Leo	
Neptune 26½ Scorpio	Mars 25⅔ Leo	
Pluto 25⅔ Virgo	Moon 25 Aries	Pluto 26 Cancer
N.Node 27⅔ Aries	Jupiter 28 Sagittarius	Uranus 28⅔ Aries
Asc. 16 Capricorn	Saturn 16 Leo	
	Sun 16½ Taurus	
M.C. 29⅔ Libra	Venus 30 Gemini	
(Saturn Zodiac)		
Sun 21⅓ Leo	Mars/Saturn 20¾ Leo	Saturn 21¾ Aquarius
Pluto 17 Aquarius	Saturn 16 Leo	Venus 18¼ Scorpio
Moon 5⅓ Scorpio		Moon 4 Aquarius
		N.Node 4¾ Aquarius
Venus 13 Virgo		
Mars 15 Virgo	N.Node 14 Taurus	Mars 14¾ Virgo
Jupiter 12¼ Virgo		Neptune 14¼ Virgo

*The positions are almost the same in the Neptune Zodiac.

The only favorable contacts among the many harshly conflicting aspects in this lengthy array are those between Parent and Atkins, but these are quite outweighed by the heavy afflictions. Particularly noteworthy are the Uranus-Ascendant interchanges between Atkins and Parent when his Mars Zodiac is compared with her nativity, and the Saturnian links with Manson and Atkins when Parent's Saturn Zodiac is investigated.

The main focus of this survey has been centered on the Mars, Saturn and Pluto Zodiacs since violence and the inscrutable web of destiny were the unmistakable keynotes of this lamentable episode.

Did Manson order the assassination of President Ford, attempted by Lynette Fromme, one of his followers, on 7th September, 1975? A comparison of the two men's horoscopes suggests that such an order would not have been out of character with the nature of the planetary cross-aspects between the two. Each man's Mars, for instance, squares the other's Saturn. The following contacts might be expected to produce antagonism in any relationship:

Ford
Sun 21¼ Cancer
 (conjunct Neptune 25½ Cancer)
Mars 19 Taurus

Manson
M.C. 21¾ Capricorn
Sun 19¾ Scorpio, Venus 18¾ Scorpio, Saturn 21¾ Aquarius

(the Solar Eclipse of 11th May, 1975 fell in 20 Taurus.)

Uranus 6 Aquarius
Saturn 13¼ Gemini

Asc. 7½ Taurus, Jupiter 7 Scorpio
Mars 14¼ Virgo, Neptune 14¼ Virgo

(on 7th September, 1975, the Sun was in 14 Virgo, Mars in 14 Gemini)

Before he allowed himself to be the subject of a television interview in jail some three weeks before the assassination attempt, Manson stipulated that a copy of the interview should be sent to his followers. They had their own code and the interview could have contained a hidden message to the gang.

Manson felt that Ford's policies were as unacceptable to him as Nixon's had been. Nixon's M.C. in 12½ Gemini and Ascendant in 14 Virgo, together with his pre-natal Sun in 12½ Pisces, Mars in 13 Gemini and Jupiter in 14 Sagittarius clash with Manson's Mars-Neptune conjunction. Manson's pre-natal Sun in 14½ Pisces joins in the pattern.

Associate Angles

When the associate angles are calculated, those for Susan Atkins show a large number of contacts with the birth planets of Manson and Parent. On the other hand, while Manson's associate angles fall on a number of Atkins' planets, there is only one contact with Parent. Below is a selection of the more striking contacts based on the associate angles in Susan Atkins' nativity.

Atkins (Associate Angles)	**Manson (Natal Positions)**	**Parent (Natal Positions)**
When Uranus is on the M.C. 24½ Virgo rises	Sun/Pluto 23 Virgo Merc./Mars-Nept. 23¾ Virgo Saturn/Uranus 25¼ Pisces	M.C. 22½ Virgo
When Sun is on the M.C. 21½ Leo rises	Saturn 21¾ Aquarius	Sun 22¾ Aquarius
When Sun is on I.C. 26¾ Capricorn rises	Pluto 26 Cancer	
When Moon is setting 28 Cancer is on the M.C.	Pluto 26 Cancer	
When Moon is on M.C. 4½ Leo rises	Moon, N.Node 4¾ Aquarius	Mercury 4 Aquarius
When Venus is on M.C. 0 Libra rises		Saturn 1½ Libra
When Venus sets 19 Libra is on M.C.		Neptune 19⅓ Libra
When Mars is on M.C. 18 Scorpio rises	Venus 18¼ Scorpio	
When Mars rises 21 Taurus is on M.C.	Sun 19¾ Scorpio	Sun/Pluto 20¾ Taurus
When Mars sets 8½ Sag. is on M.C.		Asc. 9 Sagittarius
When Pluto is on M.C. 7½ Scorpio rises	Asc. 7½ Taurus Jupiter 7 Scorpio	Moon 7 Taurus
When Uranus rises 4¼ Pisces is on M.C.		Sun/Mars 3½ Pisces
When N.Node is on M.C. 19⅔ Leo rises		Pluto 18½ Leo
When N.Node sets 23½ Leo is on M.C.		Sun 22¾ Aquarius

A MALE-FEMALE RELATIONSHIP

Let us now approach the relationship horoscope from another angle. Below is the horoscope of a male-female relationship, calculated for the midpoint in space and time between two nativities. What can we learn from the relationship horoscope?

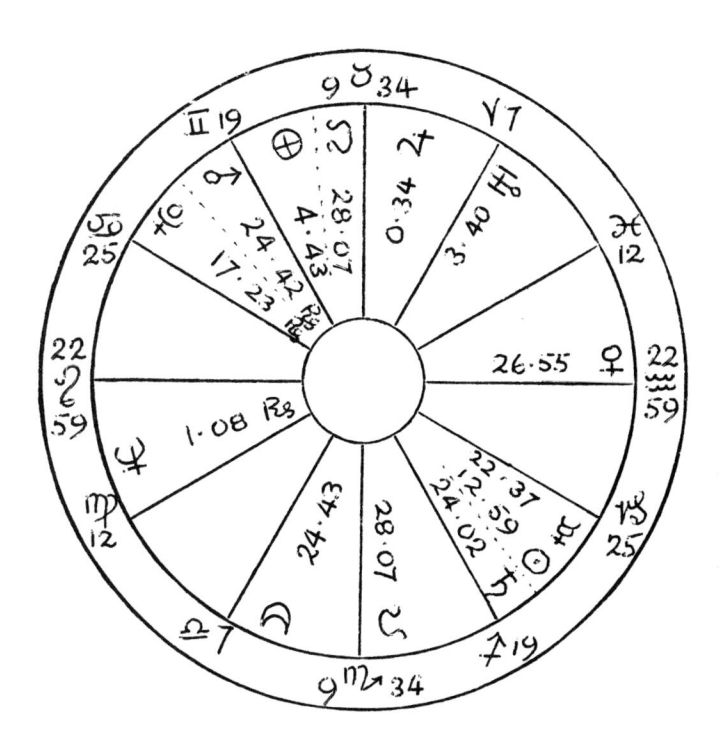

Relationship
3 January 1929

51N34, 1W52
7.46 p.m. G.M.T.

Venus in the seventh house is in trine to the Moon in Libra, and Mars in Gemini completes the grand trine. Here are the ingredients of a very harmonious and compatible relationship. The Sun, ruler of the Ascendant, is close to the Moon/Uranus mid-point and opposes

Pluto. This places the relationship on a more fragile basis, indicating the possibility of a good deal of tension at times, yet a relationship in which great depth of feeling is possible (Pluto in Cancer opposition Sun). Saturn opposes Mars, being in sextile to both the Moon and Venus. The stabilizing influence of Saturn is linked with the Ascendant by a trine aspect. Mars is in sextile to the Ascendant, which therefore holds a rather uneasy balance between the two malefics. The opposition, however, is prominently placed in the fifth and eleventh houses, suggesting difficulties in actualizing the ideal concept of partnership that both partners may cherish. Such an opposition can indicate some disagreement regarding whether or not to have children or difficulties involving children. The Sun-Pluto opposition, which lacks a mediating influence, also suggests that the partners may have to solve major problems in the course of their relationship, in which each may be challenged to effect some kind of self-transformation if the partnership is to survive. That every effort should be made to place the relationship on a high spiritual level is shown by the debilitated Neptune rising in opposition to Venus in the seventh. Fortunately an elevated Jupiter in trine to Neptune modifies this opposition, making possible a greater degree of mutual understanding.

Thus there are strong elements of attraction and yet marked problem aspects present in the relationship horoscope. The former might reasonably be expected to signify marriage between the two, while the latter pose obvious problems in maintaining the marriage relationship on an even keel. While the relationship horoscope on its own gives clear-cut indications of the way in which a partnership is likely to develop, further information is provided when we compare the nativities of both partners with the relationship horoscope. In this case there is the following build-up:

Relationship Horoscope	Husband	Wife
Uranus 3½ Aries	Venus 4½ Capricorn	Asc. 4¼ Libra
Pluto 17½ Cancer	Jupiter 18⅓ Capricorn	Venus 18 Aries, Uranus 17 Ar
	Sun 18 Scorpio	Pluto 20 Cancer
	Saturn 17 Scorpio	

The principals in this relationship are Richard Burton and Elizabeth Taylor. Elizabeth Taylor's close Venus-Uranus conjunction in Aries in the seventh house indicates a tendency to attract to herself partners who will challenge her to exercise her initiative to an extraordinary degree in maintaining harmony with them. While Jupiter in Leo in trine to this conjunction from the eleventh house shows that a sense of idealism would encourage an enlightened attitude towards marriage and partnership, the square from Pluto in the tenth house suggests that great emotional tentions is likely to build up through her efforts to maintain harmony while adverse publicity over marital problems could have a harmful effect upon her professional standing. As Venus is the ruler of her Ascendant, she is shown to be greatly influenced by the behaviour of her partner.

Richard Burton's Sun-Saturn conjunction in Scorpio, denoting great emotional intensity, falls in quincunx to her Venus-Uranus conjunction, thus testing the strength of his partner's ability to maintain a stable relationship. His seventh house Jupiter in Capricorn squares her seventh house conjunction, suggesting that his desire for a prestigious partner could add to her doubts about the permanency of the partnership. The relationship Pluto very closely squares her seventh house conjunction and warns of the emotional problems that would have to be confronted and solved in order to give greater solidity to the partnership.

Normally, the square of Richard Burton's Venus to his wife's Ascendant could be considered a favorable factor in the relationship, even though Venus is debilitated, but the position of the relationship Uranus on Elizabeth Taylor's seventh cusp provides a composite Ascendant-Venus-Uranus T-square that serves to place additional stress on her natal Venus-Uranus conjunction. Burton's Fortuna falls on the Midheaven of the relationship figure.

The stresses in the relationship horoscope therefore take on a greater significance when the individual horoscopes of the two partners are superimposed on it.

Both partners have a seventh house benefic in debility. Though Burton's Jupiter here is in opposition to Pluto, it is well supported by sextiles from the Sun, Saturn and Uranus and a trine from the

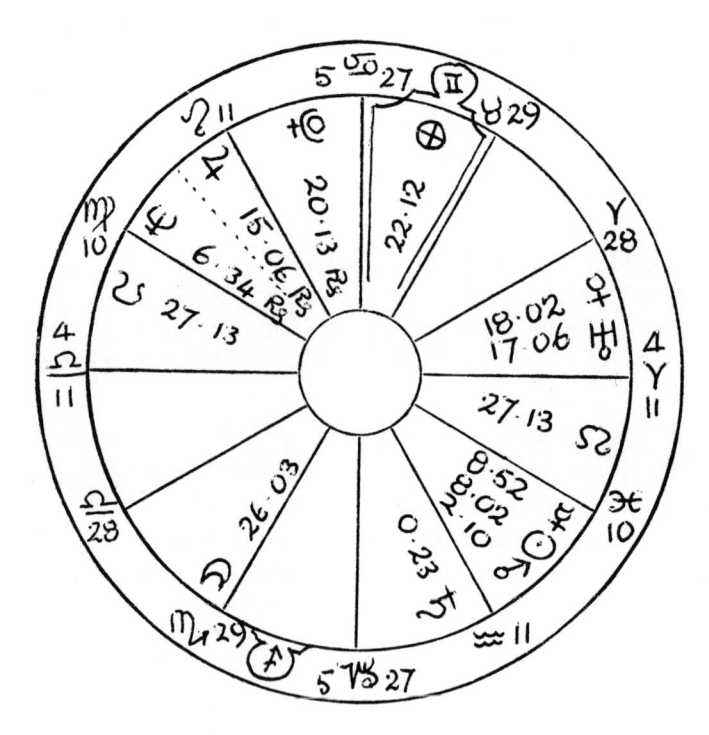

Elizabeth Taylor
27 February 1932

London
7.57 p.m. G.M.T.

Moon. Saturn rules Burton's seventh house and its close conjunction with the Sun in the fifth indicates some likelihood of a self-doubting tendency and a lack of self-confidence which can lead to attempts at over-compensation, and a need to subject himself to rigorous tests in order to dispel such doubts.

Elizabeth Taylor's Sun/Mars mid-point is opposed by Neptune, and the Sun in Pisces is on the sixth cusp. Mars, close by, rules the seventh. Thus the general and specific indicators of the husband are both in Pisces, and indicate the possibility of health or addictive problems affecting the partner.

UNDERSTANDING HUMAN RELATIONS

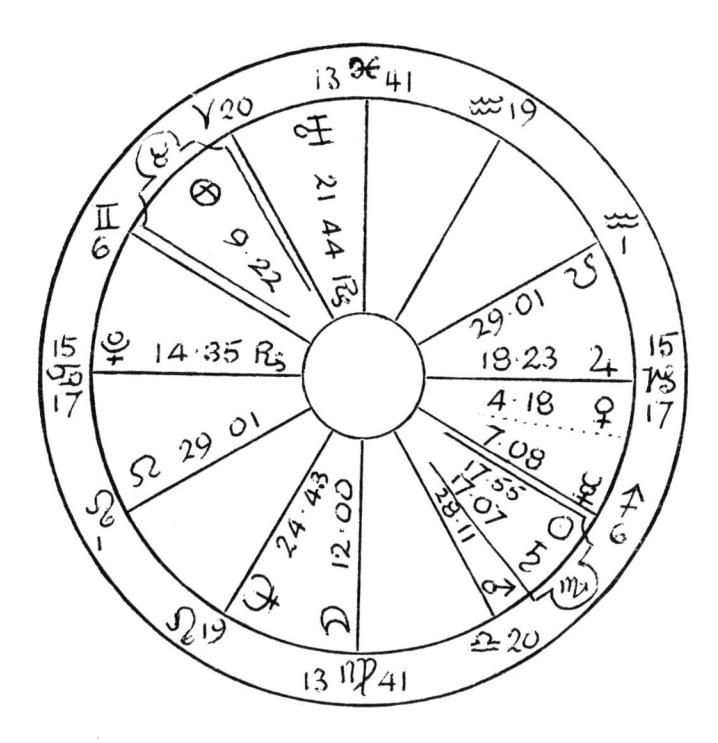

Richard Burton
10 November 1925

Port Talbot, Glamorgan
7.58 p.m. G.M.T.

The elements are distributed in more or less the same way in each nativity, each having a majority of planets in water and only one planet in air. While Miss Taylor has three planets in fire, however, Burton has three in earth, showing her to be the more vivacious and active of the two. Both have their planets fairly evenly distributed between the Triplicities. Taylor has a Mutable Water and Burton a Fixed Water synthesis, in itself an excellent indication of compatibility and a guarantee of a depth of feeling on both sides.

One or two of the cross-aspects have already been mentioned. Those that remain show a number of powerful links, including the classic Sun-Moon contact:

Burton	Taylor
Sun 18 Scorpio, Jupiter 18⅓ Capricorn	Pluto 20¼ Cancer
Saturn 17 Scorpio	
Moon 12 Virgo, Mercury 7¼ Sag.	Sun 8 Pisces, Mercury 9 Pisces, Neptune 7 Vi
Venus 4 Capricorn	Asc. 4 Libra, M.C. 5 Cancer, Neptune 7 Virgo
Neptune 24¾ Leo	Moon 26 Scorpio, Sun/Jupiter 26½ Scorpio
Asc. 15⅓ Cancer, Pluto 14⅔ Cancer	Venus 18 Aries, Uranus 17 Aries

There are three main contacts by antiscion degree:

Burton (Radical)	Taylor (Antiscion)
Mars 27¾ Libra	Mars 28¼ Libra
Moon 12 Virgo	Venus 12 Virgo
M.C. 13¾ Pisces	Uranus 13 Virgo

These contacts all relate specifically to the area of marriage and courtship as Venus and Uranus occupy the seventh house of Elizabeth Taylor's nativity. Mars in Libra focuses the energies upon maintaining harmony, and can indicate quarrels. The two latter contacts indicate strong physical attraction and are often productive of much tension, here projected into Burton's domestic fourth house.

There are three mutual receptions between the two nativities. Elizabeth Taylor's Moon in Scorpio pairs with Burton's Pluto in Cancer, her Sun in Pisces is matched by his Neptune in Leo, and her Venus in Aries with his Mars in Libra. The involvement of both Sun and Moon in these interchanges is significant and the links underline the strong sympathy between the two horoscopes and the predominance of water signs in each.

The Luminaries also feature in another type of pairing, where the sign position in one nativity is matched in the other by an aspect between that luminary and its dispositor:

Taylor	Burton
Sun Pisces (opposition Neptune)	Sun square Neptune Leo
Moon Scorpio (trine Pluto)	Moon sextile Pluto Cancer

In addition, Elizabeth Taylor duplicates her husband's Sun-Neptune and Moon-Pluto contacts. Other pairings of this nature are:

Taylor	Burton
Venus Aries	Venus sextile Mars
Mars Pisces	Mars sextile Neptune
Jupiter Leo	Jupiter sextile Sun
Saturn Aquarius	Saturn trine Uranus
Pluto Cancer (angular)	Pluto sextile Moon (both angular)

Burton	Taylor
Sun Scorpio	Sun sesquiquadrate Pluto
Mars Libra	Mars semisquare Venus
Saturn Scorpio	Saturn semisextile Mars
Uranus Pisces	Uranus trine Jupiter
Neptune Leo	Neptune opposition Sun
Pluto Cancer	Pluto trine Moon Scorpio

Of the mid-point contacts, only the first is definitely helpful, though in square to Miss Taylor's seventh house conjunction:

Taylor	Burton
Sun/Moon 17 Capricorn (square own Venus/Uranus)	Jupiter 18⅓ Capricorn
Sun/Jupiter 26⅔ Scorpio (conjunct own Moon)	Neptune 24¾ Leo
Sun/Saturn 18¾ Aquarius	Sun/Saturn 17½ Scorpio, 9th cusp 19 Aq
Sun 8 Pisces	Mars/Pluto 7¾ Virgo
Neptune 6½ Virgo	Mars 7 Sagittarius
Venus/Pluto 4 Gemini	
Mars 2 Pisces	Moon/Neptune 3½ Virgo

The square of the two Sun-Saturn mid-points is particularly revealing, especially as Burton's ninth cusp is involved. Some basic inability to share the same philosophy of life could give rise to considerable problems.

Elizabeth Taylor's Sun, Mercury and Mars fall in Burton's ninth house and her Neptune falls in his third. His third house Neptune is in Leo, hers is in Virgo, so that an intellectual rapport would not be easy to achieve. Her Pluto falls in his Ascendant, and while the same will apply to all his contemporaries, such a contact involving someone close to the native means that she will be instrumental in causing him to become more aware of the hidden motivations that underlie his outward behaviour, especially the type of behaviour that could lead to mutual tension. Her Saturn on his eighth cusp could also tend to make him very much aware of any of his character shortcomings and, because of the square between the Sun/Saturn mid-points of the partners, play on any guilt complex inherent in his nature. Her Saturn is also conjunct his South Node, suggesting that she might have played such a role in a previous incarnation.

Her Jupiter falls in his second house, while his Mars falls on her second cusp, bringing mutual benefits through each other's earning capacity. Her Moon in his fifth house is a happy augury. The proximity of her Venus-Uranus conjunction to his eleventh cusp is a stimulating and happy contact though one subject to sudden and unexpected fluctuations, to the extent that the partnership fails to actualize the high ideals that each aspires to reach in the married state. His Neptune in her eleventh house, often the sign of a relationship calling for an easy-going tolerance on both sides, shows that he is able to appeal to her idealistic impulses, though such a position sometimes means that the partner whose Neptune is involved requires the compassionate understanding of the other in respect of some physical or psychological difficulties.

His Venus and Jupiter in her fourth house will assist in the building of a happy domestic atmosphere in which both can flourish. Jupiter here often means that the partner whose planet is involved will adopt a rather parental attitude towards the other. His Venus also squares her Ascendant, suggesting a tendency to over-indulgent behaviour towards her.

His Moon on her twelfth cusp and his Uranus in her sixth house indicates some facility on his part for identifying any weak points in her psychological make-up, which could operate to make the relationship more fragile, while his health problems would give her cause for concern.

His Pluto in her tenth house shows that her prestige and career are a matter of keen concern to him and suggest that he may be able to encourage her to cultivate a more definitive attitude towards her aim in life. Both have an angular Pluto, indicating that their relationship is likely to be a matter of total involvement for each of them. His Mercury in her third house encourages communication on an everyday level, but its square to her Mercury-Neptune opposition implies that his way of thinking would rarely coincide with her more subtle approach.

His Sun-Saturn conjunction, one of the key configurations in his nativity, falls in her second house. This conjunction is often an indication of a sense of inadequacy, based on self-doubt and, falling in his own fifth house of courtship, it may have led him to compensate for any imagined shortcomings in this direction by showering lavish gifts on his partner, thus operating through her second house of possessions and financial resources.

Uranus is the most elevated planet in Richard Burton's horoscope and is in trine to his Sun. As there is a close conjunction between Venus and Uranus in Elizabeth Taylor's marriage house it is not surprising that Burton's planets transposed into his Uranus Zodiac produce the most striking cross-aspects to the planets in her nativity. In her case, it is the Nodal Zodiac which has the greatest number of significant cross-aspects to the planets in his nativity. His key Sun-Saturn conjunction receives notable cross-aspects from several of the subsidiary zodiac positions in Elizabeth Taylor's horoscope:

Burton (Tropical Zodiac)	Taylor (Venus Zodiac)
Sun 18 Scorpio Saturn 17 Scorpio	Neptune 18¼ Leo **(Draconic Zodiac)** Jupiter 18 Cancer **(Pluto Zodiac)** Sun 17¾ Scorpio Mercury 18⅔ Scorpio Neptune 16⅓ Taurus **(Mars Zodiac)** Venus 16 Taurus Uranus 15 Taurus Neptune 18 Leo

There is a similar build-up on Elizabeth Taylor's important Sun/-Jupiter mid-point involving her Moon:

Taylor (Tropical Zodiac)	Burton (Solar Zodiac)
Moon 26 Scorpio Sun/Jupiter 26⅔ Scorpio	Asc. 27⅓ Scorpio Pluto 26⅔ Scorpio M.C. 26 Cancer **(Uranus Zodiac)** Sun 26¼ Scorpio Saturn 25 ⅓ Scorpio Jupiter 26⅔ Capricorn

The Burtons were married on 15th March, 1964. The progressed Sun in their relationship horoscope was in 17 Aquarius, in sextile to Elizabeth Taylor's seventh house Venus-Uranus conjunction and in square to Burton's Saturn. The progressed Ascendant in 18 Virgo had just passed the trine of his seventh house Jupiter. Converse Venus was in 15 Capricorn, conjunct Burton's seventh cusp. Converse Mercury was in 26 Scorpio, listed above as a 'key' area. The converse Midheaven was in 3½ Aries, conjunct radical Uranus, in square to Burton's Venus and in opposition to Taylor's Ascendant. Converse Mars in 7 Cancer was in trine to her Sun.

On the wedding day Venus was in 9 Taurus conjunct Relationship M.C.
Sun was in 25 Pisces square Relationship Mars
Mercury was in 27 Aries sextile Relationship Venus
 in the seventh house
Jupiter was in 23½ Aries trine Relationship Ascendant
Pluto was in 12½ Virgo trine Relationship Sun
Saturn was in 0 Pisces sextile Relationship Jupiter
 opposition Relationship Neptune

When they were divorced in 1974, the secondary progressed Midheaven of the Relationship Chart was in 25 Gemini conjunct Mars(r.) opposition Saturn(r.) (the most disruptive aspect in the radix). The converse Sun was then in 27 Scorpio. The converse Venus was separating from the square of converse Uranus having just passed the conjunction of Burton's Venus(r.). To complete the array of disruptive aspects, the secondary converse Midheaven was in square to the progressed Mars.

The contacts through associate angles cast for London are not as numerous as in some cases but contain several very significant links:

Burton (Associate Angles)	Taylor (Natal Positions)
When Sun/Saturn rises 6 Virgo is on M.C.	Neptune 6½ Virgo Sun/Mars 5 Pisces
When Sun/Saturn sets 20¾ Capricorn is on M.C.	
When Uranus is on M.C. 21 Cancer rises	Pluto 20¼ Cancer
When Mars is on I.C. 15 Leo rises	Jupiter 15 Leo Mars/Saturn 16 Aquarius
When Venus is on I.C. 4 Libra rises	Asc. 4 Libra

(Natal Positions)	(Associate Angles)
Sun 18 Scorpio	When Sun is on I.C. 19 Scorpio rises
Uranus 21¾ Pisces*	When Sun rises 21½ Sagittarius is on M.C.
Sun/Jupiter 18 Sagittarius	When Mars rises 19 Sagittarius is on M.C.
Uranus 21¾ Pisces	When Venus rises 20¾ Pisces is on M.C.
Sun/Saturn 17½ Scorpio	When Pluto is on I.C. 17 Taurus rises

*Planets in square to Associate Angles may also have significance.

ADOLF HITLER AND EVA BRAUN

This is a particularly rewarding case for study. Although both were apparently very much attracted towards each other, and Eva was the only woman whose name was linked romantically with the Fuehrer for any length of time, they did not marry until two days before their suicide in the Berlin Bunker. The ritual of marriage was therefore a final gesture before their entry into the next world and not the prelude to a more meaningful relationship in this one.

Both nativities have seventh house afflictions. Eva Braun was born with Saturn on the seventh cusp squaring her Sun, a classic indication of delay in or denial of marriage, and often of an attraction to an older man (Hitler was her senior by nearly 23 years). Additionally she had Mars in the seventh in trine to Uranus, so that there was a strong likelihood of her involvement in liaisons, even if they did not result in marriage. Hitler had four planets in the seventh. Mercury, close to the cusp, was opposed to Uranus, almost a built-in guarantee of instability in relationship, in complete contrast to Eva's Saturn square Sun in fixed signs, showing a pre-disposition for her to seek security in partnerships above all else.

Her Saturn was 3° from his Venus-Mars conjunction (both in their seventh houses) and in almost exact square to his Saturn in Leo. The importance of this square is given dramatic emphasis by the fact that their relationship horoscope has a Midheaven of 12 Leo 39.

The importance in the relationship of Hitler's afflicted seventh house Mercury is underlined by the position of the Lunar Nodes in Eva's nativity, with the North Node in 25 Aries 12.

Valuable evidence is often present in the Pre-Natal Epoch. Eva has her pre-natal Sun in 24 Aries exactly on Hitler's Descendant. Her Epoch contains many strikingly appropriate features relative to her friendship with Hitler but apart from the position of Saturn in 7 Taurus 43 in close trine to Hitler's natal Moon-Jupiter conjunction (of which Saturn is the dispositor) it will suffice to mention only her pre-natal Jupiter in 11 ⅔ Scorpio and S. Node in 11 Scorpio conjunct her natal Ascendant, and in square to Hitler's radical Saturn.

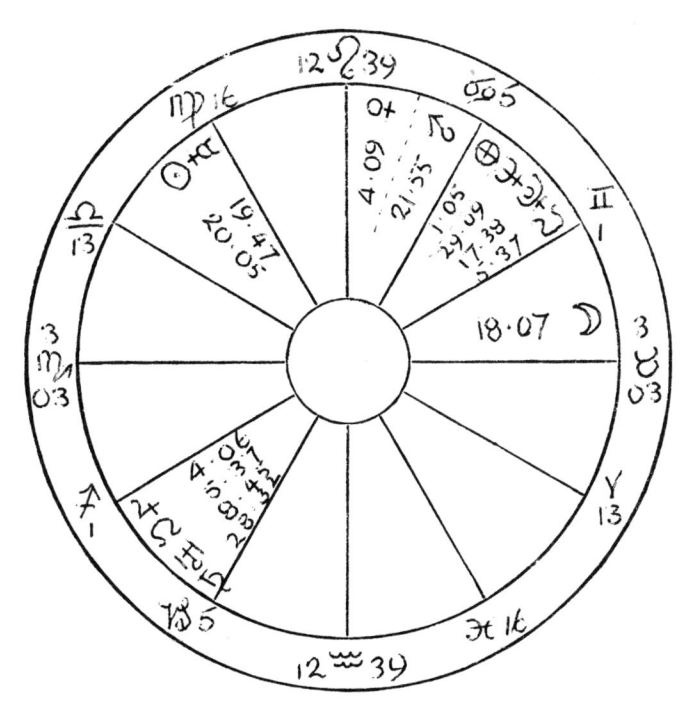

Hitler/Braun Relationship
13 September 1900

48N01, 12E17
8.43 a.m. G.M.T.

The Relationship Horoscope

Eva's seventh house Mars falls on the mid-point of Hitler's Neptune-Pluto conjunction in his eighth house. Both have Pluto in the eighth. Eva's Pluto in 27 Gemini 08 is closely involved with Neptune (29 Gemini) opposition Saturn (28½ Sagittarius) in the relationthips horoscope. The two first met in 1929, when the relationship horoscope was 29 years old (the degree number of the relationship Neptune). The converse Midheaven of the relationship horoscope was 28 Gemini at the time of their suicide and the converse Ascendant 28 Virgo (conjunct Eva's Moon). On the day of the suicide, April 30th, 1945, Mars was in 28 Pisces. Translated into terms of the

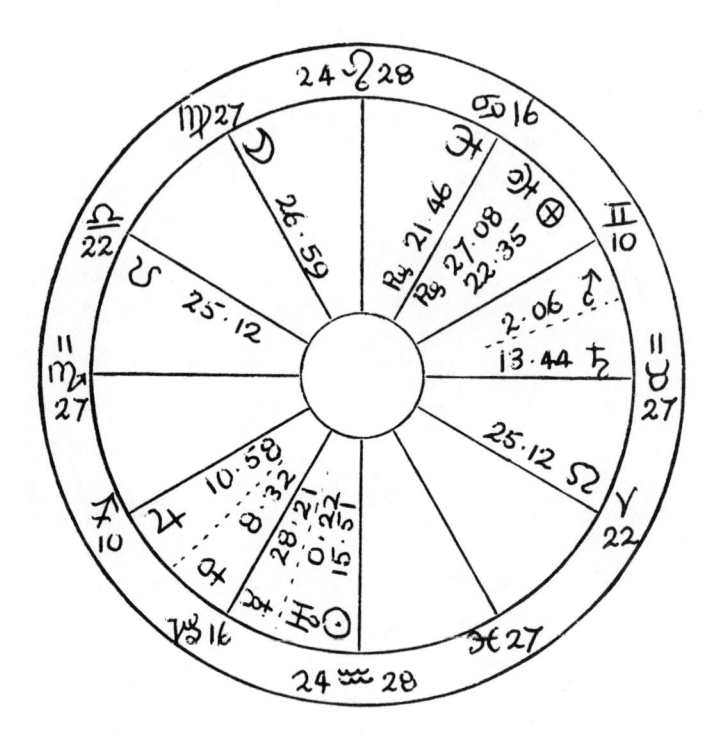

Eva Braun
6 February 1912

Munich, Germany
1.02 a.m. C.E.T.

Venus Zodiac Hitler's Mars was 29½ Pisces, his Saturn 28 Gemini.

The relationship horoscope has strong connections with Hitler's eighth house Pluto in 4 Gemini, for Jupiter is in 4 Sagittarius and Venus in 4 Leo. The progressions of the relationship horoscope measuring to marriage are Asc.(p.) conjunct Jupiter(r.) trine Venus(r.).

A classic indication of attraction and sympathy is furnished by the close conjunction of Eva's Venus with Hitler's Moon-Jupiter conjunction in the third and in trine to his Sun/Venus-Mars midpoint, facilitating easy communication, while Eva's Mercury-Uranus

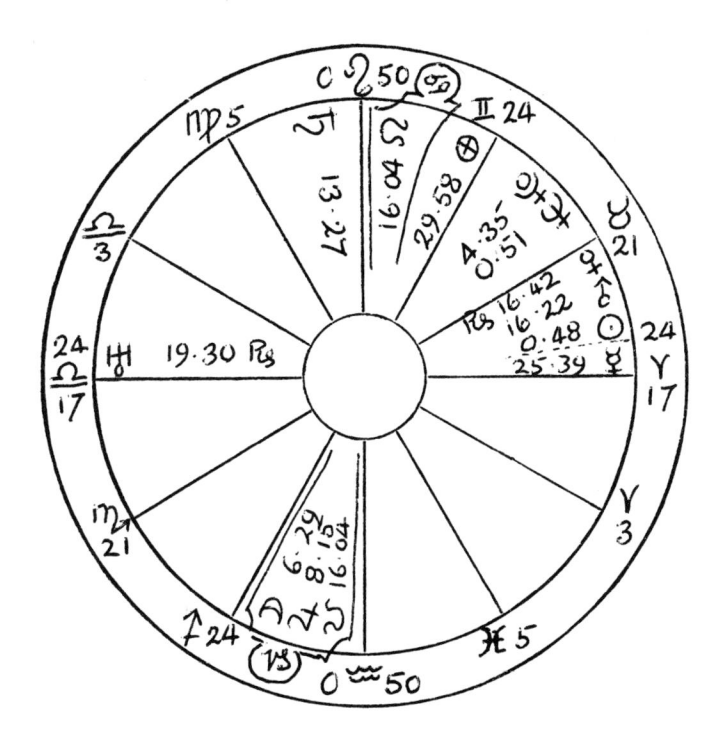

Adolf Hitler
20 April 1889

Braunau-am-Inn, Austria
6.25 p.m. C.E.T.

conjunction, falling on his lower Meridian, echoed his own Mercury-Uranus opposition involved with the other main axis of his horoscope.

Her Sun square Saturn in fixed signs built up a T-square with his Venus-Mars square Saturn, firmly linking their destinies yet denying formal marriage until almost the last moment. Her Uranus in square to his Sun and in opposition to his M.C. may have caused him to doubt whether marriage to her would have served to uphold his political image and she was kept very much in the background. Even when her friendship with Hitler was well known to the Fuehrer's intimates and the upper echelons of the Nazi Party, the general public were deliberately kept in ignorance of the liaison. She was not favorably accepted by some of the Hitler clique, who referred to her contemptuously as the "little clerk." (When she first met Hitler she was working as a clerk in a photographer's studio.)

Hitler had eight planets in Earth and Air, so did Eva. Both had Cardinal and Fixed signs represented equally but Hitler's minority in Mutables was compensated by Eva's majority in that quadruplicity.

At a time when the Russians were almost literally knocking on the doors of the Berlin Chancellory the marriage between Eva and the Fuehrer was perhaps not much more than a last gesture of defiance and a belated, though somewhat bizarre, recognition on Hitler's part of Eva's uncomplaining loyalty and devotion during the latter years of their relationship, when she had been forced to remain in comparative obscurity without enjoying the status of wife. On April 28, 1945, close to midnight, the two were married in the Bunker beneath the Chancellory that had been their refuge for some days past, even though Hitler had previously ordered Eva to leave Berlin for her own safety. The Sun was in 8 Taurus (Eva's Sun in the Venus Zodiac was 7¼ Taurus) at the mid-point of Hitler's seventh house Sun and Venus-Mars conjunction and closely squared by transiting Pluto in Leo. Neptune in Libra was squared by Saturn. Venus in 18½ Aries opposed Hitler's rising Saturn. When they first met the relationship Sun had progressed to 18 Libra.

The Ascendant of the wedding horoscope could well have been 28 Sagittarius, squared by Mars two days later at the time of their suicide. This would have given the Sun square Pluto an angular position in the marriage chart.

Eva's Midheaven in 24½ Leo suggests a conscious aim to establish herself in a position of importance. That this was only partially satisfied is shown by the conjunction of the Midheaven with the mid-point of her own Moon and Neptune (an unsatisfied yearning to fulfill her wifely role and to have it publicly acknowledged). Her Midheaven degree also stands in square to the mid-point between two of the most significant conjunctions in Hitler's horoscope, Venus/Mars and Neptune/Pluto.

It was when she felt that Hitler's affection for her was waning that she made her two suicide attempts. The mid-point of her close conjunction between the Moon and Pluto falls on Hitler's Saturn.

Hitler's debilitated and afflicted Saturn fell in Eva's ninth house, while his rising Uranus squared her ninth house Neptune. He no doubt did his best to indoctrinate her in his own dictatorial way, probably leaving her more confused than illuminated. Her Venus falling on his Moon-Jupiter conjunction in his third house made her a willing and sympathetic listener, even though she might not have understood the deeper implications of the Nazi philosophy.

Eva's Uranus on his fourth cusp suggests that she was a threat to his public image and a complication in his domestic life that brought problems, but her Sun, also in his fourth, showed her later role as hostess at Berchtesgaden when the party dignitaries gathered there.

His Moon-Jupiter conjunction fell in her second house, while her strong Jupiter fell in his second, so that she was assured of financial security as a result of her friendship with him. Eventually, through his agency, she was installed in her own villa on the outskirts of Munich. Later, she had her own quarters in Berchtesgaden and was allocated enough money to buy whatever she wanted.

His Mars and Venus fell in her seventh house, too close to her Saturn for comfort, while his Neptune and Pluto fell on her Mars in the same house. Thus four of his planets fell within the area of her seventh. His Uranus fell close to the cusp of her twelfth house (self-undoing), and his downfall was the cause of their suicide. Her Moon in his eleventh house no doubt sustained the partnership and its trine to her own Mercury and Uranus would have made her a lively companion. Her South Node on his Ascendant suggests that they had worked closely together in previous lives, though her Mercury/Neptune mid-point falling in the same degree indicates that a similar lack of total fulfillment in their relationship may have been present then.

Eva's Sun in Aquarius and Hitler's Saturn in Leo were in mutual disposition as well as being in opposition, a strong bond but not one which promised any consummation of the partnership.

A comparison of Hitler's planets in signs with Eva's planetary aspects shows the following correspondences:

Adolf Hitler	Eva Braun
Saturn Leo	Sun square Saturn
Moon Capricorn	Moon sesquiquadrate Saturn
Jupiter Capricorn	Jupiter quincunx Saturn
Mercury Aries	Mercury trine Mars
Neptune Gemini	Mercury opposition Neptune
Pluto Gemini	Mercury quincunx Pluto

Hitler's chart has only two such aspect correspondences, in this case involving the planets in Eva's nativity that were in mutual disposition:

Eva Braun	Adolf Hitler
Venus Capricorn	Venus square Saturn
Saturn Taurus	

In view of the pattern of their relationship, this isolated correspondence is highly significant.

The most impressive interplay between the two horoscopes, however, is the following:

Adolf Hitler	Eva Braun
Asc. 24½ Libra	N.Node 25½ Aries
Antiscion Pluto 25½ Cancer	Pre-natal Sun 24 Aries
Sun/Uranus 25⅔ Cancer	Mars Zodiac Moon 26 Cancer
	Mars Zodiac Pluto 25 Aries

CHAPTER 11

Conclusion

With a clear understanding of the various comparison techniques set forth in the foregoing pages, the student should now be in a position to make a very fair assessment of the degree of compatibility between any two people. Having made such an assessment he must then decide how to deliver his judgment in such a way as to render the greatest assistance to those seeking his aid.

The psychological make-up of an individual is often complex and intricate and he does not always function at the same level of consciousness, so that his motivations may vary considerably from time to time. To some extent this tends to make him unpredictable, though the more he has learned to exercise self-control, the more "predictable" he may be. It follows that any relationship between two people, carrying within their psychological make-up such an element of unpredictability, may not be quite as cut and dried as we should like to believe; nevertheless, provided in both cases the time of birth is known, we shall stand a fair chance of arriving at a reasonably sound estimate of the quality of their relationship.

Even when two horoscopes show a high degree of compatibility, the matter does not rest there for, just as each individual can actualize the potentialities of his own nativity according to the effort and understanding he is able to bring to the solution of his own problems, so both individuals must contribute their due share to bringing into being what on paper may appear to be a true affinity. Just as the Sun in trine to Jupiter in a nativity may show a tendency to drift while riding one's luck and so frittering away valuable opportunities, such mutual configurations should also not not be allowed to diminish the amount of effort, by both partners, to live up to the best and highest expressions of the possibilities indicated by the more benefic aspects. This is especially so when the marriage partnership is involved.

It sometimes happens that two members of the opposite sex will gravitate towards each other through some natural magnetism (not necessarily related entirely to the physical, emotional or mental planes) and that there is a high degree of affinity and compatibility between them. On the other hand, if the attraction is less deep-rooted and to some extent superficial, then an exercise in synastry between the two nativities and an examination of the comparison horoscope may well show marked areas of stress between the two personalities. In such cases it will be the astrologer's task to point out the areas of harmony that can be strengthened and built up, and to indicate areas where difficulties are likely to arise, so that these can be reduced to a minimum through conscious effort on both sides.

It is the awkward predicaments we meet in life that teach us most about ourselves and, if we learn our lessons properly, enable us to strengthen our characters in the process of dealing with them. Such predicaments usually arrive in the course of our transactions with other people. When possible problems are foreseen in the relationship of two people, especially a married couple, these need not occasion alarm, for they may merely indicate that each partner has valuable lessons to teach the other. To avoid such lessons may not be the best method of promoting soul-growth and, provided there is a good basic harmony between two nativities, there should be no undue concern about the presence of a number of stresses which may in any event, not relate to the personal side of the partnership but to difficult circumstances brought about as a result of illness, poverty, enforced separation and so on.

It may sometimes happen that two people contemplating marriage have very few indications of real affinity present in their charts. Even so, the astrologer must be very careful not to "interfere" with the intended course of events (though usually such betrothed couples are fairly strongly determined on their course of action before they reach the stage of consulting an astrologer, often in the hope of receiving some final and definitive confirmation that they were made for each other!).

When, on the strength of the astrological evidence before him, he has misgivings about the desirability of such a marriage, the astrologer's best course is to set out as frankly as possible the strengths and weaknesses of the partnership as they appear to him and not to suggest in as many words that the marriage should not take place unless the circumstances are so exceptional as to warrant such an extraordinary course of action. In any case, the astrologer should endeavour to set forth as complete a picture as possible, always leaving the final decision to the couple themselves. He should try to avoid painting an extreme picture, either of the highlights or the shadows of such a partnership.

It is well to remember that while one couple may abhor any kind of disagreement between themselves, another may thrive on the occasional argument, which they will often use as a very healthy safety-valve should tensions accumulate. However, when a partnership appears to contain certain explosive elements, and the relationship has existed for a sufficient length of time for these to have manifested in severe emotional disturbances, it is possible that the only really satisfactory solution is for the couple to part.

True compatibility is compounded of many indefinable and sometimes elusive elements that are dependent upon the mysteriously fluctuating complexities of human nature. To be linked by a permanent bond to an incompatible partner is one of the most traumatic experiences a human being can be called upon to undergo, while a heart-breaking love affair can leave deep emotional scars or at least give rise to a disturbing emotional crisis. Consequently the determination of an affinity between two people, or its absence, is one of the most important functions of astrology.

Glossary

Co-Latitude
The difference between the latitude of a place and 90°.

Cross-Aspect
An aspect from a planet or angle in one nativity to a planet in another nativity.

Debilitated
A planet in a sign opposite to the sign which it rules, or in which it is exalted, is said to be debilitated.

Final Dispositor
A planet in its own sign, which also rules the signs in which the other planets in the nativity or the dispositors of the other planets are placed.

Fortuna
The Part of Fortune. This marks the point where the Moon would be if the Sun were placed exactly on the Ascendant (which symbolically represents illumination). It suggests the way in which the personality must be re-oriented before illumination can be gained. It is therefore an important factor in the chart.

It is calculated according to the formula:
Longitude Asc. + Longitude Moon − Longitude Sun.

Horizon
The plane in which lie the points where the Sun rises in the East and sets in the West, and a general term for the Ascendant/Descendant axis (cusps of the first and seventh houses.)

Local Mean Time
The time at any place relative to G.M.T. and determined by the distance in longitude of that place from Greenwich. Each degree

West of Greenwich means that the Local Mean Time is 4 minutes earlier; each degree East of Greenwich means that the L.M.T. is 4 minutes later. Unless a place is exactly on a Standard Time Meridian, the L.M.T. will not be the same as the Standard Time operative in that zone.

Part of Marriage

A point as many degrees above or below the Ascendant or Descendant as Venus is below or above the Descendant or Ascendant. It is calculated according to the formula:
Longitude Ascendant + Longitude Descendant − Longitude Venus.

Piscean Age

One of the twelve subdivisions of the Great Year of Precession of 26,000 years during which the First Point of Aries in the Tropical Zodiac regresses through the Zodiac of the Constellations (due to the rotatory movement of the earth's axis). The present Piscean Age began in 221 A.D.

Quadruplicities

The subdivision of the signs according to their quality, Cardinal, Fixed or Mutable. E.g. the Cardinal Quadruplicity is Aries, Cancer, Libra, Capricorn.

Re-domification

The placing of a planet belonging to one person's horoscope in the appropriate house of another's horoscope according to its zodiacal longitude.

Singleton

Usually, the sole occupant of one hemisphere of the horoscope either above or below the horizon or to the east or the west of the meridian. Occasionally, the sole occupant of a quadrant of the horoscope.

Triplicities

The division of the signs according to their element, Fire, Earth, Air, Water. E.g. the Fire Triplicity: Aries, Leo, Sagittarius.

Vertex

Strictly speaking, the Vertex is the Zenith, but the term has lately been used to designate a point where the plane of the ecliptic intersects the Prime Vertical, thus creating, together with the Midheaven and Ascendant, a "three dimensional" horoscope.

To find the Vertex, calculate the co-latitude of the birthplace, turn to the Tables of Houses for this latitude and take out the Ascendant when the degree of the I.C. of the nativity is on the Midheaven. This ascending degree will be the Vertex for that horoscope.

Zenith

The point above the earth 90° from the horizon. This point rarely coincides with the Midheaven. It is the cusp of the tenth house by Equal House Division.

Bibliography

C.E.O. Carter, *Essays on the Foundations of Astrology,*
The Theosophical Publishing House, London, Ltd.

Rodney Collin, *The Theory of Celestial Influence,*
Samuel Weiser Inc., New York

R.C. Davison, *The Technique of Prediction,*
L.N. Fowler & Co. Ltd., London

Alan Leo, *How to Judge a Nativity,*
L.N. Fowler & Co. Ltd., London

Maurice Wemyss, *The Wheel of Life, Vols. I, II & III,*
L.N. Fowler & Co. Ltd, London

Essays, *Synastry: An Astrological Study of Relationships,*
Astrological Association, London

The author also wishes to acknowledge his indebtedness to the contributors to various magazines of articles dealing with one or other of the many aspects of synastry and notably to the *Astrologer's Quarterly,* published by the Astrological Lodge of the Theosophical Society in England, and to *Horoscope Magazine.* An idea gleaned here and a hint picked up there have enabled him over the years to gain a greater grasp of the principles of synastry and to elaborate his own system along the lines presented in the foregoing pages.

INDEX

ADLER, ALFRED .... 268 et seq.

AIR ELEMENT 71
   combined with air 78
   combined with water 79
   combined with earth 77
   combined with fire 75

ANGULAR PLANETS 85
   combined with
      angular 86
      succedent 87
      cadent 87

ANTISCIONS 60, 260, 261, 274

ASPECTS (see also cross-aspects) .... 89 et seq.

ASSOCIATE ANGLES .... 61, 266 et seq., 296, 307

ATKINS, SUSAN .... 284 et seq.

BRAUN, EVA and Adolf Hitler .... 308 et seq.

BURTON, RICHARD and Elizabeth Taylor .... 297 et seq.

CADENT HOUSES 86

CARDINAL SIGNS 81
   blended with
      Cardinal 82
      Fixed 83
      Mutable 83

CHANGE OF RESIDENCE
   AND LOCALITY HOROSCOPE 51

CHILDREN AND THE FIFTH HOUSE 47

CROSS-ASPECTS
   To Sun 100-113
   To Moon 114-121
   To Mercury 122-126
   To Venus 126-134
   To Mars 134-142
   To Jupiter 142-145
   To Saturn 145-151
   To Uranus 151-154
   To Neptune 154-156
   To Pluto 156-157

DEGREE AREAS 274-277

DIVORCE 24

DOMAL ANALOGUES 59

DRACONIC ZODIAC 256-258, 275-277, 293, 306

EARTH SIGNS, planets in 70
   blended with
      Air 77
      Earth 76
      Fire 74
      Water 78

FATHER FIGURE 4, 12, 18

FINAL DISPOSITORS 57

FIRE SIGNS, planets in 70
  combined with
    Air 75
    Earth 74
    Fire 73
    Water 77

FIRST MEETING HOROSCOPES 35

FIFTH HOUSE and CHILDREN 47

FIXED SIGNS, planets in 81
  combined with planets in
    Cardinal signs 83
    Fixed signs 84
    Mutable signs 84

FORD, President 295

FREUD, SIGMUND 268

FROMME, LYNETTE 295

HITLER, ADOLF and Eva Braun .... 308 et seq.

HORARY CHARTS 44

HOUSE CUSPS 159

HOUSE INTERCHANGES
  Sun in another's houses 164-173
  Moon in another's houses 173-182
  Mercury in another's houses 182-187
  Venus in another's houses 182-193
  Mars in another's houses 193-200
  Jupiter in another's houses 200-207
  Saturn in another's houses 207-216
  Uranus in another's houses 216-224
  Neptune in another's houses 224-233
  Pluto in another's houses 234-243

HOUSES, Significations
    First to Fourth Houses 161
    Second to Eighth Houses 162
    Ninth to Twelfth Houses 163

HOUSE, TWELFTH and Jig-saw Puzzles 262

INCEPTIONAL CHARTS 42

JUNG, CARL GUSTAV . . . . 268 et seq.

JUPITER,
    Cross-aspects to 142-145
    In Libra 26
    In seventh house 16
    Significations 99, 200

JUPITER ZODIAC 259, 260

MANSON, CHARLES . . . . 282 et seq.

MANVILLE, TOMMY 23

MARRIAGE elections 39
    horoscope 38, 40, 41, 42
    vow 48

MARS,
    Cross-aspects to 134-142
    In Libra 25
    In seventh house 15
    Significations 99, 193

MARS ZODIAC 294, 295, 306

MERCURY,
　Cross-aspects to 122-126
　In Libra 25
　In seventh house 14
　Significations 98, 182

MERCURY ZODIAC 275

MID-POINTS 97

MOON,
　Cross-aspects to 114-121
　In Libra 24
　In seventh house 13
　Significations 98, 173

MOON-URANUS isolated by hemisphere 56

MOTHER FIGURE 4, 13

MULTIPLE MARRIAGES 23

MUTABLE SIGNS, planets in 82
　combined with planets in
　　Cardinal signs 83
　　Fixed signs 84
　　Mutable signs 85

MUTUAL RECEPTION (Mutual Disposition) 302, 314

NEPTUNE,
　Cross-aspects to 154-156
　In Libra 27
　In seventh house 20
　Significations 100, 224

OPPOSITION ASPECT 96

ORBS in comparison 97

PARENT, STEVEN EARL 289

PART OF MARRIAGE 28

PHYSICAL MAGNETISM 5

PLANETARY PATTERNS .... 62 et seq.

PLANETARY SIGNIFICATIONS (see under individual planets)

PLANETARY ZODIACS (and under individual planets) 59

PLANETS IN CANCER 28

PLANETS IN LIBRA 24-28

PLANETS IN SEVENTH HOUSE 12-23

PLUTO,
    and Psychoanalysis 270
    Cross-aspects to 156
    In Libra 28
    In seventh house 22
    Significations 100, 234

PLUTO ZODIAC 275-278, 294, 295, 307

PRE-NATAL EPOCH 65, 262, 263

QUINCUNX 97

RAPHAEL, comments on
    Duke of York's nativity 250
    Edward VIII's nativity 250

RELATIONSHIP CHARTS
Atkins/Parent 292
Burton/Taylor 299-301
Freud/Adler 279
Freud/Jung 280
Hitler/Braun 309, 310
Jung/Adler 281
Manson/Parent 290
Windsors .... 264, et seq.

RELATIONSHIPS with
Brothers 32
Employees 32
Employers 32
Friends 32
Neighbors 32
Relatives 32
Sisters 32

SATURN
Cross-aspects to 145-151
In Libra 26
In seventh house 17
Significations 99, 207

SATURN ZODIAC 259, 275, 276, 293-295

SEPARATION 24

SEPHARIAL, comments on
Edward VIII's nativity 252

SOLAR ZODIAC 258, 275-277, 293, 294, 306

SUCCEDENT HOUSES, planets in 86
combined with planets in
    Angular 87
    Succedent 86
    Cadent 87

SUN,
- Cross-aspects to 100-113
- In Libra 24
- In seventh house 12
- Significations 98, 164

TATE, SHARON 284

TAYLOR, ELIZABETH and Richard Burton .... 297 et seq.

TIME DEGREES 283

TWELFTH HOUSE and jig-saw puzzles 262

UNITED KINGDOM horoscope 251, 261

UNITED STATES horoscope 251

URANUS,
- Cross-aspects to 151-154
- In Libra 27
- In seventh house 19
- Significations 99, 216

URANUS ZODIAC 306

VENUS,
- Cross-aspects to 126-134
- In Libra 25
- In seventh house 14
- Significations 98, 187

VENUS ZODIAC 255, 256, 306, 310

VERTEX 263

WATER SIGNS, planets in 72
    combined with
        Air 79, 80
        Earth 78
        Fire 76
        Water 80

WINDSOR, DUKE and Duchess of .... 246 et seq., 249 et seq.

YORK, DUKE of 249, 250, 251

AURORA PRESS

Aurora Press is devoted to pioneering books that catalyze personal growth, balance and transformation. Aurora makes available in a digestible format, an innovative synthesis of ancient wisdom with twentieth century resources, integrating esoteric knowledge and daily life.

Recent titles include:

COMING HOME
Deborah Duda

CRYSTAL ENLIGHTENMENT
Katrina Raphaell

CRYSTAL HEALING
Katrina Raphaell

SILVER DENTAL FILLINGS • THE TOXIC TIMEBOMB
Sam Ziff

AWAKEN HEALING ENERGY THROUGH THE TAO
Mantak Chia

TAOIST SECRETS OF LOVE
Mantak Chia

THE LUNATION CYCLE
Dane Rudhyar

SELF HEALING, YOGA AND DESTINY
Elisabeth Haich

For a complete catalog write:

AURORA PRESS
P.O. BOX 573
SANTA FE NEW MEXICO 87504
(505) 989-9804

Wisdom of the Tarot

by Elisabeth Haich

Wisdom of the Tarot relates the path of higher consciousness through the color, shape and symbolic forms on the 22 cards. Detailed study of a Tarot card may release instinctively all that is involved with each level towards the light. These cards may be used in conjunction with the text or separately for meditation. When studied individually, a card may reveal the necessary steps to be taken to find one's essential path. Tarot cards, or symbolic representations of truth, have always been used to help man relate not only with his mind, but instinctively through the feelings evoked by the colors and forms.

Included in *Wisdom of the Tarot* are 5 color gold Tarot cards designed and colored by Oswald Wirth.

Paper 174 pp.

The Planetarization of Consciousness

by Dane Rudhyar

The Planetarization of Consciousness is Rudhyar's major philosophical and psychological work, the concentrated outcome of a lifetime of thinking concerning the most basic problems of human existence and the meaning of the radical social-cultural and psychological crisis mankind is experiencing. Rudhyar has been for years an apostle of world integration based on the interpretation of Eastern and Western concepts and attitudes to life. He sees emerging a global society, and through the worldwide interaction of all cultures, a new type of "planetary" consciousness which for the first time will reveal in its fullness the potential of man.

"The holistic world-view which I present here is meant to be an incentive to think greater thoughts, to feel deeper, more inclusive feelings, and to act as "agents" for the Power that structures human evolution—however we wish to image this power."

The Planetarization of Consciousness is essentially an act of faith in Man. Man as a microcosm of the universe, Man as a reality that transcends the physical organism, all localisms and nationalisms, and in whom spirit and matter can unite in a "Divine Marriage" productive of ever new and greater creative tomorrows.

Rudhyar, an accomplished and innovative painter, composer, poet, astrologer and philosopher has actualized a "humanistic" yet deeply spiritual approach to existence.

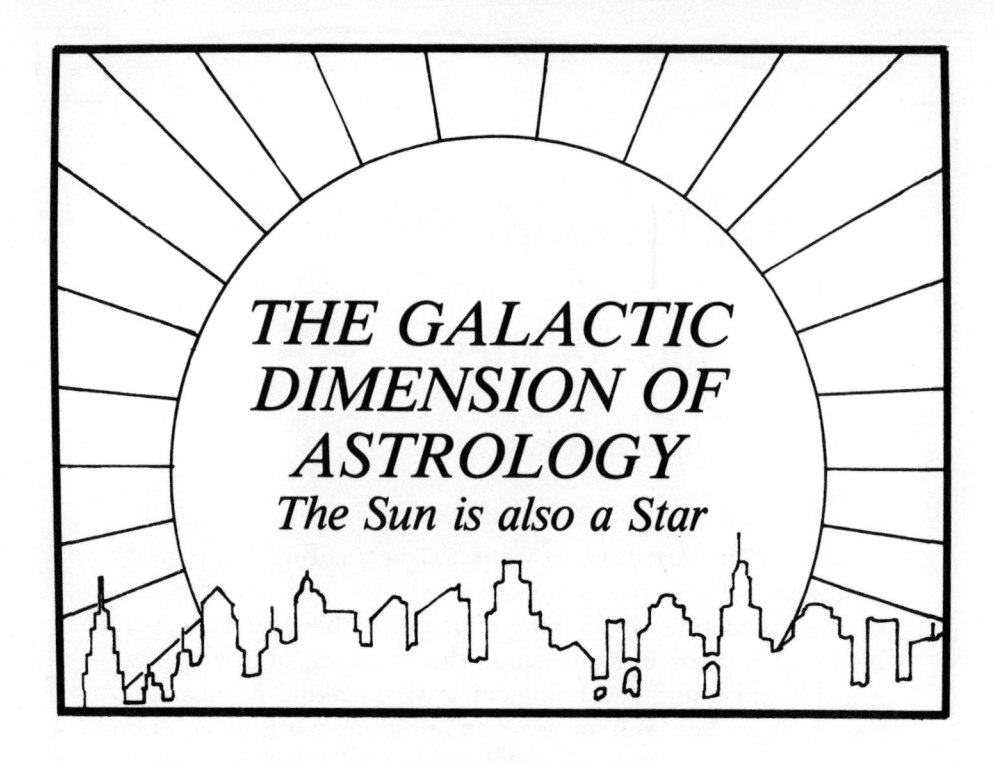

THE GALACTIC DIMENSION OF ASTROLOGY
The Sun is also a Star

by Dane Rudhyar

Rudhyar expands traditional astrological philosophy by introducing a galactic view of the solar system:

"When the Sun is seen as the star it fundamentally is, a galactic frame of reference takes form in the consciousness of man, and it brings to all the patterns and events of our traditional solar system a potentially new meaning. The planetary facts at first remain what they were. The orbits, the speed of revolution, and the cyclic interrelationship between their positions in the sky seen by human eyes do not change; but the interpretation of these facts is altered.... The entire solar system is seen in a new light, the light of the relationship it has to the Galaxy."

Rudhyar shows how a deepened understanding of Uranus, Neptune and Pluto can guide us towards experiencing the galactic level of consciousness. The "challenge of galacticity" to humanistic astrology releases new perspectives when applied to individual horoscopes. His new interpretations of the trans-saturnian planets provide a vehicle to transform how we use astrology in our daily lives, and for the evolving planet we live on.

Paper 224 pp.

ASTROLOGY

Astrological Insights

By Dane Rudhyar

Astrological Insights provides a penetrating, sensitive, poetic and visual insight into the 12 qualities required for the spritual life. Using the astrological signs and houses, Rudhyar builds a framework for impregnating the seeker with an awareness of how to use basic life challenges, as a process through which an individual human being evolves.

Twelve exquisite artistic renderings evoke the archetypal, intuitive level of each sign. Parts of this book were previously published as *Zodiacal Insights* and *Astrological Themes for Meditation*; new material has been added, enlarging the themes creating a whole view of the spiritual dimension of astrology.

A treasure for both astrologers and non-astrologers alike, this is the ideal gift book.

Paper 160 pp.

TRIPTYCH

Gifts of the Spirit

The Way Through

The Illuminated Road

by Dane Rudhyar

In Triptych Rudhyar extracts from traditional astrology a great wealth of psychological and spiritual meaning. New interpretations of the zodiacal signs, the houses and the planets are presented shedding light on the three basic phases of the great ritual which constitutes the spiritual unfoldment of the human being.

"To become whole by assimilating that which completes our particular being—to realize that individual existence is a process of repeated emergence out of a number of typical conditions which test the individual's strength, resilience and faith, and having realized this, to be victorious over the negative trend which is met at every step of the way."

Triptych is a book to read and reread! Each chapter stands by itself, yet as a part in a vast symphony of revealed values and inspired imagery.

"I am particularly pleased because Rudhyar's whole trend of thought is in the spirit of psychosynthesis. From different starting points and using a different terminology he arrives at the same basic conclusions on important issues such as: harmonizing the opposites in individuals and in society; the central importance of purpose; the need of a new humanistic psychology." ROBERTO ASSAGIOLI